THE RELIGIONS OF MANKIND

KANSAS SCHOOL OF RELIGION
University of Kansas
1300 Oread Avenue
LAWRENCE, KANSAS 66044

THE RELIGIONS

OF

MANKIND

Hans-Joachim Schoeps

TRANSLATED FROM THE GERMAN BY
RICHARD AND CLARA WINSTON

DOUBLEDAY & COMPANY, INC.

Garden City, New York

1966

This book was published in Germany under the title
RELIGIONEN: WESEN UND GESCHICHTE.
© C. Bertelsmann Verlag, Gütersloh 1961, 1964/54.

PREFACE

RELIGIONS: PATHS TO SALVATION

RELIGIONS are paths to salvation. They attempt to answer man's fearful questions, and to liberate him from the toils that hinder communion with divinity. That was the case even in the early stages of history, when magical notions prevailed. In religion man encounters a power superior to himself. Therefore he seeks to obtain the favor of the deity, whose protection he needs against dangers, whose consolation he desires. He craves peace and truth and hopes for the attainment of immortality.

A society without religion is inconceivable. Religion has always occupied a prominent place in social organization, in philosophy and in history. Today, when the very existence of humanity is threatened by nuclear warfare, man seems to live without fixed ties, solely in the present. In his existential anxiety he strives restlessly for success, happiness, prosperity. But within his deepest self he seeks a firm ground; he wishes to see some meaning to his existence. Men are filled with longings for peace and for redemption.

The object of this book is to present as inclusive a picture as possible of man's religions. To that end, we must first clarify the nature, origin, and forms of religion. This is also helpful if we are to understand the minds of primitives. Religion begins with belief in fetishes, powers, spirits, with sacrifices to images of gods. It can also include magic. Man knows himself to be dependent on an unknown power. That power arouses fear, love, and hope. Among the basic forms of relationship between man and deity, which occur all over the world, are sacrifice, prayer, ritual acts. Certain figures in the world of religion, such as founders, prophets, priests, mystics, and reformers, develop special traits in the different religions.

The concept of religion embraces the whole vast realm from belief in objects imbued with mana to selfless devotion to a per-

sonal God. Diverse and often contradictory answers are given
to the question of the nature of supernatural power. Religions
are numberless, as are the names of the gods to whom men have
prayed; but all share certain elements, such as fixed rituals, moral
requirements, expectations of judgment and redemption.

The questions and the ideas of long extinct religions, which
are by no means to be dismissed as primitive, still influence our
present world. That is true for the religions of Babylonia, Egypt,
Persia, for the civilizations of the Aztecs, Mayas, and Incas,
and for the extinct religions of Europe.

The great religions of the East proceed from concepts of immutable laws of existence. They manage either entirely without notions of personal gods, or link the nature of their gods
with other ideas which are alien to the religions based on the
Bible.

Judaism, Islam and Christianity are religions of biblical revelation. Among them, too, there are common elements and great
differences, which must be examined in order for us to attain an
understanding of the special message of each. The religions of
revelation have it that they were established in the world by
God at a certain point in history; that God made Israel his Chosen
People and concluded a covenant with that people on Mount
Sinai. In Islam, Mohammed is the recipient of revelation who has
transmitted to men Allah's will and doctrine. To the Christian,
God revealed himself in Christ, who is "the way, the truth and
the life."

Each religion necessarily claims to be the true one; if it did not
do so, it would have no right to the name of religion. But we as
individuals should consider the various forms of religion and try
to understand them.

The author has seen his task as that of presenting the most
important facts of general religious history. He has not dealt in
detail with scholarly disputes—although there are few matters in
this branch of scholarship on which complete unanimity prevails.
However, he has mentioned important points at issue. To be sure,
the reader will recognize where the author is advocating his own
opinions. The author has, nevertheless, endeavored as far as possible to set forth certain facts and avoid hypotheses.

The author wishes to thank his assistant, Kurt Töpner, for con-
tributing the chapter entitled "The Second Vatican Council."

Contents

Preface   v

THE SCIENCE OF RELIGION:
ASPECTS AND PROBLEMS

What Is Religion?   3

    What Is the Science of Religion?   4

    Theology and the Science of Religion   5

The Origin of Religion   7

    The Animistic Theory   7

    The Preanimistic Theory   8

    The Theory of Original Monotheism   8

Basic Ideas of the Science of Religion   11

    Holiness   11

    Mana   13

    Taboo   15

    Sacred Kingship   17

The Thinking of Primitive Peoples   20

    Magical Thinking   20

    Magic and Religion   23

    Shamanism   25

    Early Age-classes and Leagues of Men   26

    Totemism   27

BASIC MODES OF RELATIONSHIP BETWEEN MAN AND
DEITY   30

    Offering   30

    Prayer   34

    Ritual   37

TYPICAL PERSONALITIES IN THE WORLD OF RELIGION   40

    The Founder   40

    The Prophet   42

    The Mystic   44

    The Priest   46

    The Reformer   47

    Classification of Religions   48

EXTINCT RELIGIONS OUTSIDE OF EUROPE

RELIGION IN BABYLONIA   53

    The Gods   54

    Mythology   56

    Piety and Morality   58

    Babel and Bible   59

    The West Semites   60

THE EGYPTIAN RELIGION   63

    History   63

Gods 65

Amenophis IV, the Reformer 70

Pharaohs, Priests, and Monuments 72

Ideas of Death and the Last Judgment 74

THE RELIGION OF THE PERSIANS 76

The Word of Zoroaster 77

The Doctrine of Last Things 78

Iranian Dualism 80

Ritual and Funeral Customs 83

Zervanism 84

Cult of Mithra 85

Manichaeism 86

End of Persian Religion 89

RELIGIONS IN PRE-COLUMBIAN AMERICA 91

The Aztecs 91

The Mayas 94

The Inca 94

EXTINCT RELIGIONS WITHIN EUROPE

THE RELIGIONS OF THE TEUTONS 99

Teutonic Gods and their Cult 100

Teutonic Belief in Fate 101

The Magic of the Runes 103

Ideas of Death and the Ultimate End 105

Conversion of the Teutonic Peoples 108

The Religion of the Celts and Slavs   110

   The Celts   110

   The Slavs   112

The Religion of the Greeks   117

   Historical Introduction   117

   The World of the Greek Gods   118

   The Mysteries and Their Gods   124

   Organization of Worship and the Polis   127

   The Cult of Heroes   129

   The Classical Enlightenment   130

The Religion of the Romans   134

   Etruscans and Latins   134

   The Roman Pantheon   135

   Character and Organization   138

   Development   140

THE GREAT RELIGIONS OF THE EAST

Indian World-view   147

Hinduism   148

   The Veda   148

   The Bhagavadgita   150

   The Gods of Hinduism   151

   The Doctrine of Karma   152

   Caste   153

Developments in Hinduism 155

Modern Hinduism 158

BUDDHISM 161

   The Life of the Buddha 162

   The Doctrine of the Buddha 165

   Buddhist Monasticism 168

   Evaluation of the Buddha's Doctrine 169

   Developments in Buddhism 172

   The Present State of Hinayana Buddhism 174

RELIGION IN TIBET 176

RELIGION IN CHINA 181

   Chinese Buddhism 181

   Chinese Folk Religion 183

   Lao-tse and the Tao-te-king 185

   The Doctrine of Confucius 188

   Developments in Taoism and Confucianism 192

RELIGION IN JAPAN 197

   Japanese Buddhism 197

   Shintoism 199

   The Present Situation 203

THE RELIGIONS OF BIBLICAL REVELATION

JUDAISM 207

   The Jewish Creed 209

Jewish Ritual and Worship   211

Jewish Ethics   214

The Talmud   216

Development of Jewish Mysticism   218

Recent Religious History of Judaism   221

Judaism and Christianity   223

THE RELIGION OF ISLAM   227

Foundations of the Islamic Religion   227

Life of the Prophet and Origin of Islam   229

The Message of the Prophet   234

Mohammedan Mysticism   236

The Five Pillars of Islam and the Koran Tradition   237

History of Islam   238

The Present   240

CHRISTIANITY   242

The Creed of Christendom   242

The Life and Message of Jesus   243

Jewish Religious Parties in the Time of Jesus   245

John the Baptist   247

The Kingdom of God   249

The Passion   251

The Gospel of John   253

Paul's View of Christ   254

The Growth of the Christian Church   255

The Sacraments   257

The Ecclesiastical Offices   258

The Papacy 260

Spread and Persecution 261

Christianity as the Religion of the Empire 263

Sin and Penance: the Great Struggle 265

Monasticism 266

Development of Theology and Dogma 268

Christological Doctrinal Disputes 271

Augustine 274

Brief Sketch of Medieval Church History 275

The Schism 276

World Power and Political Decline of the Papacy 277

The Crusades 280

Christian Art and Scholarship 281

Symptoms of Decay 283

The Reformation 285

Zwingli and Calvin 290

The Counter Reformation 294

Catholicism Today 296

The Second Vatican Council 299

Christianity Today 302

The Present Situation and the Need for Tolerance 304

INDEX 313

The Science of Religion:
Aspects and Problems

WHAT IS RELIGION?

RELIGION may be defined, in its broadest sense, as the relationship between man and the superhuman power he believes in and feels himself to be dependent on. This relationship may be expressed by feelings such as trust or fear, by ideas such as legends, myths, or dogmas, and by actions, such as special rites and the carrying out of religious precepts. Jakob Burckhardt has offered this definition: "Religions are the expression of the eternal and indestructible metaphysical craving of human nature. Their grandeur is that they represent the whole supersensual complement of man, all that he cannot himself provide. At the same time they are the reflections, upon a great and different plane, of whole peoples and cultural epochs."

The theme of religion is redemption from the powers that prevent man from communing with the divine. What Friedrich Schleiermacher called the "feeling of absolute dependence" is an important component of religion, but is by no means all of it. In fact, Hegel rather ridiculed this definition: If religion, let alone Christianity, were merely a matter of this feeling, then dogs would be the best Christians, for dogs exhibit this feeling to perfection.

The religious impulse springs from a longing for truth, peace, and a life after death. The words for union with God are, in all the languages of the world, limited and imperfect. The languages of Christian peoples have taken over the Latin word *religio*. Cicero derived it from *relegere*, meaning "to consider." St. Augustine, on the other hand, preferred to define the word as meaning the finding again of something that has been lost, while Lactantius saw it as a derivative of *religare*, "to tie"; thus religion meant the tie, or the knowledge of being tied, to a higher power.

Definitions have often been attempted, but the concept eludes precise formulation. Nor are formulas necessary for our purpose. We may best sketch in a definition as follows: The impulse toward religion is an essential part of man's endowment. Religion manifests itself as a sum of beliefs relating to a reality which is not provable by experience, but which is nevertheless an unconditional certainty to the believer. This reality represents an ultimate standard in the life of the believer and prompts him to certain modes of action. The concern of the science of religion is to examine these interrelationships.

WHAT IS THE SCIENCE OF RELIGION?

By the science of religion we do not mean theology or its offshoots. We do mean a discipline independent of creed that aims at objective statement. It has two branches: a general history of religions, and so-called comparative religion. General history of religions deals with the growth and development of specific historical religions. It studies the stages in the development of religions and tries to understand how these arise out of the premises of each faith. It is interested in the inward shaping of each religion, in the evolution of piety, in change of forms and expression in worship and myth. The history of religions includes the outward and the psychological development of particular religious communities; it takes in questions of dogma, ritual, veneration of founders and saints. The emphasis in this discipline is distinctly on facts.

The science of comparative religion builds on the findings of its sister science. It seeks to analyze the varieties of religious experience and by comparing religions to recognize typical developments, characteristic traits and consistent laws. Before it can determine the fundamentals underlying various aspects of religion, the central features in historical religions must be uncovered. We may put it this way: that the science of comparative religion, or religious phenomenology, takes cross sections through the various religions, while the history of religion takes longitudinal sections. The line of a longitudinal section reveals the spiritual direction of each religion, its consistent and unchanging character, whereas the cross section shows common stages or the common elements in different religions.

Subsidiary branches of these disciplines are the sociology of religion, which deals with the forms of religious communities and the influence of social forms on the development of religion; the psychology of religion, which investigates what happens in the psyche in the course of religious experience; and finally the philosophy of religion, which attempts to determine the place and function of religion in the whole of human knowledge and existence.

THEOLOGY AND THE SCIENCE OF RELIGION

The basic distinction between theology and the science of religion rests upon the fact that theology sets up rules. Unlike the science of religion, which studies the facts, theology poses and attempts to answer the question of What Is and the question of truth. Theology is not pure search for knowledge; it is the pursuit of knowledge in the interests of a creed. Thus theology is always denominational; it takes its own religious faith for its absolute. In other words, theology is patterned on the church. The nature and truth of its own particular religion, as revelation, is stated by dogma. The religious scientist, on the other hand, pursues questions which are in no way linked to his own creed. His approach is marked by objectivity. To the historians of religion, religion is not the manifestation of revelation, whose claim is that it is unique. However, such a historian may take revelation as a legitimate subject for investigation. Yet the goal of the science of religion must not be mere description and explanation of the facts. Rather, it must try to show how the facts sprang from that fundamental drive toward structuring experience which has been brought to light by the history of religions.

The German philosopher Wilhelm Dilthey (1833–1911) was a pioneer in the development of religious history as an independent discipline. He emphasized that this study must be practiced non-theologically, as part of the history of ideas. The method of religious history is the same as that of historiography in general. Nevertheless: "Among all the factors on which the objectivization and organization of the mind is founded, religion assumes a special, central place. . . . The element that leads beyond life is established in life itself" (*Gesammelte Schriften*, VII, 266).

All human things—and consequently religion, too, as it appears in man and among men—constitute the document, Dilthey said, which records the infinite potentialities of our existence. Faced with the bewildering plethora of phenomena, we must forever endeavor to understand them rightly. "Understanding does not mean carrying our own standards of evaluation to the object. Rather, the things we experience must themselves yield the clue to their meaning on their own terms" (V, 152 f.).

But the supernatural, the element in our lives which goes beyond all experience, remains unanalyzable and transposes itself into historical understanding of the unknown nature of man. Thus we can understand forms of religion that are alien to us and wholly remote from us. As Dilthey has beautifully put it: "Metaphysics falls silent, but from the stars, when night's stillness descends, there reaches even to us that harmony of the spheres which, the Pythagoreans said, is only drowned out by the noise of the world. That harmony is an unanalyzable metaphysical mood that underlay all proofs and will outlive them all" (I, 564 f.).

THE ORIGIN OF RELIGION

T HE ORIGIN of religion remains hidden from our knowledge. We possess no evidences of the beginning of religion. But wherever men live on earth, religion springs into being. The science of religion encounters the fact that nowhere on earth have peoples been found who do not possess a religion in the sense described above. Ethnologists, anthropologists and prehistorians know of no men without religion. But we know nothing of its origin because the time span known to historians is but a brief period in comparison with the thousands of years in which archaeologists deal, let alone the billions of years of the geologists and astronomers. By far the greater part of the story of mankind lies entirely in darkness, or at best in a dim twilight which can never be fully illuminated.

A number of interesting theories of the origin of religion have been posited. Ever since Charles Darwin introduced the concept of evolution into biology, the science of religion has developed a number of evolutionary theories of its own. We shall mention here:

THE ANIMISTIC THEORY

According to this theory, man in his early stages assumed the presence of a soul (Latin *anima*) in all things and began venerating certain spirits or souls as personified causes. The souls of the dead were especially venerated—in other words, ancestor worship was practiced. The soul was regarded as a shadowy image of man, a spirit which could be embodied in animals and things. Conceptions of individual gods were of later date, and point back to a primitive phase of belief in ghosts and spirits. This theory, first posed by the English scholar Sir Edward Burnett Tylor in his epoch-making book *Primitive Culture* (1871), long dominated the science of religion, and has its devotees today. But it has also met with widespread skepticism. The late Rudolf Otto tersely expressed one major objection: No one has any religious relationship to ghosts.

THE PREANIMISTIC THEORY

This theory of religious evolution was long ago questioned by Tylor's own pupils, R. R. Marett and Andrew Lang, as not in accord with the facts. In the so-called primitive stage, mythologies dealing with gods can be shown to have existed side by side with belief in departed souls and animate nature. Moreover, there are peoples who seem devoid of belief in individual spirits. According to Marett, the origin of religion must be sought in the dynamistic conception of a general impersonal power which manifests itself in unusual phenomena and can cause extraordinary effects (belief in mana). The power so experienced can be conceived as an active will. Along with this primeval experience, Marett argues, goes the instinct that dangerous powers (negative mana) must be fended off (idea of taboo).

The objection has been raised that the concept of power is never experienced as an abstract, impersonal force, but always as the faculty of persons or a quality of objects. The possession of "power" and its application to magic acts might explain the origin of magic, but not of religion as a belief in divine powers. No succession in time of preanimism and animism can be demonstrated; it would rather seem that both forms of religion existed simultaneously, side by side.

THE THEORY OF ORIGINAL MONOTHEISM

This theory was developed from observations by Andrew Lang, who was able to demonstrate that the concepts of high gods in the sky developed by primitive Australian tribes were original with them. The theory was systematically worked out by the Jesuit father Wilhelm Schmidt (*Der Ursprung der Gottesidee*, 12 vols., 1912–1955) and his culturo-historical school of ethnology. At the beginning of all religious development, the argument runs, stood the belief in an omnipotent supreme being. In the course of cultural and historical degeneration, more recent peoples lost this belief and developed a cruder mythology of polytheism and spirits.

Thus, the argument goes, evolution has been from monotheism to polytheism because man, with increasing culture, felt the need for special deities as aids in his manifold enterprises. Then Jesus Christ came and taught men to believe in the Heavenly Father once more. But belief in a supreme being had been an essential component of the oldest cultures, for among Australians, Polynesians, Zulus, Bushmen, Congo tribes, and Mongolians can be demonstrated the worship of a "Primal Father." Father Schmidt further attempted to divide cultures into classes—herdsmen, hunting, cattle-raising cultures, and so on, and argued that there had been a number of original "cultural spheres." Similar opinions on belief in a supreme God have been advocated by R. Petazzoni, N. Söderblom, and G. Widengren.

The opposing school of ethnologists and religious scientists has contended that such observations have been limited to contemporary primitives, and that to equate these savages with primitive man of tens of thousands of years ago is pure speculation. Moreover, certain Christian "prejudices," such as the doctrine of revelation, lurk in the background of this theory. The facts lend themselves to a great diversity of interpretation. For example, in ancient Greece Zeus was not the original supreme god from whom the other gods developed. On the contrary, polytheism clearly marked the beginning of the Greek religious evolution. Hence the Dutch scholar van der Leeuw and others have argued that the concept of a single God is a latecomer in the history of religions.

We know, in fact, nothing certain about the origin of religion and its primitive stages. Perhaps we may well fall back on the old Latin dictum for the origin of the gods: *primo omen, deinde nomen, postea numen* ("first the sign, then the name, then the divinity"). All evolutionary constructs are unproved and unprovable. Nor can they help us to any conclusion, because every historical religion must obviously be understood in terms of its own tenets and its own peculiarities. To set a beginning for any religion, historically or individually, is an untenable procedure.

Man always stands in the midst of a historical development that has already determined him. In no respect does he create beginnings—nor can he, in religion either. This observation applies equally to so-called primitives. We never discover a primal religious experience, no matter how far back in time we pursue the written sources of history or the archaeological monuments of prehistory. We never encounter a first religious experience, or the birth of a divinely directed primal emotion. On the contrary, always and everywhere we find an existing, institutionally developed religion, and people whose life is already lived within religious institutions.

If we examine the essential content common to all the developed religions we know, we might perhaps cautiously suggest that everywhere we find the striving for a lost unity. Religion always proceeds from an existential dichotomy between man and the world, between man and God or the gods. Man longs for unity, longs to overcome the dichotomy; wholeness rather than division seems to him necessary for living. But—and this is the crucial element—he can never achieve in reality the unity he seeks. Thus the essence of religion may be seen as springing from contradiction, at the focus and source of which stands the dichotomy of life itself.

BASIC IDEAS OF THE SCIENCE OF RELIGION

THE COMMON feature of all religions is that they move men to the depths of their beings, because religious feeling is rooted in the core of human existence. For religion's sake, man is prepared to assume any burdens; for religion he practices renunciation and asceticism. Most of the great monuments of art have sprung from religious impulses. For religion's sake, wars have been fought and men crucified. Religion governs man's whole being; but religion does not have its origin in the depths of the human soul. Rather, the soul's depths must be touched and moved by something else. Rudolf Otto, the great German student of religions, has called this something from outside "holiness." Certainly, the religion a person holds is some indication of the kind of person he is; but this is true only insofar as he has a distinct relationship to some kind of holiness, which it is necessary to understand.

HOLINESS

Just as the central concept in art is beauty, in ethics goodness, so in religion it is holiness. Rudolf Otto in his famous book *The Idea of the Holy* has described holiness as the basic experience of all religions. By way of illustrating his meaning, he refers to the biblical account of Jacob's awakening from his dream of the ladder (Genesis, 28: 17 ff.). "And he was afraid, and said, 'How awesome is this place. This is none other than the house of God, and this is the gate of heaven.'" Jacob has discovered something about the place that he had not previously observed. His discovery entails a feeling of awe. To this is joined a statement of his conclusion: This is the house of God, the gate of heaven. That sentence expresses the reality of holiness. The biblical text continues with the description of an act of ritual: Jacob pours oil over the stone on which he slept, and sets it up as a pillar, for the discovery of holiness brings in its train the act of veneration.

Holiness is always experienced as a dual feeling, both attracting and repelling, delighting and frightening, as *fascinosum* and *tremendum*. Man finds in it the fulfillment of his longings, and at the same time the very opposite. Rudolf Otto sums up these elements in the concept of "the numinous." In the account of Jacob's dream the word *awesome* could be replaced by *numinous*. Holiness is filled with power; to touch it is dangerous. The children of Israel may not approach the vicinity of Mount Sinai. Even Moses, at the burning bush, is enjoined: "Put off the shoes from your feet, for the place on which you are standing is holy ground." There are many other examples in the Bible of the "fear of God."

But this must not be misunderstood as did the Roman writer Petronius, who coined the phrase: *timor fecit deos* ("fear created the gods"). Before fear comes, there must be something that is feared, something from which man protects himself or even hides, as the prophet Isaiah hides his face when the glory of Yahweh appears in the temple. And on the other hand, the people of Bethshemesh are "smitten" by the divine presence when they look curiously into the ark of Yahweh instead of saluting it reverently (I Samuel 6: 19).

Among primitive tribes and in many popular religions, holiness is dispersed among a variety of objects. The deities are holy, but so are the places where they live—trees, mountains, caves, springs, temples, altars. Persons who serve the gods are holy—magicians, priests, prophets—as are ritual acts: signs, words, sacrifices, implements and images of the gods. But holiness never confronts the observer as a quality linked with many others. Rather, it is always felt to be the mysterious total "otherness," infinitely superior, sublime power, the absolute.

Finally, we must consider the ambiguity of holiness, which is also expressed linguistically: Latin *sacer*, Hebrew *kadosch*, and Arabic *haram* mean both holy and accursed, as well as impure. In the Talmud, which is a collection of Jewish laws and religious traditions, the statement is made that the holy scriptures stain the hands of those who carry them. Both holiness and impurity can be dangerous to man, and both are therefore avoided. Originally they were polarities; only later developments—in the Prophets and the New Testament—converted them, by a process of ethical differentiation, into antitheses. In any case, depending on man's maturity, holiness appears to the religious sense in various guises, and is venerated with greater or less appropriateness.

Nathan Söderblom in his article "Holiness" in the *Encyclopedia of Religion and Ethics* has put the matter in a nutshell:

> Holiness is the great word in religion; it is even more essential than the notion of God. Real religion may exist without a definite conception of divinity, but there is no real religion without a distinction between holy and profane. . . . An idea of God without the conception of the holy is not a religion. Not the mere existence of the divinity, but its *mana*, its power, its holiness is what religion involves.

Consequently, the definition for piety should read: "That man is pious to whom something is holy." It is holiness that first awakens reverential awe, the fear of God.

MANA

Everywhere in the wide world of religion, holiness is understood as a mysterious power linked with certain beings, events, or modes of action. The concept of holiness held by the ancient Germanic peoples shows this with particular clarity. Holy, hail, hale, and whole all derive from the same word; to hail a person is to wish him the power of haleness. It expresses more than congratulations or admiration. Essentially, the Melanesians of the Pacific mean the same thing when they speak of *mana*. Everything that goes beyond normal human capacity or the natural course of things can be or have mana. Among the Melanesians, mana is both a noun and a verb. Transitively, the verb *manag* means: to communicate mana or influence by mana. An object which contains mana is said to mana; that is, the verb is also used intransitively. A man, on the other hand, has mana; he cannot very well be said to mana or to be mana. Melanesian religion consists in snaring this mana for oneself in order to use it for one's own advantage. We would have to call this magic, since for us, an indispensable element of religion is that man approach the power or powers with awe or reverence. Among Melanesians and Polynesians that is not the case; they treat mana merely as a means or instrument. But on the primitive level of religion it is scarcely possible to draw a sharp distinction between religion and magic. In the original conception of mana, sorcery and magic, reverence for holiness and religious worship, exist side by side, unseparated. On the one hand, the concept of mana probably fostered the development of personal divinities; on the other hand, it is also the root for pantheistic notions of supernal powers. In the sphere of Semitic religion, the concept of mana was absorbed by the experience of God's holiness, which is at once feared and desired.

The classic description of Melanesian mana was written by Robert Henry Codrington, a missionary to Melanesia, in a letter to Max Müller, the Anglo-German Orientalist and religious scientist. Müller published this letter in 1878. Codrington described mana as a supernatural, invisible force possessed by the strong man—above all the chief and the medicine man. It can, however, also be communicated to animals, plants, and stones. Mana is potential energy, comparable to an electric charge. It is contagious and thus transmissible, and in the Melanesian view can be harnessed. Objects possessing mana are called fetishes—a Portuguese word introduced at the end of the eighteenth century by Charles de Brosses. Fetishes are striking objects, unusual stones, chains, and so on, which confer supernatural powers upon their possessors because mana is stored up in them. Amulets, talismans, mascots, all of which fend off misfortune, occur the world over as expressions of fetishism, and in all stages of religious development.

The American Indians also have ideas, corresponding to belief in mana, of a mysterious vital power permeating all things. Among the Sioux this is called Wakanda, among the Iroquois, Orenda, and among the Algonquin, Manitoo. Recent, chiefly American, research tends to identify mana and parallel beliefs less with a free-floating, mysterious primal power than with a power connected with persons, a talent for producing unusual effects.

TABOO

As we have seen, mana can also be dangerous. This property of danger leads to the concept of *taboo,* which means literally something marked out as forbidden, in contrast to ordinary things (*noa*) which can be freely handled. The word comes from the Tonga dialect, which is spoken on the Friendly Islands. Taboo may be regarded as negative mana.

Notions of taboo occur in almost all religions. For example, the entire Taharoth, the laws concerning cleanness and uncleanness in the Old Testament, are based on taboos. Leviticus 5: 2–3 reads: "If any one touches an unclean thing, whether the carcass of an unclean beast or a carcass of unclean cattle or a carcass of unclean swarming things, and it is hidden from him, and he has become unclean, he shall be guilty. Or if he touches human uncleanness of whatever sort the uncleanness may be with which one becomes unclean, and it is hidden from him, when he comes to know it he shall be guilty." Here breach of the rules of taboo is regarded as a sin against the deity, which makes the man guilty. We can clearly perceive the age-old notion that any contact with something taboo, that is, forbidden or unclean, is in itself dangerous, whether that contact occurred wittingly or unwittingly. For example, the fact that the pig is unclean to the Jews does not mean that it is a profane and indifferent animal. If it were, it could be used and eaten without fear. Rather, it is—or was—a demonic animal in the negative sense. Obviously, a taboo was at one time connected with the pig.

Naturally, anything may become taboo; but taboos arise above all about such beings and things which arouse instinctive repugnance in men. Thus we find that corpses have become taboo in almost all the religions of the world. Numbers 19: 14–16 reads: "This is the law when a man dies in a tent: everyone who comes into the tent, and everyone who is in the tent, shall be unclean seven days. And every open vessel, which has no cover fastened upon it, is unclean. Whoever in the open field touches one who is slain with a sword, or a dead body, or a bone of a man, or a grave, shall be unclean seven days."

The dead person and everything that pertains to him is probably taboo because death represents the great breach in the course of earthly life. There are peoples who cannot believe that death ensues from natural causes. They regard death as a mysterious evil force and take the same view of sickness. For fear of contagion is genuinely primitive. The ancient discovery, basis for many a taboo, that cadaveric poisons can be dangerous to the living, was adopted in ancient Israel into a ritual context, cleanness being made the indispensable prerequisite for participation in public worship.

Another common feature among most peoples is the fact that certain persons are taboo at times—for example, women during their periods, during pregnancy, and in childbed; or bride and bridegroom are taboo to one another until the day of the wedding. In Polynesia they were kept strictly segregated from all associates. There are also permanent taboos, with which kings, chiefs, priests or the images of gods are surrounded. Such a taboo applied to the Israelite high priest, who was not allowed to be present even at the funeral of his father or his mother, so as not to incur uncleanness (Leviticus 21: 11). Similarly, the *flamen dialis*, the priest of Jupiter in Roman religion, was surrounded with an extensive system of tabooistic rules. Prescriptions regarding taboo, and the ritual of purification when taboos were infringed, often formed the basis for the entire social order.

Both holy and unclean things can be taboo and must be avoided because they are dangerous. Often infraction of a taboo is automatically punished by a kind of autosuggestion. Söderblom tells of a Negro who learned that he had eaten a forbidden animal; he instantly fell ill and died. In other cases the community inflicts the punishment. That is why medicine men and priests are indispensable to primitive peoples; they alone know all the perils that threaten men from the infection of taboo things, and they alone know the rites which protect against such dangers and attract beneficent forces.

Finally, there are holy places such as the *marae* (Polynesian temples), graveyards, and so on which have been declared taboo and designated as such by stone markers. Most religions have such *loci sacri*. Not only are there taboo places; there are frequently taboo days also, consecrated to the gods, when trade and legal proceedings must cease: *dies nefasti*. Among the Romans it was the fifth day in the week. Among the Babylonians, the seventh day was sacred to the god Marduk. The Jews, in choosing this day for their Sabbath, raised it to a higher religious sphere.

SACRED KINGSHIP

The original position of chieftains and kings belongs among the notions connected with taboo. Frequently these rulers were regarded either as gods themselves or as the representatives of the gods. In the Near East, especially in Egypt, Babylonia, and Iran, we encounter the conception of sacred kingship. Vestiges of it existed in ancient Israel. It was also well established among African herding peoples, such as the Shilluk Negroes on the White Nile. The king is venerated as a concentration of power, and surrounded by strict taboos so that the power will, on the one hand, not run away and, on the other hand, not endanger people by its emanations. If the mana of a ruler was considered to be exhausted, he would, among many peoples, be put to death (sacral regicide).

Among the Jews the Mishna tract known as the Sanhedrin (2, 5) set forth a number of such taboos for the king. No one was allowed to ride on the king's horse, sit on his throne, grasp his scepter. It was not permissible to see him sitting naked, or when he had his hair cut, or when he was in the bathhouse, and so on. Similar rules applied to the *flamen dialis*, the priest of Jupiter. Many kings were shut up inside special palaces, where no one except a few select persons was permitted to see him or come into contact with him. Such was the case with the emperor of Japan, who until 1868 was required to stay inside his palace, while the royal dignity was actually exercised by the shogun. The young emperor Mutsuhito (1868–1912) was the first to break with this custom; he took over the government himself, moved the capital from Kyoto to Edo, which is now called Tokyo ("eastern capital"). As is well known, until 1945 the Japanese emperor was regarded as the son of the Sun and literally a god on whom the welfare of the whole people depended.

Among some primitives, the tribesmen must not even speak of the chieftain's head in which mana is incarnate with especial strength. No one may eat leftovers from the king's dishes; they must be destroyed.

The ancient Roman customs, which surrounded the king with a great many taboos, are likewise illuminating. The king was not allowed to remain with ordinary persons and not permitted to walk on the ground, since that would make it sacred. Instead, he had to be carried in a litter. He was not allowed to eat in the presence of others. Similar rules applied to a number of African chieftain-kings. The explorer Stanley recalled that when he met King Mtesa in Ganda, the king came forward toward him only the length of the leopard skin that was laid before him so that his feet would not touch the ground. The red carpet still laid down from a railroad train to the waiting automobile when royalty arrives is a vestige of this ancient taboo. A similar taboo underlay the ancient court ceremonials of Austria and Spain which required subjects to drop to the ground before the king: the taboo in this case being that the subjects were not supposed to see the king. This same custom existed in Egypt, Babylonia, and Persia. Until 1945 in Japan the people had to turn their backs on the emperor when he rode through the streets on rare occasions.

In ancient China the emperor was called the Son of Heaven. Among the Incas of Peru, the rulers were regarded as sons of the sun. Among the Aztecs in Mexico they were venerated as gods. When they acceded to the throne, they had to take an oath that they would let the sun shine, would give rain to the clouds, and would command the earth to bear fruit. We find similar notions in Babylonia, where the accession of the king was called his "grasping of Marduk's hands." In the Persian Avesta we find the concept of *hvarena,* the mysterious gift of power inherent in a king (charisma). The word might be rendered as "radiance of fortune"; its possession proved that a man was destined to be legitimate ruler of Persia.

Similar views and rites probably existed in ancient Egypt. The Upsala school of religious scientists maintains that the celebration of the king's accession originally meant that he was being placed on the throne as Yahweh's son and representative. The editors of the biblical texts expunged this Canaanite tradition, but traces of it may still be found. Thus there are certain psalms which may once have been sung at the king's accession, such as Psalm 2, in which God speaks to the earthly king: "You are my son, today I have begotten you." Perhaps the words of the prophet Isaiah (42: 1) refer to the consecration of the king, Yahweh himself saying: "Behold my servant, whom I uphold, my chosen in whom my soul delights; I have put my spirit upon him, he will bring forth justice to the nations."

THE THINKING OF PRIMITIVE PEOPLES

IT IS erroneous to speak of a special form of religion reserved for primitives—meaning by that term the "savages" of the interior of Africa, Australia, and the Pacific islands. It would be more to the point to speak of a special magical way of thinking which can be observed among present-day primitives and which we may assume existed in the earlier stages of ancient thought. According to Wilhelm Dilthey, the sixth century B.C. may be regarded as a dividing line. Before that time, he maintains, the dominant view of the world was a magical one which produced myths. These myths, he argues, emerged "out of the daily petty traffic with objects." Man sought some support against the aspects of the world he could neither understand nor control; to his mounting fear of life he opposed substantial images. The world in which "primitive" man lives has been compared to an electrically charged atmosphere. Thunder and lightning are everywhere, and the lightning may strike at any moment. The actual charge is numinous rather than electrical; that is, the atmosphere is charged with divine forces. Out of such generalized awe and dread both taboos and myths seem to have arisen.

MAGICAL THINKING

This precursor of rational consciousness has frequently been called magic. It has also been called prelogical, prerational, or mythic. The French ethnologist Lévy-Bruhl discussed it in an epoch-making book published in 1909. He pointed out the mystical character of mythic ideas, their prelogical nature, and the law that the part is equivalent to the whole. In other words, in such early thought, the bird's feather is regarded as the same as the bird. Primitive peoples, of course, were not yet able to submit their associations of ideas to the test of logic. Nevertheless, the opinion has gained ground in recent decades that there is no fundamental difference between primitive logic and our own; that both are merely early and later stages of the same development.

One of the characteristics of our mode of thinking is that we can think in species and in generalities. We speak of trees, mammals, birds, meaning all the various kinds of trees, mammals and birds on earth. Primitives are said to be unfamiliar with this kind of generalizing. To us, a camel is always a camel, whether it is male or female, young or old, whether it walks, stands, or runs. To the primitive all these are quite different phenomena, for which reason he frequently uses entirely different words for the various guises of the same animal. On the other hand, primitives see relationships where we do not. To us, a bird and a tree are two separate things; but if a bird always nests on the same tree, the primitive regards the bird and tree as belonging together and will identify them with the same word. Similarly, for almost all primitives there exists an identity between a living being and inanimate things that belong to it. A snipped fingernail or a clipped hair is identical with the person to whom they belonged; what happens to the nail or the hair happens to the person. Hence the widespread custom in lower stages of culture of carefully hiding or burning nail-parings, hair, excrement, and so on.

Primitives have the same feeling about their own names. In a man's name is his whole ego. Someone who knows his name might acquire power over him by using magic spells. The fairy tale of Rumpelstiltskin embodies this notion. Hence, many primitives do not pronounce their names before strangers, or they use a false name. The underground Communist movement still avails itself of this psychological precaution, though it may also have its practical side as well. Similarly, some peoples conceal the names of their gods, so that unauthorized persons will not obtain power over the gods. The name becomes taboo and cannot be pronounced. In ancient Israel only the high priest knew the sacred name of God; he whispered it into the ear of his successor, for which reason we do not know today how it was actually pronounced. To this day the Jews circumlocute the name, using

"Lord" or "the Name," and at any rate never pronouncing the four consonants, YHWH, that compose the name.

Another aspect of magical thinking is the idea of the soul, which is identified with the life-force. For all of nature, animals, mountains, plants, rivers, are regarded as animated, and all natural events as filled with spiritual forces. Hence the soul is equally present in all parts of the human body. If a girl procures a lock of her sweetheart's hair, she has him entirely in her hand. If he breaks faith and she burns the lock of hair, the faithless lover will die.

The substance of the soul or the life-force can be transmitted by the spoken word. That is why blessings play so great a part in primitive thinking. If the hand is laid on someone's head and a blessing spoken, spiritual force is transferred to that person. This blessing can never be taken back, as the story of the blessings of blind Isaac shows. Intending to give his firstborn son Esau the blessing, Isaac is tricked by Rebecca into blessing Jacob. The blessing cannot be recalled, for when it was spoken Jacob received the vital force as a permanent possession.

The case of curses is similar. A curse pronounced inevitably leads to the doom of the person accursed. For that reason curses, insults, war songs mean so much to primitives who are setting out to make war on another tribe. Before battle they must assemble and sing songs of hatred against the enemy, who will thus be robbed of vital force.

Mythic-magical thinking is based on the principle of effect by similarity. For example, water must be poured out if rain is to fall. Furthermore, there are contagious acts. Contact transmits strength; hence, to be struck with a shoot from a flowering tree will communicate vitality. Finally, there are acts of sympathetic magic. The spears hurled into the air during a war dance will strike the most distant enemies; inflicting injuries on a doll, or piercing an image, will cause pain or death to the person depicted.

In all these notions we are dealing with forms of early logic which preceded the rise of a rationalistic culture. This can be called "magical," since the law of inner necessity always is characteristic of magic. Remnants of this kind of thinking are found to this day in the popular beliefs of many tribes and peoples.

Magic has often been conceived as a precursor of religion and also as a degenerate competitor of it. Both views are incorrect. Magic has nothing at all to do with religion; it is neither preliminary stage nor decadent variant. Magic belongs to an early view of the world that did not yet distinguish between the living and the lifeless, the organic and the inorganic. Sir James G. Frazer went so far as to term magic the primitive's effort to practice science by reversing the principle of causality in his efforts to direct natural forces. That is conceivable, for the magical view does not reckon with causalities in our sense, but with forces and effective influences which embrace both the spiritual and the material realms. Religion arose out of the failure of such activity, Frazer holds—as an expression of magic's incapacity to actually master the phenomena of the world.

This is a seductive argument—but it cannot be reconciled to the facts of the history of religions. Nowhere has magic ever graduated into religion. As Rudolf Otto commented in regard to this theory: "It is turning matters upside down to attempt to derive numinous power from magic power; for before the magician can acquire it and before he can manipulate it, it has long since been perceived as numinous in plants and animals, in natural processes and natural things, in the dread of bones and also independently of all these." The veneration for strangely shaped stones in early times, Otto argues, must be attributed to the experience of mysterious, numinous powers. Magic only begins where religious worship is passed over and man uses the power of the stone to cure illnesses, say; in other words, where he makes it serve his ends and reduces it to a profane power. The magician is equipped with supernatural secrets, but he does not venerate them; he employs them.

The difference between religion and magic consists, according to Nathan Söderblom, in precisely that: in religion man venerates the deity, while in magic he attempts to coerce the divine principle for his own purposes. In religion, the deity is the master; in magic, man is the master. To be sure, magic also can have dealings with spirits and gods. But characteristically, the deity is regarded as a mere instrument in the hands of the magician, not as a power above men.

Religion and magic, then, are magnitudes of different qualities. In the early history of mankind they may have been interlaced; but later magic became pure sorcery, and the evolving of religion repressed the magical elements. Magic was seldom completely extirpated, however. The biblical account of Saul's visit to the witch of Endor reveals that even in so-called high religions there is always the chance of a relapse into magic.

The real contrast between magic and religion appears most clearly in the higher stages of the history of religions, for then magic is branded as the most dangerous enemy of religion. The essence of religion is humility and trust. The essence of magic is bold self-glorification. There is an element of megalomania in magic, for the magician thinks himself capable of making rain fall and changing the course of the heavenly bodies. Religion in the true sense begins when man feels his full insufficiency in the face of a power that fills him with fear and reverence. Religion comes to life in a man only when recognition of his own faults and limits has forced him to his knees before the supernatural; only—as Söderblom puts it—when he finds genuine dignity in submission to the elementary existential power of God.

Ultimately, magic is an ideology, and no religion can develop out of an ideology—at most a substitute for religion. And something inherently ersatz will never become something genuine, any more than chicory can be transformed into coffee. Thus magic may be the framework within which the oldest religion evolved, but it is neither a preliminary stage nor the "root" of religion.

On the other hand, religion and magic can often overlap, resulting in a degeneration of religion into magic. The rituals and formulas of prayer tend to become impious means of coercing the gods. Such characteristics developed in the later stages of Egyptian religion, in Chinese Taoism and elsewhere. The history of revelation in the high religions has usually been the story of liberation from magical elements, even though a good many survivals of the magical mode of thought were carried along with the religion for a long time. The distinction between magic and religion may then be summed up as follows: In religion man "encounters" a power that stands above him and summons him. In the summons and in man's obedient response lies the essence of religion. In magic, on the other hand, man seeks of his own accord to dominate reality, and believes in coercive effects and influences.

SHAMANISM

The religious magic of primitives is practiced by consecrated specialists, usually wise old men—medicine men, priests, shamans. Because the shaman has mana at his disposal, he can also command spirits, as in Siberia, Central Asia, among the Kirghizes, the Lapps and the Eskimos. The shaman's chief instrument for summoning spirits is, among the Lapps, for example, the magic drum on which heaven and earth are depicted. The spirits are forced by spells to enter this drum. The shaman transports himself by wild dances into an artificial ecstasy, a kind of self-hypnosis, and in this trance he travels through heavens and hells where he obtains various information from the ghosts of ancestors. The shaman's high prestige among Asiatic peoples depends on this "supernatural" knowledge he has. Frequently, the frenzied dances which continue to the point of utter collapse are the mark of an epileptic disposition which is transmitted hereditarily to his successors in the office. This disposition is often developed and intensified by an apprenticeship and by the practice of asceticism or the use of narcotics. The capacity for visions, hallucinations, and trances may be psychopathic in nature. The shaman typically develops a high degree of alienation from his own ego. In ecstasy, in speaking with tongues and in possession, the subject feels that a god or demon is saying something to him. Such experiences, of course, run through all phases of religion. In shamanism, however, a good deal of cunning and worldly shrewdness often mingle with the magical arts. Shamans usually are well versed in the properties of medicinal herbs.

With the evolution of religion to a higher stage, in which the cult of the gods becomes dominant, the shaman or magician develops into a seer and priest whose pre-eminent characteristic is knowledge of ritual and dogma. In those religions that stress destiny, the seer has the gift of learning the will of the gods of fate. Usually he becomes a prophet whose powers permit him to probe the whims of destiny. The priest, on the other hand, is more a functionary of public worship who must above all know how to venerate the gods and how to celebrate their rituals.

On the primitive level of magic or sorcery, we usually distinguish between white and black magic. White magic concerns itself with fertility, rainmaking, hunting success, spells to cure illness and attract love; black magic is concerned with war, revenge, harm, and killing. Both kinds endeavor to make the supernatural powers obey the will of man, either for the benefit or injury of the community. Shamanism, too, and the whole of primitive religion, must be regarded against the background of daily life in village and tribe. The forms it takes are governed by the uncontrollable happenings of everyday life in primitive communities. Hence it is often difficult to determine what is purely ethnic custom and what is religious. Shamanism undoubtedly partakes of both elements. That is also true for the very widespread institution of leagues of men.

EARLY AGE-CLASSES AND LEAGUES OF MEN

Among primitive peoples reception into the community of the tribe is accompanied by a variety of ceremonies, usually puberty rites. The attainment of male maturity is confirmed by symbolic or realistic ceremonies: tests of courage, circumcision and magical acts intensify the "true life" in the young men. A significant and extremely common rite is the novice's symbolic death and resurrection as a new man, often with a new name, and physically changed by minor mutilation. The groups of initiates form so-called age-classes within the tribe, and in herding, hunting, and agricultural tribes these classes may band together into the leagues of men. If uninitiates are in the majority, the league becomes a secret society. Secret knowledge is transmitted to members only, and magical procedures are communicated only to the initiates. Such secret cults are simultaneously magical and religious. Fertility ceremonies are particularly important in these leagues, in which pederastic practices are common. In the beliefs of primitives, such leagues are guardians of magical powers to produce rain or fertility in men and animals.

TOTEMISM

The intimate connection between man and nature is expressed with particular force in the phenomenon we call totemism. It occurs principally among hunting and herding peoples who are completely dependent on nature. Certain rites are intended to equate man with the natural world and its growth processes, and thus assure man's security. Totemism springs from a view of the world permeated by a sense of the unity of all living things.

The word totemism comes from the language of the North American Ojibway Indians and the kindred Algonquins. Two etymologies have been proposed. The English writer J. Long, who in 1791 introduced the word and concept, gave *Totam* as the term for the now familiar totem pole which stood before the Indians' tents and symbolized the protective spirit of the clan. The Indians of the clan would not hunt, kill or eat the animal represented by the totem. Others, however, derive the word from *ototeman*, which in the language of those tribes means "of the clan of his brother's sister."

The oldest description of the tribes was written by Peter Jones, a baptized Ojibway chieftain who became a Methodist priest. He relates:

"The Ojibway explanation for the division of their tribe into various clans is that many years ago the Great Spirit gave his red children their toodaims so they would never forget their kinship and so they would remember to help one another in times of hardship and war. When a travelling Indian runs into a strange band, he must always first find out whether they carry the emblems of his own clan. If this is so, he can be sure of a friendly reception. In the past, it was considered unlawful for carriers of the same toodaim to intermarry, but later on this was forgotten. Each Indian tribe has its own animals or things as toodaims; the Ojibway Indians have the following: reindeer, otter, bear, beaver, birch-bark, white oak, bear's liver, and so forth."

In this description, written in 1856, we find all the characteristic elements of totemism. Man feels himself to be in closest relation to nature, which is frequently represented by an animal, more rarely by a plant or natural object. He must not kill or eat the animal because it is his nearest kin. Frequently he calls it his father or brother and regards it as his guardian spirit. Finally, the totem is the symbol of the social group to which the man belongs. In Australia especially, the entire social structure of many tribes depends upon an often extremely complicated totemistic system.

There are various varieties of totemism. In individual totemism, each person has his own totem from puberty on. In tribal totemism every tribe has its special totem. Half-tribal totemism divides the tribe into two halves—the men and the women. Finally, in territorial totemism the totem rules over a particular area, independently of blood relationships, while in cult totemism various cultic groups have their own totems. In tribal and half-tribal totemism, the totem is almost always inherited through the mother, who symbolizes participation in the communal life. In other forms of totemism, the father's totem is passed on to the sons. Totemism is usually linked to exogamy; that is, marriage with a woman of the same totem is forbidden.

Sir James Frazer demonstrated (*Totemism and Exogamy*, 1910) that totemism was originally not inherited. Any totem can be embodied in any member of a clan, so that father and mother, son and daughter need not necessarily belong to the same totemic community. Frazer calls this totemism based on conception. Tribes in the interior of Australia are said to be in a state of transition at this very time from the totemism of conception to hereditary totemism. Frazer defines totemism as an artificial sociological structure for magic purposes, an organized and corporative system of sorcery intended to afford the members an ample supply of the goods of life and to protect them against threatening dangers in their environment.

No one has been able to determine how totemism originated. Totems, of course, must not be conceived as deities. In the strict sense, totemism has nothing to do with religion. Totemism and animal worship are also entirely different phenomena. In animal worship, man is conscious of his tremendous distance from the animal he venerates as holy, and to which he offers his sacrifices. Totemism, on the other hand, establishes alliance and kinship between a clan and a specific species of animal. The totem animal is regarded as a member of the clan, is frequently considered a helper and protector, and may be appealed to in time of need, or before sleep. Totemism unites all members of a clan with all members of a whole animal species, whereas animal worship—for example, in Egypt—is addressed to an individual animal. What is venerated is not the likenesses but the differences from the species. Totemism, we repeat, is not religion but a social phenomenon. At best we can say it is a social tie in early stages of religion. Frazer and other scholars consider the totem a more binding tie than blood relationship because it expresses a mystic link on the part of groups of human beings to the numinous vital force of an animal or even a plant.

BASIC MODES OF RELATIONSHIP BETWEEN MAN AND DEITY

M AN has always attempted to enter into a personal relationship with the power he fears, with the deities he worships and wishes to placate. The basic modes in which this relationship is expressed are offering, prayer, ritual acts.

OFFERING

We can discuss only the most important of the many types of offering: gift, sacramental, primitial (offering of first fruits), and expiatory:

Gift offering. By this form of offering, which arose early in the history of religion, we mean a gift made to a deity or power on the principle of *do ut des*—I give so that you will give. We may also speak of votive offerings: gifts promised, for example, by a man in moments of peril if the god helps him out of the emergency or fulfils some other urgent desire.

The basic idea of the gift offering is that the deity needs the things the man is presenting, and will therefore provide protection in return. But the idea goes deeper than the superficial appearance of a swap would suggest. An act of communion is intended which will bring the giver into an intimate union with the recipient of the gift. A primitive feels that his offering incorporates a part of his soul. By giving, he places himself wholly within the power of the deity; his offering is intended as a pledge of the protective relationship or the mercy of the deity. This kind of offering was as common in ancient Hindu religion as in the Babylonian Gilgamesh epic in which the gods were regarded as materially dependent on the gifts. Among the ancient Israelites, minha was the special gift offering. The Mohammedans make votive offerings only if their prayers have been effective.

The most consistent notions about this kind of offering are probably to be found in Hinduism. By the gift offerings which "nourish
and strengthen" the god, the Brahmin wins power over him. If
the gods drink the offered soma, they undertake an obligation
toward the donor. Such notions constitute, in Max Weber's
terminology, "coercion of the deity" in contradistinction to "service of the deity."

Sacramental offering. This is closely akin to the conception of
gift offering. Communal eating of the offering is supposed to
create the same vital and spiritual substance, so that the donor
will share in the soul-substance of the one to whom the offering
is made. This idea underlies many clan and community feasts
which play so great a part in the lives of primitives everywhere
on earth. Those who are taken into the communion of the feast
belong to the community of the clan. The same principle is
present in the worldwide custom of breaking bread with a
stranger when he first enters a house, or serving him bread and
salt. This act makes him sacrosanct; he can henceforth feel absolute security.

There are two kinds of sacramental offering. One is the communion meal in which the sacrificed animal is eaten together
with the deity; the donor thereby partakes of its vitality. In the
second type, the sacrificed animal transforms itself into the
deity, so that the donor eats the god himself. The most exalted
form of this "communion offering" is the Catholic Mass, which
probably derives from Jesus' Last Supper with his disciples. In
this sacrament, when the priest speaks the commemorative
words, bread and wine are transformed into the real flesh and
blood of Christ, which the partakers of communion are then
given to eat, for in the Catholic view, at the moment of consecration the bread and wine are miraculously and realistically
transformed into the flesh and blood of Christ. The Calvinist
view holds that the sacramental act has only symbolic value,
while Lutheran doctrine stands midway between these extremes.
It has been said that different religious modes hang on this
factor: the symbolic view makes religion a matter of developing
ideas, whereas the realistic view changes the very situation of
man: after receiving the sacrament into which the deity has

entered, he becomes different from what he was, filled with vitality and blessing.

The celebration of a sacramental meal occupies a central place in all ancient mystery religions. "To dine at the table of the Lord Serapis," is the wording of an invitation from the Serapis-Isis mystery cult. The Attis mysteries likewise had a holy feast; the Eleusinian mysteries included a holy drink called *kykeon;* and in the Mithra mysteries the feast was celebrated with bread and wine in memory of the god Mithra's last meal on earth. The basic principle of the sacramental offering is always that physical contact with the consecrated elements will bring about spiritual union with the deity present in the sacrament.

Primitial offering. This form of offering is also very ancient. It consists in man's offering the first fruits of the harvest and field, or of the animals he has raised or the game he has killed, as a sacrifice to the deity—because the deity has a claim on them. Sacrifice of the first fruits was particularly widespread during the nomad stage of culture and in patriarchal pastoral societies. Once the offering is made, all the rest may legitimately be kept. The Bible reveals traces of this view, when, for example, Yahweh speaks to Moses: "Consecrate to me all the first-born; whatever is the first to open the womb among the people of Israel, both of man and beast, is mine" (Exodus 13: 2). This passage is of interest because it shows that the primitial offering was originally applied to man as well. Later, among the Israelites, the rigor of this demand was mitigated and an animal sacrifice was substituted for the child. To this day, among Orthodox Jews, the firstborn must be redeemed in the synagogue by an offering of money placed in the poor box. Incidentally, Abraham's offering of his firstborn may symbolize the transition from human sacrifice to animal sacrifice. So, at any rate, rationalistic Bible interpretations hold.

Expiatory offering. Another widespread practice is for man to make an expiatory offering in order to escape punishment after infringing the commandments of the deity. An animal is sacrificed in place of the man himself, and suffers as his representative. The spilling of blood is always an important element in such sacrifices, since in ancient times blood was envisaged as the bearer of life or even as life itself. Among the Greeks and many other peoples, the expiatory offering—especially offerings to the gods of the underworld (chthonic deities)—took place in the following fashion: the head and throat of the victim were pressed into a pit, so that the blood could run into the ground after the arteries were cut. The blood of the victim would then purify the man himself of all his sins. The ultimate version of this sacrifice is represented by the Christian doctrine of Christ's expiatory offering: the idea that Jesus Christ was sacrificed for the redemption of the sins of all men. "The blood of Jesus his Son cleanses us from all sin" (I John 1: 7).

The expiatory offering has given rise to many other rites and ideas, most of which involve the notion that blood has the property of cleansing. On this premise in both ancient Nordic religion and among the Israelites the walls of the temple and of ritual objects, or the doorposts of houses, were sprinkled with blood. In the latter case (Exodus 12: 7 ff.) it is explained that the Israelites in Egypt sprinkled their doors with blood so that the angel of death would pass over their houses.

Another type of expiatory offering was the practice of making an animal or even a man the recipient of all evil substances, and then killing it or him. Thus the Israelites would lead the scapegoat around their entire camp on the Day of Atonement, so that it would gather up all evil. The animal would then be driven out into the desert. Its death was intended to atone for the sins of the people. There were similar expiatory offerings to the god Marduk in Babylonian religion, among the Greeks in the festival of Apollo at Athens, when a criminal was hurled into the sea from the Leucadian cliffs. There are additional forms of expiatory and substitute offerings in which, for example, a part of the person is sacrificed. Possibly circumcision and even the tonsure of monks go back to such ideas.

Curiously, even the purity of the body can be sacrificed to the deity, as was done by temple prostitutes and minions; such practices were rejected by the Old Testament as *toebah* (abominations) in the eyes of the Eternal. Sacrificial excesses usually drew forth severe criticism, such as the fulminations of the Israelite prophets. Thus Isaiah 1: 11: "What to me is the multitude of your sacrifices? says the Lord. I have had enough of burnt offerings." Or Hosea 6: 6: "I desire steadfast love and not sacrifice, the knowledge of God, rather than burnt offerings."

A still more important link between man and deity is prayer—which, to be sure, is often found in close association with sacrifice, as in the Akkadian psalms, in the Vedas, and in Persian texts. In the advanced religions, prayer counts for more than anything else. "Devoutness and prayer are one and the same," said Schleiermacher, the German theologian and philosopher. And the Romantic poet Novalis wrote: "Prayer is in religion what thinking is in philosophy. Praying means practicing religion. The religious temperament prays just as the brain thinks."

That is true for all forms of religious life, for even among the most primitive peoples prayer occurs in the form of an address by man to the will he knows to be above himself. Prayers have been recorded among the Bushmen, among the Bataks of the Pacific, among the Cora Indians in Mexico. In the advanced religions prayer is always an appeal to God or man's answer to God's summons. Hence prayer is usually couched as dialogue and runs the whole gamut from the most servile humility and timid supplication to hearty confidence. We may classify prayers by content as prayers of petition, penitence, praise, and thanksgiving. The outward forms are as various as the religions of men. The Mohammedan squats on his prayer rug and frequently touches his forehead to the ground. In India the believer likewise prays in a squatting posture; in Christendom he kneels or stands with folded hands. Jews usually pray standing, the men with covered head. The direction of the prayer (*kibla*) in Islam is toward Mecca, among Jews toward Jerusalem, in the Mithra cult toward the sun, and among the early Christians toward the East.

According to the researches of Friedrich Heiler, prayer in the major religions may be divided into naive, prophetic, mystic, and liturgical prayer.

In naive prayer the individual human being spontaneously declares his wishes to the deity, appeals to it for help in hours of need, and at the higher stages of religion commends his soul to it. Such prayer always has the character of a dialogue and is addressed to a personal god. Fate cannot be worshiped, only adjured. And one does not surrender to a blind, impersonal power.

By prophetic prayer Heiler does not mean the prayers of the prophets, but the kind of praying that takes place in prophetic religions. Man's longing for perfection, his lamentations and sorrow over impurity, guilt, and his inability to do God's will, are the chief content of such prayer. Intercessory prayer is a common corollary of the type.

Mystic prayer springs from the mysticism present in all world religions. Mysticism tends to regard the deity as impersonal and to conceive the total immersion of individuality in the deity as the ultimate goal of salvation. "Prayer is nothing but a dissolution of the soul in God," says Tauler, the German mystic. God and man conduct a dialogue, but petition for anything specific ceases entirely. Such prayer is also often conceived as spiritual training in which the human soul lifts itself above the limitations of earthly life, and the petitionary prayer becomes devout meditation. In the literature of Catholic mysticism we may read of three successive ways or stages. First there is a stage of purification (*via purgativa*) in which the soul releases itself from the world of the senses and from sins and desires. In the second stage (*via illuminativa*) the soul is more and more illuminated by God's will, and prays that its own will may wholly coincide with God's will. Finally man experiences the third stage (*via unitiva*), total union with God in the sense so well expressed by Lutheranism's greatest mystic, Gerhard Tersteegen (1687–1769) in one of his psalms:

> I sink myself in Thee
> I in Thee, Thou in me.

Or:

> Dearest, burn what parts us
> Until we melt into oneness.
> Let me vanish utterly,
> See and find naught but Thee.

Liturgical prayer, of course, arose originally out of spontaneous prayers which were fixed once and for all for the purposes of public worship. Naturally, reducing prayer to rigid formulas may mean a sapping of its inner vitality; but this is not necessarily the case, for the supplicant can also couch his deepest emotions in well-established forms of expression. Still, there has been a grave degeneration of the original impulse when, as in Tibet, for example, prayers are transcribed on strips of paper and hung on poles to flutter in the wind, or are fastened to prayer wheels. The theory is that the prayer is pronounced whenever the paper flutters or the wheel turns. In such cases religion has been completely overgrown by magical elements, for the real character of prayer as direct address to the deity, as submission to the divine will, has certainly been lost.

But we may not legitimately draw conclusions about actual prayer from its degenerate forms. Real prayer, both individual and collective, always presupposes belief in a living God who speaks to man and can be spoken to, who enters into real dialogue with man. Friedrich Heiler has given a fine definition of prayer: "There are three elements that determine the internal structure of prayer as an experience: belief in a living, personal God; belief in his real, immediate presence; and the dramatic intercourse into which man enters with God. . . . In that living intercourse the forms of human social relationships are reflected."

Finally, we must mention some subsidiary forms of prayer which glide over into magic. There is prayer as a *magic formula*, as a word of power or a weapon—because the word is in itself powerful. Examples of that may be found among many primitive peoples, as well as among the ancient Germans and Romans. Thus, for example, the famous tenth-century Merseburg spells are formulas for conjuring. A spell always implies coercion. The *invocations* common in rituals, such as the primitive Christian *maran atha* ("Lord, come soon!"), lies somewhere midway between real prayer and magic spell. Finally, there is the oracle, which is found among primitives (Bushmen and others), in Chinese Taoism, among the Babylonians and Etruscans, among the Greeks and the Roman augurs. The oracle transmits messages from the power venerated in ritual prayer. The deity is supposed to reveal its will and answer questions from the priests—questions that usually concern the future. Here, too, we come back to the distinction between religion and magic; the key factor is whether the deity dominates the priest or the priest the deity.

Offering and prayer belong in a larger context, that of public ritual, which has almost as many components and modes of expression as there are religions and sects. Ritual gives dramatic form to the veneration of the deity and the form of the mutual relationship. Holiness "takes place" and is observed. Usually, the offering and prayer form the heart of the ritual, but it may also consist of dances, processions, sacred games, hymns and music. Ordinarily, rituals are limited to specific sacred places and times, and often special utensils, robes and masks are requisite.

In the masked dances of many primitive peoples, the dance represents spirits or gods and some event involving them. Thus the ritual dance to honor or delight the deity becomes an act of worship in which each participant has a share. The sacred dance was an essential part of the ritual, especially in the mystery religions. Rhythmic singing or instrumental music is an accompaniment of liturgy in nearly all cults and religions, the exceptions being Israel and original southern Buddhism.

Dance as prayer, aimed at achieving direct connection with the deity, can lead to ecstasy, in which the soul seems to be freed from the body and carried into the immediate presence of the god. "Drink the drink of ecstasy, burn in the fire of love," sings Omar Khayyám. The dancing god Dionysus, dancing satyrs and maenads on Greek vase paintings, or Eastern Jewish Chassidim, exemplify this sort of union with the deity sought by many peoples. Another form of it is glossolalia (speaking with tongues), a phenomenon of many religious movements in ancient and modern times; "it" speaks out of men, who no longer control their own speech. Such speech is usually gibberish, whose meaning must be extracted by interpretation. Paul the Apostle, who was familiar with these experiences, thought it preferable to speak five words with a clear mind than ten thousand words of glossalia (I Corinthians 14: 8–19).

Procession, too, is basically a form of dance, aimed at mobilizing the religious community. "Every procession is as it were sacramental, in that it places something sacred in motion and spreads the power of the holy thing over a certain area. In the sacramental procession, such as is practiced by the Roman Catholic Church, the blessing locked within the sanctuary spreads out over village and town, over field and meadow" (Gerard van der Leeuw).

Procession may evolve into religious drama. In the festival calendar of the ecclesiastical year, the Christian Church relives again and again the life and death of its Lord. It presents the events of salvation and redemption in its services as a symbolic drama. The Greek Orthodox Church does this with particular impressiveness. So also the death and resurrection of the vegetation god in Babylonia and Syria, or the sham battles fought between the adherents of the god and his adversaries in the Egyptian cult of Osiris, or the mystery of the sacred wedding in Eleusis and elsewhere, were intended as real, ritual links between the believer and the deity. Of course, magical notions also entered in—as, for example, among the ritual ball games of the Aztecs; it is thought that the imitative action will actually create what is represented and thus permit man to participate in salvation. Images and the veneration of images are also intended to be vivid representations of the presence of the god at the site of worship; veneration of icons in the Eastern Church is an impressive example of this practice. The Jews alone do not permit pictorial representation of God; Yahweh's ark was an empty divine throne. To the Jews, God might sometimes be heard but never seen.

Among the rituals of the biblical religions, finally, is the reading of scripture; that is, the solemn reading aloud of the Word of God, to which man responds with the *laudatio*, the praise of the Lord. Man can, however, also answer by the holy silence of deep emotion, thereby making it possible for "it" to speak within him. It has been well said that "silence in ritual does not mean empty moments of piety, but the moments of fulfilment." Wordless, inner prayer or "waiting silence" exists not only in the services of the Quakers, but also in the Hellenistic mystery religions and in the Chinese cult of Heaven. Above all, however, silence is the mystic's expression of true absorption; according to Meister Eckart, utter silence gives birth to the "hidden word" through which man attains to "illumination." Gnosticism even has a deity of silence: Sigé. Silence in religious ritual, then, can signify transmission of the highest revelation; it can also be a means to spiritual equanimity and, as in Buddhism, serve to overcome the passions and desires. The Lutheran hymnist Tersteegen sings: "By silence are they known for sure, who bear their God within the heart."

TYPICAL PERSONALITIES IN THE WORLD OF RELIGION

Among the *homines religiosi* who are forever reappearing in the world of religion, we may distinguish the following personalities: the founder, the prophet, the mystic, the priest and the reformer. They are all representatives of the religious message in their own fashion, and embody a number of the principal types of piety.

The founder determines the nature of the religion and exercises a decisive influence on every phase of its development. Not all religions are founder religions, but the group comprises some of the most important, such as Judaism, Christianity, Manichaeism, Mohammedanism and Buddhism. Every religion takes its start in a unique event projected into historical effectiveness by the divine gift (charisma) of the man who has experienced it. A religion is not founded like a religious club or a political or social movement. Its inception always has a monarchic character; those who are affected by the new historical reality gather around the founder as an intimate following. Primarily, the founder is the witness of revelation. He has seen or heard something; thereafter, the force of his charisma works creatively to form something new. The classically simple form is the founding of the Israelite religion, as told in the story of the burning bush—the appearance of God as a flame in the desert. Only one thing is essential to this story: God speaks, and the founder hears. The narrative in Exodus 3 reads: "God called to him out of the bush, 'Moses, Moses!' And he said, 'Here am I.'" What follows is likewise characteristic: "Do not come near," God says, and Moses removes his sandals and shrouds his face. The voice speaks: "I am the God of your father, the God of Abraham, the God of Isaac, and the God of Jacob. . . . I have come down to deliver Israel out of the hand of the Egyptians." This is the God of the forefathers who manifests his will in history, and here announces it to the founder. Moses' role is to fulfill the historical task imposed by his God. Henceforth, obedience is incumbent upon Moses, and loyalty upon his people.

With the one exception of Moses, all founders of religions have themselves become objects of religious veneration and adoration. Thus we find a cult of the founders in Christianity, Buddhism, Mohammedanism, Zoroastrianism, Manichaeism, Confucianism and Taoism.

Usually, a luxuriant growth of legends begins to twine around the life of the founder. A common theme is that the circumstances of his birth are not natural; the stories concerning the mothers of Buddha and of Mohammed are strikingly parallel to the Annunciation of Mary. Furthermore, there are similar accounts of temptations and transfigurations, of the assembling of a circle of disciples, and of miracles surrounding the death of the founder. Again, there are a wealth of parallels between the farewell addresses of Jesus according to the Gospel of John and the last words of Gautama Buddha. Within all these religions, there are contending conceptions of the nature of the founder. We need only think of the christological disputes in the early Christian church, the prophetological discussions in Islam, and the debates between Hinayanists and Mahayanists on the personality of Buddha. Frequently, the message of the founder is obscured by the interest in his personality.

All the founders of religions at first felt themselves to be merely emissaries who had a mission to carry out. Jesus declares that he was sent by the Father; Mohammed was a *rasul* (messenger) of Allah; the Tao speaks through Lao-tse; and Buddha, too, does not claim to have attained his Enlightenment entirely by himself. From the psychological and characterological points of view, these personalities were highly unlike each other. Nevertheless they all share the common trait of an inner composure; they all reject extremes and excesses. Even Mohammed, more inclined than the others to emotional radicalism, was no exception. More even than Mani and Zoroaster, he felt his mission to be the establishment of a definite political and social order in his own Arabic world. The other great founders were more concerned with the clarification and deepening of their religious message.

Every founder was venerated as the Master by his disciples. To the Master the disciples always have a threefold meaning: they are the representatives of humanity; they are his companions, personally close to him; and they are apostles who will proclaim his doctrine to the world. To the disciples, the existence of the Master represents a tremendous demand: that of total devotion. A profound saying of Jesus, recorded in the apocryphal Acts of John, expresses the essence of the matter, for he says to his favorite disciple: "For what you are, I show you. But what I am, I alone know, none other. Let me have what is mine; but see what is yours through me."

The relationship of Jesus to his disciples, of Mohammed to the fellows of the "League of Allah" and of Buddha to his followers differed greatly in point of detail, even though the structure of the group of disciples and the historical effects and spread of the doctrine present some surprising sociological similarities. But even as we note these, we must remind ourselves that the great founders of religions were always individuals, which is to say, personalities who cannot basically be compared with one another. They share a common affliction: that they are sorely pressed by the question of God or the Absolute. The founder's life itself points the way to an answer to that question. The founder shows the spot where eternity is to be discovered within the realm of space and time.

THE PROPHET

The prophet is the enunciator or the interpreter of a divine message imparted to him in visions or in "auditions," that is, in the hearing of divine voices. The distinguishing mark of the prophet is that he has been summoned. Thus almost all the prophets of the Old Testament were called, frequently against their will, into the service of the deity. For example, Jeremiah reports the summons he received from Yahweh as follows: "'Before I formed you in the womb I knew you, and before you were born I consecrated you; I appointed you a prophet to the nation.' Then

I said, 'Ah, Lord God! behold, I do not know how to speak, for I am only a youth.' But the Lord said to me, 'Do not say, "I am only a youth," for to all whom I send you, you shall go, and whatever I command you, you shall speak. . . . Behold, I have put my word in your mouth.'" This is the characteristic appointment of a prophet. A prophet is not equipped for his office by tradition and training, but by divine predestination and the call of the Holy Spirit. He is by no means the functionary of some organization. His task, from which he shrinks, is imposed upon him by the deity, which has chosen a weak man for its mouthpiece.

The mythical ideal king Yima of Mazdaism is similarly summoned: "And I spoke to him, I, Ahura Mazda: 'Handsome Yima, Son of Vivanhvat, be you a judge and propagator of my religion.' And handsome Yima answered me: 'I am not suited and not learned enough to be a judge and propagator of the religion.'" Zoroaster, too, is a prophet who must be compelled by Ahura Mazda to assume his task. Prophets, then, become such under duress of their deity: "O Lord, Thou has deceived me, and I was deceived; Thou art stronger than I, and Thou has prevailed," Jeremiah cries.

Jeremiah, Amos, Hosea are not real visionaries and ecstatics, but Ezekiel and the early band of prophets in the time of Elijah were. They dance themselves into a frenzy, behaving like shamans and medicine men. In fact, their ecstasy is infectious, as we may read in I Samuel 10: 10–11: "When they came to Gibeah, behold, a band of prophets met him; and the spirit of God came mightily upon him, and he prophesied among them. And when all who knew him before saw how he prophesied with the prophets, the people said to one another, 'What has come over the son of Kish? Is Saul also among the prophets?'"

As in early Israel, in Canaan, Babylonia, Assyria, Egypt, and especially in the primitive religions, there were also ecstatic prophets who believed that the spirit of the deity had entered into them and transported them into their ecstasy. But the religion of Israel produced a new phenomenon: great individuals who emerged from the ranks of these ecstatics, to interpret the history of the nation and cry warning. The new prophets of reform and revolution came forward with messages from Yahweh that contradicted the official religion of the country and opposed the desires and expectations of the people. Frequently they proclaimed what no one wanted to hear: judgment and doom, rather than good fortune and victory.

The prophetic personality is voluntaristic and purposeful, because the personal God is will and power. Allah's will, as proclaimed by Mohammed, is so exaggerated that it becomes almost a tyranny to which the believer fatalistically submits. According to the Old Testament prophets, Yahweh, the Holy One of Israel, has a propensity for raging and rejecting. He is an unapproachable mysterious God before whom the believer can only prostrate himself. The distance between god and man is strongly felt and stressed in prophetism.

Prophetic religion is involved with history. In particular, it looks forward to the close of history, to the end of all things. This element of future perfection may already be found in Zoroastrianism; Yasna 30: 2 reads: "When the judgment comes upon these blasphemers, then will your kingdom be prepared by Vohu Manu, O wise Lord." And a glance at the Koran reveals a similar motif. The most glorious title of Allah, the god with a thousand names, is "Lord of the great Judgment" (Sura 1: 2). Islam is the typical prophetic religion. The message of prophets is always disturbing, because it is directed against decadent or lifeless traditions and creeds. The fate of prophets, too, is typical: they are attacked and persecuted, and often martyred by their own people.

THE MYSTIC

While the figure of the prophet represents a clearly definable type of piety, the nature of mystical piety is considerably harder to grasp. It has been said that the mystic strives for the soul's emancipation from its physical bonds in union with God. Consequently, the mystic strives to kill all affective stirrings in body and soul. The ego itself must be destroyed in order for the apex of ecstatic experience to be achieved: the *unio mystica*, perfect mingling with the deity. Mysticism seeks abdication of being, "annihilation"; it is "cessation of outward seeing for the sake of inner perception," as Heinrich Zimmer once defined Yoga.

In contrast to the personal, voluntaristic god of the prophet, the god of mysticism is impersonal. He is described in terms of emptiness, absence of qualities and similar negatives. The nature of mysticism is usually quietistic, passive, concerned with pure inwardness. "Mysticism is esoteric; it tends to keep its insights secret and undertakes no missionary work" (Mensching). It is often quite indifferent to denominational distinctions. But above all, mysticism is wholly unhistorical and timeless, prophetism is extraordinarily concerned with history as the sphere in which the divine will is realized—its demands being expressed through the mouth of the prophet.

The mystic strives for the deepening and fulfillment of religious values within himself. "If Christ were born a thousand times in Bethlehem and not in you, you would be lost forever," writes Angelus Silesius. These words express the mystic's view of the salvational content of his religion. In transposing that content from the objective to the subjective realm, he revivifies it. Similar phenomena can be observed in all religions. Rudolf Otto has carefully compared the Hindu mystic Shankara and the German mystic Meister Eckart and shown how much they have in common, although their mysticism is rooted in an entirely different history and cosmology. Even Islam has produced mysticism. The nature of the religion would seem to obviate this. Nevertheless there are Mohammedan monks, which means meditation and hence the contemplative life.

There are, of course, many varieties of mysticism, extending all the way from pantheism to revelatory religion. Tor Andrae, the Swedish religious scientist, has written a book on the psychology of religion in which he distinguishes twenty-six different forms. All are marked by the spiritual attitude that results from a deliberate turning inward. Probably, the fundamental difference between prophetic and mystic piety may be traced back to two manners of cognition. Ordinary cognition consists in a cleavage between subject and object. One sees a tree; the retina of the eye is influenced. That happens to the mystic, too, of course. But he stares at the tree for so long, and expends so much psychic energy in contemplating it, that at last the experience of confronting an object vanishes and the tree enters into him, as it were. A merging of subject and object takes place. Transposed to the sphere of religion, this means a kind of absorption in God, the *unio mystica animae cum deo* (mystic union of the soul with God). Compared with the normal mode of access, with God always an object of human cognition, the mystic access represents a rare event, a reaching out to the limits of human potentiality.

THE PRIEST

The priest as a type is antithetical to both the prophet and the mystic. With the emergence of established cults and rituals, the priest develops out of the sorcerer or magician of primitive religions. Bound to rigid custom, the priesthood easily succumbs to the perils of degeneration and secularization. Criticism of the priesthood as such is a familiar theme to us. We have met it in the prophets of the Old Testament and Jesus, but we find it also in the preaching of Zoroaster.

As a religious leader, the priest is naturally counterposed to the laity (from Greek *laos*, "people"). Usually the priests form a closed caste arranged in a hierarchical order. As representative of the community, the priest is chiefly empowered to watch over the administration of public worship in general and sacrifice in particular. Sacrifices without priests are unknown in the history of religions. In addition, the priest can also be a seer, as was the case among the ancient Arabs and the Hebrews. The same word that in Hebrew means priest of the sacrifice (*kohen*) signifies oracular priest or seer in Arabic (*kahin*). After the taking of the land, the Levites became both sacrificers and takers of auspices, using for the latter purpose the holy lots, the Urim and Thummim. In daily life the priests also had judicial functions and were the representatives of the king in the temple. Gradually they acquired the privilege of alone performing the rites. Ultimately the Jewish high priest assumed all the religious duties of the king. The Levites, as the tribe of priests, were assigned the task of standing before Yahweh, of ministering to him, and of giving blessings in his name (Deuteronomy 10: 8). Their role was to transmit the blessing of Yahweh, the *berahka,* to the community. According to Numbers 6: 22 f., the climax of the entire divine worship was to be the priestly blessing. This blessing of the kohanim and the Levites is still part of the religious proceedings of the synagogue.

Priesthoods can be hereditary; they can also be conveyed by consecration and laying on of hands. A special priestly costume is customary. Not only in ancient Israel, but in Babylonia, in Egypt, in Rome and among the Sikhs of India, the priesthood assumed an extremely important position. In the Catholic Church, the consecration endows the priest with an "indelible character" which qualifies him for distributing the sacrament.

In every religion, the priestly type represents the conservative element, which tends to persist through all changes in culture and ways of life. Often the forms of ritual do not change for thousands of years. We need only think of the Catholic liturgy of the Mass or the Jewish service whose prayers have remained basically unaltered for between two thousand and twenty-five hundred years. This persistence is also manifested in the costume of the clergy. Present-day Franciscans still wear the dress of the thirteenth century. Frequently secular costumes become sacerdotal by thus being adopted by the clergy. Once these costumes become established, no one lifts a hand to change them, even though there are good reasons to do so—as in the case of Protestant clerical robes, which are simply the one-time gown of scholars.

THE REFORMER

We have finally to consider the type of the reformer. He is an innovator who combats old traditions for the sake of a still older truth. Often he considers himself the restorer of the primitive tradition. Cases in point are Zoroaster, the reformer of the Persian popular religion; Ramanuja, the preacher of divine love and religious justice in India; Shinran, the fourteenth-century reformer of Japanese Buddhism, who like Luther sparked a revolution by taking a wife, thus breaking with the old monastic ideal of asceticism. This break with religious custom in order to restore original truths characterizes all reformers. Even Buddha, who unlike the religious leaders of his age urged the restoration of the original ideal and called his disciples the "true Brahmins," was in this sense a reformer.

The effort to recall a church to its origins was particularly marked in the Reformation of Luther and Calvin. The reformer would in fact be closely akin to the founder were it not that his efforts are directed at reinterpreting existing tradition. Reformers always try to justify the novelties they propose as true traditions, and to discount the traditions they condemn as misconceptions. The Egyptian king Ikhnaton was just as much of a reformer in this sense as the Augustinian monk Martin Luther or the above-mentioned Far Eastern personalities, to whom we should add the lamaistic reformer Tang-Khapa of the beginning of the fifteenth century. The reformer always stands at the crossroads of tradition and innovation; his reinterpretation has two faces. The old is understood anew as a result of his rediscovery, while at the same time his revision of old views launches a new phase in religious evolution.

CLASSIFICATION OF RELIGIONS

We have distinguished various types of *homines religiosi*. Similarly, typical modes of religious association can also be discerned and traced through all known religions. Thus we might investigate congregations, orders, sects and churches, these being the four basic forms of organization which recur in the history of most religions. To define and compare these forms belongs to the special discipline called the sociology of religion, and would lead us far beyond the subject of this book. We must confine ourselves to classifying the types of religion. There are a number of approaches to this problem. Thus Gustav Mensching has suggested a triple classification into nature religions, folk religions and world religions. There is much to be said both for and against this classification.

By "nature religions" we mean the religions of primitive peoples who still live in close dependence on nature, whence they draw their religious objects. These religions are polytheistic, or rather polydemonic. Their world is filled with innumerable forces, or populated with formed and half-formed divine beings who are objects of local veneration. Unfortunately, the term is difficult to work with, since the sense of what is "nature" and "natural" changes greatly in the course of time. To the Papuans, nothing is more natural than that old people should be buried alive, whereas we regard the practice as an atrocity.

"Folk religions" is a term that is something of a catch-all for the religions of many civilized nations. There are folk religions whose gods represent natural cosmic forces, and hence serve as guarantors of existential order. The religions of Greece, Rome, Babylon, Egypt, ancient India, ancient China and of the ancient Germanic peoples fall into this category.

There are also folk religions which rest upon an older tradition and were given their shape by the personalities of founders. In the distinctly revelatory religions the deities appear as living, personalized powers, entirely separate from the cosmos. They manifest themselves in history. Such religions are molded by historical figures who acquire great personal authority. An example is the religious community of Israel, where an original nature religion was renounced as a result of a unique historical experience: the revelation of a personal God, the God of Abraham, who directs the destinies of the universe toward a specific end. He comes as judge and savior and establishes a divine dominion.

Most of the religions of the Orient do not exert a moral influence upon the course of history. In Israel, however, expectation of the redeemer runs through the whole of the national religious tension. The anticipated goal is a lasting kingdom of God. This tension was passed on to Christianity and Islam.

The "world religions"—most of which likewise spring from a founder—differ essentially from the folk religions in breaking out of the cultural and historical limitations of a given community. They are no longer restricted to a people or a sect, but appeal directly to individuals. The sanctity of God as the Lord of history is avouched by the historical revelation of the founder. There are, however, salvational religions which do depend on revelation and which are unhistorical in substance. Such are the Far Eastern religions: Buddhism, Taoism, Confucianism.

Other classifications might be set up in lieu of the one outlined here. Folk religions can be opposed to world religions, revelation religions to natural religions, primitive religions to advanced religions, founded to unfounded religions. There are also missionary religions as against those that disparage missionary activities. It is also possible to group those religions that believe in the one God hailed in the Bible as the creator of heaven and earth. Judaism, Christianity and Islam come under this head. Such monotheistic religions could be set apart from the polytheistic religions of Greece, Rome or the ancient Germans. A third group might be the "religions of the eternal world-law" in India and the Far East, which manage well without any concept of a personal God: Buddhism, Confucianism, original Taoism. A category would still have to be found for monotheistic currents in Hinduism, or for Zoroastrianism as a mean between two extremes, insofar as it advocates a consistent dualism and its supreme god, Ahura Mazda, is not the God of the Bible.

For our purposes, however, we shall choose two somewhat superficial aspects as the basis for our classification. We distinguish between dead or extinct, and living, still effective religions. Furthermore, we shall approach the problem geographically, recognizing that some of the living as well as the dead religions have remained limited to a particular continent, whereas others, starting on one continent, have sought to penetrate others. Hence we shall first consider the extinct religions outside of Europe, the religions of Babylonia, Egypt, Persia, and pre-Columbian America, then turn our attention to the extinct religions within Europe, those of the Greeks, Romans, Teutons, Celts and Slavs. From these we move on to the great religions of the East, the living religions of Asia: Hinduism, Buddhism and the religions of China and Japan. Finally, we shall turn to the religions of biblical revelation, which started in Asia but spread beyond that continent: Judaism, Islam and Christianity. Christianity, in particular, has of course become a world religion which nowadays has its strongest bastions in Europe and the Americas.

*Extinct Religions
Outside of Europe*

RELIGION IN BABYLONIA

Sumerians and Akkadians. One great source of the religions of Asia has been the fruitful delta of the Tigris and Euphrates rivers, the so-called Land of the Two Rivers, Mesopotamia, or as it is called from its ancient capital on the Euphrates, Babylonia. Toward the end of the fourth millennium B.C. that land was peopled by a race of unknown origins called the Sumerians, while further to the north, around 2600 B.C., the East Semitic Akkadians established themselves. The Sumerians developed the first advanced civilization of the Near East. They are also credited with the invention of cuneiform writing. Very early in their history, apparently, they merged a multitude of local cults into a theocratic system headed by the high god Enlil, "father and king of the gods." But since the Sumerians mingled around the middle of the third millennium B.C. with seminomadic Semitic immigrants from the north, it is impossible to trace clearly the various elements that went to form their religion. Later, waves of Cassites, Hittites and Aramaeans poured into the country. In the second millennium B.C. an Assyrian Empire was founded in northern Mesopotamia. For several centuries—from about 1100 on—it was a world power. Consequently, we speak today of a "Babylonian-Assyrian" religion—which represented a spiritual force in the vicinity of biblical Israel. The Neo-Babylonian Empire that arose after the collapse of Assyria and the fall of Nineveh (612 B.C.) flourished briefly under Nebuchadnezzar (605–562), but was conquered in 538 by the Persian king Cyrus and thenceforth disappeared from world history as an independent kingdom.

A large part of our knowledge of Babylonian-Assyrian religion we owe to Assurbanipal (668–626 B.C.), whom the Greeks called Sardanapalus, for this king had all the literary works and inscriptions available to him copied on clay tablets in cuneiform script for his palace library in Nineveh. In the middle of the nineteenth century these tablets were excavated by English archaeologists. The greater part of them are now in the British Museum. They provide an invaluable supplement to the references in the Old Testament and the statements of such classical authors as Herodotus and Strabo.

THE GODS

The Babylonian-Assyrian religion was distinctly polytheistic, and much closer to the world of Homer than to that of the Old Testament. It grew out of the local cults of many nature gods, since Babylonia originally consisted of a number of independent city-states. Apparently, each one claimed to be the image of the cosmos and the seat of the supreme god. Of the more than six hundred gods that were originally worshiped, the majority merged. The god of the more powerful city-states achieved hegemony over the others—as had been the case with the local gods of Egypt. Thus the dominion of Enlil in Nippur was replaced by that of Marduk, the city-god of Babylon, when King Hammurabi (circa 1955–1913 B.C.) made Babylon the political capital and religious center of the empire. Marduk, as god of Babylon and king of the gods, was a priestly creation in whose honor the existing astral system was revised. Incidentally, the Tower of Babel, mentioned in Genesis 11, was an actual structure. Excavations indicate that it was nearly three hundred feet high. It was part of the principal sanctuary of the god Marduk.

Assur, the belligerent local god of the city of that name, underwent a similar transformation. The Assyrians attached all the other gods to him by declaring them members of his court. The worship of Assur was practiced with particular intensity by King Sanherib or Sennacherib (705–681). In the Assyrian version of the creation myth, Assur became the principal figure in the New Year festival celebrated at the spring equinox. Furthermore, the Babylonian-Assyrians inherited from the Sumerians the blue-bearded moon god Nannar of Ur in the Chaldees, the starting point, Genesis tells us, of Abraham. Nannar had his principal seat in Haran under the name of Sin. The Akkadian Shamash (Sumerian Utu) was the sun god who presided over civil order and justice; he was worshiped at Sippur in the north and at Larsa in the south. He was considered the son of Nannar-Sin, which would indicate that the cult of the moon god was the older. Furthermore, the Babylonians worshiped the sky god Anu in Uruk, the city of the seven spheres. Ea (Sumerian Enki) was the lord of the fresh-water ocean, and Nergal the god of the underworld and the realm of the dead.

It is striking that divine trinities are prominent in this religion —which, however, contains no salvational elements. Thus, even in Sumerian times the Babylonians recognized the cosmic triad of static being: Anu, Enlil, Ea—Heaven, Earth and Water. Later they worshiped the astral triad of cyclical movement: Shamash, Sin, Ishtar, who represented the sun, moon and stars.

Ishtar, the Queen of Heaven (Sumerian Inana of Uruk; later in Syria, Astarte), is frequently identified with the planet Venus. Ishtar was the mistress of Arbela, where she had a famous oracle. She later became the goddess of Nineveh. She is particularly interesting because she absorbed several fertility goddesses and was worshiped by the Assyrians as the goddess of hunting and war and also of motherhood and love. Sacred prostitution was associated with her cult. She is usually pictured riding on a leopard, bearing bow, arrows and quiver; on her head she wears the indented golden circlet known as a mural crown, and above that the planet Venus. But there are also representations of Ishtar as a mother-goddess, naked, suckling an infant at her breast. Ishtar's son and lover was Tammuz—the Sumerian Dumuzi (meaning "genuine son"), who was known to the Phoenicians and Greeks as Adonis.

Tammuz increasingly assumed the character of a vegetation god, symbolizing the fading and the rebirth of plant life in the eternal round of nature. Every year Tammuz was consumed by the fire of the summer sun, just as the vegetation is parched; but his mother Ishtar was able to save him from death by a "harrowing of hell," going down for him into the "land of no return." The Egyptian Osiris myth was patterned on that of Tammuz. The hymns to Tammuz that have been preserved are lamentations in which the women chant a litany of woe over the passing of the god. The cult was still alive in the time of the prophet Ezekiel

(Ezekiel 8: 14). Later speculative theology converted Tammuz into a son of Ea and merged him with Marduk.

Finally there were Adad (West Semitic Hadad), the god of tempests, who was giver of rain and also riches; Ninurta, the Assyrian god of war and hunting; Dagan or Dagon, who appears in the Old Testament as the god of the Amorites and who was a god chiefly of the grain; and Marduk's son Nabu (Nebo in the Bible), the divine scribe who wrote the fate of men on wax tablets and who was particularly venerated in Borsippa, a sister-city of Babylon.

All these gods were either deified heroes of ancient times or personified forces of nature. If the latter, they were early anthropomorphized. Special priests administered the magical rites connected with the cults of all these gods. Thus the cults were closely linked with belief in ghosts and demons. But it must be emphasized that all the above-mentioned deities were regarded as personal gods with characters of their own, and that they were worshiped as unrestricted lords and masters. From the very beginnings of Babylonian history, the king was considered the representative of the god, and as such had priestly rights and functions.

MYTHOLOGY

The knowable cosmos was divided into a celestial, a terrestrial and an underground region, corresponding to heaven, earth and the primeval waters. The triad of gods corresponded to this tripartite universe. Among the basic concepts of Babylonian religion was the idea of correspondence between all heavenly and earthly phenomena. The stars were the secret writing of the gods, and men might learn to read and interpret that script. Consequently, the Babylonians early developed a science of the stars and carried out calculations of great precision. Both our seven-day week and our solar year of 365 days are of their devising. They assigned the seven days of the week to five planets and the sun and moon: Marduk-Jupiter (Thursday), Nabu-Mercury (Wednesday), Nergal-Mars (Tuesday), Ninurta-Saturn (Saturday), Ishtar-Venus (Friday), Shamash-Sun (Sunday) and Sin-Moon (Monday). The connection they established between the planets and the gods, whose character emerged in various myths, became the basis for the astral mythology later evolved by the Greeks and Romans. If it is assumed that a harmony exists between the events on earth and the calculable orbits of the planets or apparent movements of the fixed stars, then the planetary positions and signs of the zodiac at a man's birth must reflect his destiny. Astrological horoscopes are to this day drawn up on the basis of these age-old mythological notions, although the gods of Mesopotamia, Greece and Rome have long since faded. When science stripped away the mythologizing, astronomy was born.

Cuneiform tablets preserved a great many astrological texts. But they preserved also an Akkadian Creation Epic (*Enuma elish* = "When there above") of the time of Hammurabi which was intended as a glorification of Marduk, the supreme god, who defeated Tiamat, the female sea monster. Marduk split her body into two parts like a mussel and out of it created the two hemispheres, heaven and earth. The Babylonians annually celebrated this victory during the New Year festival, which went on for twelve days. Among the ceremonies was a procession called "seizing the hands of Marduk." The king would kneel humbly before the god in behalf of his sinful people, and may well have been appointed Marduk's deputy on earth. In addition, the library of Assurbanipal has furnished us with the myth of Utnapishtim ("he saw the life"), also called Atrachasis ("the extremely wise"), the Babylonian Noah, who builds a ship and escapes the great Flood, and who goes with his wife to the "Island of the Blessed," where he becomes immortal and like the gods.

This story of the Flood forms part of the epic of the national hero Gilgamesh, composed in the second millennium B.C., which may be regarded as the greatest poetic creation of pre-Homeric times. According to the fragmentary texts that remain (twelve tablets), Gilgamesh, an early Sumerian king of Uruk in southern Babylonia, undergoes many adventures searching for the rejuvenating plant of immortality. He finds it at the bottom of the sea, but it is taken from him by a serpent. In his wanderings the royal hero comes to the end of the world and queries his immortal ancestor Utnapishtim, who, however, is also unable to explain the mystery of life to him. At last he is given the final rejection: "Gilgamesh, whither do you fare? The life you seek, you will not

find. When the gods created man, they apportioned death to
mankind; they retained life for themselves." Finally his dead
friend Enkidu, whose ghost he has conjured up, explains to him
the dreary conditions in the land of the dead, and the epic con-
cludes on this sad note. The entire poem is permeated by a profound pessimism.

PIETY AND MORALITY

Babylonian piety was permeated by magical elements. The
power of the gods was boundless, while man was exposed to innumerable terrors. But belief in the influence of the stars upon
man's fate was necessarily connected with notions of a universal,
if unknown law governing the cosmos. The oldest preserved
ritual texts are magic spells. Gradually, these were transformed
into petitionary prayers or psalms of lament addressed to particular gods. Thus the god Sin is invoked in an Akkadian psalm:
"Who is sublime in heaven? You alone are sublime. Among all
the gods, who is like you?" Or again, penitential prayers expressed a sense of guilt that reminds us strongly of the biblical
Psalter: "Lord, my missteps are great, my sins many. Lord, look
upon me, hear my supplication."

Although the extant texts contain many references to reward
and punishment, the idea of punishment beyond the grave is absent, since life after death in the "land of no return" was pes-
simistically visualized as a drifting, vegetative existence of impotent shades. The dead wore a winged dress like bats. The realm
of the dead is wrapped in darkness, and over it all lies the dust of
decay which is the food of its inhabitants. So it is described in the
account of Ishtar's visit to hell. In another underworld vision, the
realm of the dead is described as the night side of the world,
ruled over by a personified Death who commands a sinister court
of demons that swarm out over the whole earth at night and
bring mischief upon mankind. It is therefore not surprising that
the goddess Sabitu, meeting Gilgamesh on his search for eternal
life, gives him the forceful advice that so clearly underlies the
this-worldliness of Babylonian religion: "Make of each day a festival of joy, and amuse yourself with the wife of your youth."

We must finally refer to the detailed legal codes that governed the lives of the ancient Babylonians. In 1902, in the course of excavations in Susa, a large stone stele was found bearing a relief showing the coronation of the king by the sun god and, beneath this, in cuneiform script, the laws of King Hammurabi. The stele is in the Louvre now. The king claims to have received the collection of laws, which is carefully divided into articles, from the sun god Shamash in person. Actually, the text represents a codification of still older, partly Sumerian and partly Semitic, legal views, out of which Hammurabi presumably fashioned a coherent Babylonian legal system. The code is notably short on the side of religion; it lacks those injunctions against violation of divine precepts that are so much a part of biblical legislation. But there is a well-developed *jus talionis;* penalties are determined on the principle of an eye for an eye and a tooth for a tooth. But the essential character of Hammurabi's code is revealed in the final article: ". . . in order to bring true welfare to the country and a good government, so that the strong will not harm the weak and both the widow and the orphan will receive justice."

The literary and contextual relationship of Hammurabi's code to the legal sections of the Old Testament (especially Exodus 20, 22–23, 33) has often been commented on; in fact, some scholars have contended that the biblical laws must have been derived from the much older Babylonian code. The deviations, however, are more numerous than the parallels; the latter probably due to the derivation of both codes from still older Semitic sources.

BABEL AND BIBLE

Around the turn of the century the Pan-Babylonian fad swept scholarship. "Babel-Bible" was the password of the Pan-Babylonians, who made a strong case for the intimate connection between the ancient Semitic cultures and claimed that a great many biblical stories were Babylonian borrowings. Today, a more moderate view has prevailed. It is certainly striking that the Gilgamesh epic should contain the story of the Flood, that Utnapishtim resembles Noah, that Leviathan sounds like a reminiscence of Tiamat, and the hunter Nimrod of the hunting god Ninurta. Nevertheless, the astrological mythology of Babylon is not too useful a key to the understanding of the Old Testament. Abraham, who came from Ur and Haran, centers of Babylonian astrological religion, must have been familiar with much "Chaldean wisdom." According to a tale in the Talmud, the kings of the East and the West flocked to his door because of his knowledge of the stars. But then God's summons came to him: "Go out of your astrology. You are a prophet and not an astrologer!"

The ethical monotheism of the Bible is a far cry from Babylonian henotheism—the proclamation of one god (such as Marduk) as supreme, enthroned above many others, like the Greeks' Zeus at the head of the Olympian hierarchy. The complexity of the Babylonian-Assyrian pantheon does not greatly distinguish it from the Greco-Roman; and its fate was the same. The Mosaic revelation, however, appeared to the polytheistic contemporaries of Moses as an almost incomprehensible novelty: a single God as the Lord of history opposed to the nature deities.

A more reasonable formulation of the "Babel-Bible" slogan has been expressed by Wilhelm Bousset: "What the Israelite religion borrowed from the Babylonian was raw material for elaboration and finishing. To assert that the prophets of Israel were spiritual disciples of Babylon is like maintaining that a sculptor is spiritually dependent on the quarry workers. . . . Babylonian religion with its wholly polytheistic character stood on a plane so incalculably below the Jewish religion that we can scarcely attribute to the former any influence upon the latter in central matters." We need not assent to Bousset's evaluative "higher-lower" approach; but his general statement on the question of influences seems valid.

THE WEST SEMITES

If we consider the Babylonians and Assyrians as North Semites, then the Israelites, Canaanites, Phoenicians and Syrians may be called the West Semites. The land of Canaan on the coast of the Mediterranean belonged to the Babylonian and later to the Hittite spheres of influence in pre-Israelite times. Our information on the "aboriginal inhabitants" of Canaan, the coastal plain between the Red Sea and Lebanon which the Israelites called the Promised Land, was for many years drawn solely from the Bible and such ancient writers as Philo of Byblos, Plutarch, and Lucian.

Since 1929 the excavations at Ras Shamra, the ancient Ugarit, which brought to light difficult but decipherable religious and mythological texts from the fifteenth century B.C. in alphabetic cuneiform script, have added greatly to our knowledge of the religious background of early Israel. The Israelites whom Moses had converted to the exclusive cult of Yahweh found in Canaan very old communities with well-established rituals. The Old Testament is full of denunciations of the Canaanite mountain cult. Today, temples have been excavated that provide a vivid picture of the conditions prevailing in ancient Canaan. The temple would contain the image of the god; on the height (*bama*) stood the altar of the sacrifice, hewn out of solid rock. In all of Canaan sacred stones (*masseboth*), frequently in the shape of phalluses, and wooden poles (*asheroth*) forming an enclosure, as female symbols, served as centers of religious rituals, usually involving sacred prostitution of both sexes. The temple prostitutes at the Canaanite temple in Ugarit around 1400 B.C. were only one rank lower than the priests in the hierarchy of cult attendants. They were called "holy," that is, the property of the god. Ecstatic dances and orgies in honor of Baal are mentioned in Judges (9: 27). Undoubtedly, the denunciations for lechery and the numerous prohibitions of the Old Testament are responses to the orgiastic religious rites practiced in the vicinity of the Israelites.

The supreme gods of the Canaanite cults—El, Baal, Melekh—were originally generic terms stressing the power and independence of the god; later, they took on individual personalities as a result of being identified with particular sites. Each city had its own Baal or Melekh. Thus, the Bible tells us of Melkart, king of the city of Tyrus, pictured as a bull; of Baal Peor in Moab; and Baal Sebub, the god of flies in Ekron, who in the New Testament is identified as the prince of demons, Beelzebub. Sacred kingship also flourished in the Canaanite city-states; Melchizedek, the priest-king of Salem, is mentioned in the Bible (Genesis 14). The Canaanite god El—according to Ugarit texts a god who ruled as a monarch—was absorbed into Yahweh after the Israelites took the land, whereas Baal and Yahweh continued to confront one another in irreconcilable hostility, thus reflecting the religious antagonism of the Canaanites and Israelites.

In addition to the male gods, there were female deities of great importance, such as Baalath (the Mistress), wife of El; Ashera (in Ugarit Athirat), originally a sea goddess; Anath, the sister of Alijan-Baal; and Astarte, the Babylonian Ishtar, who was long venerated in Syria as a goddess of fertility and warfare.

In the Ugarit texts the savagery and bloodthirstiness of the female goddesses of Canaan is particularly striking. According to a fragment of the Baal Epic published in 1958, Anath, one of these virginal goddesses of war, wades in blood up to her neck after she has tied on her back the heads of men she has slaughtered "from the sea-coast to the sunrise." Religion, sexuality and blood joined in a strange union in Canaan.

To judge by the Ugarit texts, the male gods of Canaan also partook largely of the character of vegetation deities. The religion of the Canaanite farmers was closely related to the annual cycle of growth and decay. Thus, in an early mythological epic the body of Alijan-Baal is equated with the grain that is sowed in the field, subsequently reaped and threshed, winnowed and finally baked into bread. Worship of Phoenician-Syrian Adonis, whose cult traveled all the way to Greece, has now been established by Ugarit texts for the middle of the second millennium. He was a vegetation god symbolizing the death and resurrection of nature, like Tammuz in Babylonia and Attis in later Syria. His death was mourned at the festivals of Adonis with such heartrending wails that Hegel dubbed the Syrian religion the "religion of sorrow."

Human sacrifice must also have been extremely widespread among the West Semites. They passed their own children "through the fire" in atonement and made great offerings of human beings to Melekh (Moloch) at the beginning of a war. The Yahwist Mosaic religion regarded this custom as abominable and fought it bitterly (I Kings 16; II Kings 5). But at as late a date as the Phoenician settlement of Carthage in the ninth century B.C. human sacrifice was practiced. Through the voyages of the seafaring Phoenicians and their colonizing activity (Sidon, Tyre, Byblos), the West Semitic deities and their cults were widely disseminated. Generally, however, the Phoenicians in foreign countries identified their own gods with the native deities. As a result, the theme of Canaanite mythologies were remarkably persistent and influenced late-classical Gnosticism.

THE EGYPTIAN RELIGION

T HE LAND of the pharaohs, with its pyramids, animal gods and picture-writing, seemed mysterious even to the ancient Greeks. Such classical writers as Herodotus, who visited Egypt around 460 B.C., and later Josephus, Porphyry, Diodorus, misunderstood many things and in addition were often hoodwinked by their Egyptian guides. As a result, they falsely equated the Egyptian gods with their own, or tried to explain elements quite alien to them in the Egyptian religion, such as the animal cults, in symbolic and poetic terms. Egypt was and remained for thousands of years a closed book. It was not until the nineteenth century and the decipherment of the Rosetta Stone that a start was made on reconstructing the beliefs of the Egyptians.

Since then, excavations have brought to light innumerable inscriptions on pyramids, funeral columns, obelisks, temple walls and sarcophagi. Thousands of papyri have been found, including the invaluable *Book of the Dead*. In addition, Egyptian hymns, rituals, spells and collections of sayings or books of wisdom have been deciphered. Poems ranking with the great works of world literature have been restored to us, such as the "Harper's Song" or the "Conversation of the World-Weary Man with his Soul"—profound and beautiful meditations on the values of life and death. From the numerous sources—monuments, inscriptions and literary texts—we can now form a fairly good picture of the Egyptian religion in its various stages and manifestations.

HISTORY

The Nile is Egypt's destiny. The Nile Valley, though flanked on both sides by desert, was rendered highly fertile by the annual flooding of the river. The ancients spoke of "the Two

Egypts," meaning Lower Egypt, the Nile delta where the land was covered by the black silt from the Nile, and the Upper Egypt in the south, the land of red desert soil. As symbol of his dominion, the pharaoh wore a bipartite crown. Egyptian history proper begins with the union of both parts of the land under King Menes about 3500 B.C. At about the same time hieroglyphic writing was invented, seemingly out of the blue. The country was then divided into forty-two districts or petty states. Egyptian history is generally divided into three periods known respectively as the Old Kingdom, Middle Kingdom and New Kingdom. The rulers from Menes to Alexander the Great represent thirty dynasties— a classification that goes back to the priest Manetho, who around 285 B.C. wrote a history of Egypt for Alexander's general Ptolemy.

The Old Kingdom begins with the founding of Memphis about 2800 B.C. and includes the first six dynasties, of which the Fourth (2720–2560) is the most famous, for to it belong Kings Cheops, Chephren, and Mycerinus, who built the three great pyramids at Gizeh. Their officials were buried in carefully ordered graves around these royal tombs. After the end of the Sixth Dynasty (2190) social disturbances and a period of decadence ensued. New kingdoms were founded, among other places in Heracleopolis. In the Eleventh Dynasty the military succeeded in reunifying the kingdom. Their base was the city of Thebes in Upper Egypt. This was the beginning of the Middle Kingdom (2040–1580). Sesostris III, of the Twelfth Dynasty, transferred the capital back to Memphis around 1860. He created a strongly centralized administration and conquered Nubia. From 1710 to 1580 the Hyksos, an Asiatic pastoral people, dominated the country. After their expulsion, Egypt became a great power. This was the period of the New Kingdom (Eighteenth to Twenty-first Dynasties; 1580–950). Under Thutmosis III (1504–1450), Syria and Palestine were subjugated. The borders of Egypt then extended from Abyssinia to the Caucasus, from Libya to Mesopotamia. Thebes became a great metropolis, the Theban god Amon the supreme god of the empire, until Amenophis IV, who renamed himself Ikhnaton, attempted to displace Amon and the host of other deities by one supreme figure, the sun god Aton. He founded Tel el Amarna in Central Egypt as a new capital; but his successor, Tutankhamen, was forced to abandon the new city after the failure of Ikhnaton's reformation. Under Ramses II (1290–1223), the pharaoh of the Israelite exodus from Egypt, the New Kingdom regained its dominant position.

After many vicissitudes Egypt, weakened by defensive wars against the Libyans, the Philistines and other seafaring peoples, fell under the rule of the Ethiopians and Assyrians. In 525 it was reduced to a satrapy by the Persian king Cambyses. Several native dynasties followed; but in 332 Egypt was incorporated into Alexander the Great's empire and thus drawn into the orbit of the Hellenistic world. In 305 Alexander's successor, Ptolemy I, assumed the royal title. The Hellenistic Ptolemaic dynasty he founded lasted for almost three centuries. In 30 B.C. Egypt became a Roman province; Christianity began to spread through the country as early as the middle of the second century A.D. In A.D. 395, when the Roman Empire was divided, Egypt was assigned to Constantinople. Byzantine rule was replaced by that of the Arabs in 641, and except for a small Coptic minority (today about ten per cent of the population) Egypt became and has remained Mohammedan. But by the seventh century the Egyptian religion had already disappeared. The splendid Serapeion in Alexandria was closed under Theodosius I in A.D. 391, and the last remnants of the cult of Isis were stamped out under Emperor Justinian in the sixth century.

GODS

After this historical survey, let us turn to the religion itself. The constellations and the forces of the earth, vegetation, animal life and the world of the dead, were early recognized in Egypt as the powers of destiny which forever inspired new mythic thinking and ritual practices. However, the Egyptians were singularly conservative. Ancient and primeval religious ideas, animism and crude belief in ghosts, were retained in times of far greater sophistication and symbolic thinking. It has been said of the Egyptians that they never forgot or abolished anything. Thus ancient animal cults were preserved along with personalistic deities. Gods were depicted with human bodies and animal heads—Isis with the horns of a cow, Horus with a falcon's head, Anubis, god of the dead, with the head of a jackal. (Such images caused great astonishment among the neighbors of the Egyptians. Greek travelers were particularly amazed.) Or, on the other hand, the huge sphinx of Gizeh has a human countenance attached to a lion's body. Hegel offered an interpretation of the sphinx as symbol of the country and of the religion: "The human head that bursts from the animal body represents Mind as it begins to raise itself above Nature. . . . without, however, being able to liberate itself wholly from its fetters." Thus the German philosopher interpreted the riddle of the sphinx as a hieroglyph of Egyptian thought.

Which species of animal was to be venerated probably depended largely on local conditions, crocodile gods being worshiped in places directly on the Nile, lion goddesses in places on the edge of the desert, and so on. But it is important to note that Egyptian animal worship is devoid of that self-identification of the individual or the clan with a particular species of animal which is the characteristic mark of totemism. Just the reverse was the case in Egypt: from earliest times the Egyptians venerated the mysterious otherness and numinousness of animals, especially bulls, cows, cats, snakes and crocodiles. These animals were assigned to particular gods, or were regarded as the embodiments of those gods.

The Egyptian pantheon was highly developed and had many ramifications, for like that of Babylonia it had evolved out of the rivalry and interpenetration of many local cults. Considering the supreme importance of the Nile for the fertility of the soil, it is remarkable that the river itself was not elevated into a deity, or that moon and star cults remained comparatively unimportant by comparison with Mesopotamia. By contrast, the importance of the sun god, who appeared under various names and guises, was greatly magnified.

The oldest and most widely disseminated name for the sun god was Re, who by the Fifth Dynasty (circa 2500 B.C.) was already being hailed as the highest of all the gods. According to the theology later elaborated in Heliopolis, Re was the father of all the gods and divine kings, who was incarnated anew in every pharaoh. Various myths relate how the sun god Re sails the ship of the day over the heavenly ocean—the firmament was likened to the Nile, a great expanse of water over which the heavenly bodies sailed in their boats, changing at evening in the west to the night ship that carried them down the great underworld ocean to a new sunrise in the east. In the course of this night voyage the dead had the opportunity to greet the god and hail him in their prayers. On, the later Heliopolis (city of the sun) in Lower Egypt near Cairo, was the principal site for the worship of Re, who was adored on a hill under the open sky. The scarab, so frequently represented on seals and amulets, was considered by the Egyptians both the symbol of death and rebirth and a manifestation of the sun god, who died and was reborn every day.

Gradually numerous other gods were joined to Re; originally these had been local sun gods with whom particular myths were associated. Among them were the god-king Horus with the falcon's head, whose temple in Edfu is still well preserved; Amon of Thebes, whose sacred animals were the goose and ram, in whose temple in the Libyan Desert Alexander the Great received an oracle; the high god Atum, who actually antedated Re as sun god. When Thebes became the new capital during the Eleventh Dynasty, the combined god Amon-Re became for almost a thousand years the almighty god of the New Kingdom. In the cult of Amon-Re, the high priest of Thebes held the highest rank after pharaoh. By the time of the New Kingdom the principal temple of Amon-Re had received so much war booty that it was the richest in the whole country, and its priesthood wielded extraordinary political influence. The beautiful remains of this ancient sanctuary of the sun, of great importance in the history of art, may still be seen at what is now the village of Karnak.

Alongside the sun gods, the creator god Ptah held a vital place in Egyptian religious life from earliest times. Ptah was worshiped in the old capital of Memphis. Patron of artisans and artists, he was the only god who was always depicted in human form. His statue represents him wrapped up like a mummy, his hands holding the rod of rule against his chest. Later, he merged with the mysterious god of the grave and the dead, Sokar or Sokaris, and also with Osiris. The lion-headed war goddess Sekhmet, who was also mistress of plagues, was regarded as his wife. Memphis was likewise the center of worship of the holy Apis bull, whose cult became widespread in the later periods of Egyptian history. Apis was also occasionally associated with Ptah. In the Hellenistic period another sanctuary, in addition to the one at Memphis, was built for him at Alexandria; the Serapeum, which had its own priestly hierarchy. There he was venerated as Serapis—probably a compound of Osiris and Apis. To date some sixty mummified specimens of this black bull have been found.

The cow goddess Hathor held high rank among the goddesses. She is always pictured with the sun's disk between her horns. She was considered the goddess of women and of free love. Mut, the goddess of sky and sun in Thebes, had a lion's head and gradually became a war goddess. It is noteworthy that the lion deities (which included Tefnut and Sekhmet in Memphis) were always represented as female. The Neith of Sais in Lower Egypt (the famous legend of her veiled image is of later origin) is said to have been originally a Libyan war goddess; her symbol was a pair of crossed arrows. The goddess Bastet in Lower Egypt, depicted as a cat-headed woman, was a goddess of joy, and was worshiped with music and dancing. Partly as a result of her cult the cat became a sacred animal of Egypt; the embalming and burying of cats in specially consecrated cemeteries became a matter of great concern to the Egyptians.

Isis ultimately raised herself above her many rivals, and in the late period of Egyptian religion occupied an almost monotheistic position in the pantheon. In the time of Emperor Caligula, her cult spread throughout the Roman Empire. A temple of Isis has been excavated at Pompeii. As the nurse of her son Horus (Harpekhred, garbled by the Greeks into Harpocrates), who was not identical with the old sun god but who was occasionally equated with him, Isis was hailed as "she who turned with her sweet maternal love to the weary and heavy-laden." Frequently depicted with the child Horus in her arms, she became the prototype of Christian veneration of the Madonna.

Among the underworld deities were the forbidding crocodile god Sobk and the jackal god Anubis; also the feared Set, whom the Greeks called Typhon: his red body symbolized the desert sands in contrast to the black humus of the fields. Set gradually became a diabolic figure. Then there was Thoth, from Hermopolis in Middle Egypt. Depicted with the head of an ibis, he may originally have been a nocturnal moon god whose development reversed that of Set, for he became the friend and helper of men and gods as the god of writing and arithmetic, and later of the sciences in general. The Greeks identified him with their Hermes, the messenger of the gods. From the second to the fifth centuries A.D. a lush religious-philosophical literature sprang up around Thoth-Hermes, under the name of Hermes Trismegistos, the "threefold great Hermes." He functions as sage and lawgiver in much "hermetic," that is, secret, writing. Many Greek and a few Latin and Coptic literary works deal with him. The hermetic literature entered the Latin West probably through the Arabs; its influence can be traced in Paracelsus.

The husband of Isis occupied a special position in Egyptian religion. He was the god Osiris, represented in human form as an ancient king. A great many texts in tombs and on pyramids record variant forms of his myth; the late account of it by Plutarch is the most detailed. According to Plutarch, Osiris was lured into a coffin by his brother Set and killed. The coffin with his body was thrown into the water and floated to Byblos in Syria. According to another version, his body was mutilated and the limbs scattered over the entire country. But his spouse Isis, after performing the ceremonial lament for the dead, set about searching for him and brought him back to life by letting him eat the eye that his son Horus had lost in battle against Set. Henceforth Osiris became ruler of the underworld, while Horus ruled on earth and thus became the ancestor of all the pharaohs, who were regarded as his incarnations.

Even in antiquity the death of Osiris was equated with the annual death of nature, and his resurrection with the spring renewal. Thus, like Tammuz in Babylonia, Attis and Adonis in Syria, Osiris was regarded as a vegetation deity. The mystery cults of the Hellenistic period made much of him. For in later times every man hoped to achieve by magical means the privilege previously reserved for pharaoh: to repeat the destiny of Osiris after death. The supposed grave of Osiris in Abydos, Upper Egypt, was the site of annual mystery games held each October.

Osiris was the most mysterious of the Egyptian gods, as King Ramses had early affirmed; but he was also the most vital and the most exalted manifestation of the religion. He was also the sole god of ancient Egypt whose cult included ethical elements in addition to the usual taboos and rituals. Osiris ultimately became virtually a national god of Egypt; but in the course of centuries his original nature as a god of the dead vanished beneath the luxuriant thickets of priestly theology. Egyptian traders and sailors spread the cult of Isis and Osiris throughout the Mediterranean world and far into the countries of the Alps and the Danube.

AMENOPHIS IV, THE REFORMER

We have mentioned only a fraction of the gods whose names are recorded in Egyptian texts. It may be argued that these texts are less pure theology than the pronouncements of certain priests, and are overlaid with a strong political tinge. Certainly we can recognize again and again the priests' tendency to establish the god of their own local cult as the supreme deity. That effort is most conspicuous in the struggle between the priesthoods of Memphis and Heliopolis, until a union of the two gods was effected in Thebes.

In the Eighteenth Dynasty young King Amenophis IV (1377–1358) attempted a reform—directed against the new god Amon-Re and his all-powerful priesthood—which was based on the cult of Heliopolis and amounted almost to a religious reformation. Amenophis (really Amenhotep: Amon is gracious) attempted to do away with all the gods aside from the disk of the sun (Aton). He called for exclusive worship of his "Father" Aton, who appeared in the sky as the living sun. Amenophis, whose personality is more present to us than that of any of the other kings of Egypt, proclaimed a form of solar monotheism. He renamed himself Ikhnaton ("pleasing to Aton") after his god. Conflict with the priesthood of Amon caused him to abandon Thebes and, as we have mentioned, establish a new capital at Tel el Amarna in Middle Egypt. During the brief period of the new capital's glory, Egyptian art embarked on entirely new paths. A new motif appeared—the glowing disk of the sun depicted with its rays terminating in hands holding the hieroglyph for "life." The representation of human figures with animal heads are noticeably absent from the art work of this period, and the names of all the other gods—even that of Osiris—were erased from the obelisks. The Amarna reliefs show graceful portrayals of royal family life. Numerous full sculptures and reliefs—especially the painted limestone busts of Ikhnaton's wife Nefertiti ("the beauty who comes from afar"), and of Ikhnaton himself with his curiously shaped skull—are among the most beautiful works of ancient sculpture, and remarkable for their naturalistic manner.

Ikhnaton also wrote poetry. His "Hymn to the Sun," found in a grave at Amarna, has often been ranked alongside St. Francis's "Hymn to Brother Sun." This glorification of Aton's divine kingship is permeated by a profound religious feeling for nature and a universalistic temper. It begins as follows:

> Thou shinest beautiful on the horizon of heaven,
> O Living Disk, who dids't live from the beginning.
> When thou risest in the Eastern Horizon
> Thou fillest every land with thy beauty.
> Thy rays embrace the lands even to the limit
> Of all thou hast created. Thou art Re. . . .
> When thou descendest in the Western Land
> The earth is in darkness like unto death.
> With covered heads men sleep in their chambers.
> The eye beholdeth not its fellow. Thieves may steal
> The goods beneath their heads. They know it not.
> The lion cometh from his den, the snake biteth,
> Darkness is, and the earth is in silence.
> He who created them hath gone to his rest.
> When thou risest at dawn, and shinest as Aton,
> The darkness is routed. The Two Lands awake
> And stand on their feet, for thou hast aroused them.
> They wash their limbs and take up their garments,
> And lift up their arms for thine adoration. . . .

But Ikhnaton's experiment with monotheism failed in the long run, probably because he did not go deeply enough. His creed made no provision for those seamy sides of life that vitally concerned Egyptians in their religious life, and he found no answers to the questions of suffering, death and injustice—in other words, the question of theodicy (the justification of God). In any case, Ikhnaton, who, as his portraits reveal, looked feeble and sickly—perhaps even degenerate—lacked the necessary personal magnetism of the reformer. Probably he also was no match for the intrigues of the Amon priesthood. His ban on the cults of the gods and his other reforms, which shattered traditions and local eccentricities in favor of a supreme nature deity, apparently struck the majority of Egyptians as base heresy. When in the course of his reign some of the Asiatic provinces were lost, the people regarded these reverses as a punishment inflicted by angry gods.

Ikhnaton's son Tutankhamen returned to Thebes and restored Amon-Re to the enjoyment of his old rights. When the twenty-year-old pharaoh died, the grateful priesthood gave him magnificent burial. When Lord Carnarvon and Howard Carter opened the rediscovered tomb of Tutankhamen in the Valley of the Kings, they came upon the greatest hoard of gold ever to be recovered from ancient times. The gold coffin alone weighed some four hundred pounds. The darkness and dryness of the tomb had preserved fabulous splendor and wealth for three thousand years.

PHARAOHS, PRIESTS, AND MONUMENTS

Egyptian divine kingship, on which the whole state religion was based, is probably the oldest institution of which we have any knowledge. The pharaoh, as the son of the sun god, was a god in his lifetime, although he usually received official worship only after his death. He was called "Horus in the palace," "living sun," "the god's image living on earth." To safeguard the divine nature of the pharaohs, they were required to marry their sisters. According to the theological ideas of Heliopolis, Amon-Re assumed the form of the reigning pharaoh in every generation. In the temple cult, the pharaoh, himself a full-fledged deity, confronted his heavenly father. In the Osiris myth he sat on the throne of the divine Horus, who had been venerated as a falcon from earliest times (his two glowing eyes probably representing sun and moon). The pharaoh alone was permitted to perform the sacrifices and the ritual of worship; the priests functioned only as his representatives.

These priests, with their smooth-shaven heads, constituted a kind of civil service, graded in a strictly hierarchic structure. They served their gods as if these were living sovereigns, waking them in the morning by opening the temples, dressing them in splendid garments, lighting incense in their honor, and bringing them food for their physical well-being. In processions the images of the gods were carried by the priests. The divine myths were symbolically represented by mystery dramas during the great religious festivals. The ritual, regulated down to the last detail, was permeated with magical acts intended to assure the welfare of the country. In dealing with Egypt, the boundaries between magic and religion are indeed difficult to trace.

Monuments such as the sphinxes symbolized the numinous power of the ruler, and were also intended to protect his tomb. In addition to these, from the Fifth Dynasty on, we find obelisks, richly adorned with hieroglyphs. Originally these "little spits"— this is the literal meaning of the word *obelisk*—stood at the entrances to the temples as symbols of the sun god. Their metallic tips were intended to reflect the rays of the sun.

The most characteristic of the Egyptian religious monuments, however, were the pyramids, which developed out of the mound tombs of the nomads. From about 2700 B.C. pyramids were built as funeral monuments for the pharaohs. The pharaohs of the New Kingdom had their graves in the Valley of the Kings, near Thebes. The gigantic pyramids were intended to protect the king's mummified corpse, which was generally placed in an inaccessible chamber, usually underground. Nevertheless, the enormous treasures these tombs contained proved too tempting and most of the royal tombs were plundered by robbers in the course of the centuries. The pyramid proper served as a site for making offerings to the dead and for ritual ceremonies to aid the king's "*ka.*" The dimensions of some of these structures are almost unbelievable. The pyramid of Cheops towers to a height of 467 feet; a hundred thousand workers spent twenty years in the building of it, piling up 29,500,000 cubic feet of stone. When it was finished, the structure could be seen for miles: visible symbol of the power of its builder.

The pyramids of the Fifth and Sixth Dynasties contain fascinating reliefs on the walls of the burial chamber depicting incidents in the lives of the kings, as well as inscriptions recording the hymns and ritual texts sung and recited at the time of burial. These so-called "pyramid texts" throw enormous light on the language and religion of ancient Egypt.

IDEAS OF DEATH AND THE LAST JUDGMENT

The pyramid texts—sacrificial formulas and magic spells, hymns to the gods, narratives of the king's ascension and his intercourse with the gods—provide a comprehensive view of the Egyptians' ideas about death and the hereafter—a subject of more concern to them than to any other ancient people. They assumed that the dead continued to live on in the grave, for which reason food was stored in the tomb, and later regular offerings of edibles were made to the deceased. The ritual embalming or mummification of the corpse, which began in the Old Kingdom, must have been linked with this idea. Plato, in the *Phaedo*, remarks with wry astonishment that the Egyptian dead thereby became "almost immortal." Hegel took a different view, commenting: "The very fact that the Egyptians attempted to provide permanence for the body indicates that they knew nothing of true immortality. For in true immortality the preservation of the body is totally unimportant."

On the other hand, the Egyptians conceived of a future life of the *ka* after death. The *ka* meant both embodiment of the vital force and the genius or protective spirit of the deceased. In addition man was thought to have a *ba*, a kind of soul—usually imagined in the form of a bird—which could rise into heaven, but which also visited the mummy in the grave. In Heliopolis it was believed that the dead continued their life in this world by sailing in the sun god's barque on the heavenly Nile, or inhabiting the realm of the dead where they received the nightly visit of the sun god. A goodly number of different notions about life after death were commingled, as the *Book of the Dead* indicates. But although Herodotus reports that the Egyptians believed in the transmigration of souls, this was not the case. Herodotus appears to have confused their beliefs with those of the Orphic mystics.

An elaborate doctrine of immortality, and expectation of a judgment of the dead to which everyone was subject, from king to day laborer, became attached to the Osiris myth. The *Book of the Dead* describes how the deceased must conduct himself on his long, wearisome pilgrimage to the judgment seat of Osiris. In Chapter 125 there is a detailed description of Osiris sitting on his throne, surrounded by forty-two assistant judges. Before him are the scales of justice, with a symbol of righteousness or truth in one pan and the dead man's heart in the other. Horus and the jackal-god Anubis weigh the heart. Thoth, the scribe of the gods, notes the result and informs Osiris.

Before the verdict is pronounced, however, a "negative confession" is required of the dead man. That is, he must swear he has not given false witness, has not refused bread to the hungry or water to the thirsty, nor neglected offerings to the gods and funeral meals for the dead.

The ethical ideas implicit in these scenes of judgment are overlaid by all sorts of magical practices and exorcisms. In the pyramid texts, particularly, the dangers of the journey to the realm of the dead are described in a manner more consonant with magic than with religion. Nevertheless, in the description of the judgment there is mention of *Maat*—also personified as a goddess —the moral cosmos, which expects of the dead person a "just heart without sin." At least the possibility of sinning has been conceived, although man's acceptance of his own sinful nature was as yet scarcely possible—would, in fact, have seemed blasphemous to the Egyptians. The myth took an alternative course: the pan of the balance containing the man's heart grew heavy and sank downward if he had sworn falsely. Thus we may see, softly foreshadowed in the Osiris myth, the idea of a supreme personal God who requires righteousness of men. Herein may lie the explanation for the early strides made by Christianity in Egypt.

THE RELIGION OF THE PERSIANS

IN THE period before 1500 B.C. Persia and India were still closely connected. In both countries certain common "Indo-Aryan" attitudes can be discerned. The Persian pantheon with its characteristic dualism may already have been a thousand years old when Zoroaster appeared on the scene to reform and reshape the Iranian folk religion. For almost a thousand years thereafter the religion of the Persians was Zoroastrianism, or, as it is also called, Parseeism. From A.D. 227 on this was the official religion of the Persian Empire, and so remained until it was overthrown by the victory of the Arabs over the Sassanid Kingdom in 642.

We learn about Zoroaster (to use the Greek version of the Persian Zarathustra) from the frequently obscure *Gathas* of the Avesta. Avesta means knowledge; Zend-Avesta, a term that keeps recurring, means "knowledge with commentary." The surviving Avesta texts are only fragments of a much larger host of writings which have been lost. We still possess a lawbook (Vendidad) which sets forth the prescribed rites for purification from demonic contamination. It outlines the ethics and jurisprudence of the ancient Persians and also describes their cosmology and some eschatological beliefs. There is also the Yasht—a collection of hymns glorifying such deities as Mithra, Haoma and so on; and the short Avesta (Khorda Avesta), a kind of layman's breviary with prayers for the entire year. Of particular value is the Yasna, a compendium of liturgical texts somewhat like a Roman missal, from which we learn many myths and legends about the gods and heroes of prehistoric times. Seven chapters of the Yasna, consisting of *Gathas*, hymns and meditations, are regarded as especially old and probably composed by Zoroaster himself.

The *Gathas* indicate that Zoroaster—his name means "owner of camels in good condition"—came from a prosperous family in eastern Iran, which in those days included what is now Afghanistan. The year of his birth was 599 or 598 B.C. according to the calculations of Altheim; his first public appearance fell in 569 or 568. If these dates are correct, Zoroaster was a contemporary of Buddha, Confucius and Deutero-Isaiah. Compared to what we know about other religious founders, prophets and reformers, our knowledge of the historical Zoroaster is sparse. Some scholars regard him as a prophet, others as a shaman or medicine man. By profession Zoroaster was a priest and liturgical singer; in psychological type he was an ecstatic visionary with a bent for speculation akin to that of an Islamic *mahdi*. His personality seems to have left few traces. In compensation, we know all the more about his doctrines.

THE WORD OF ZOROASTER

Zoroaster's creative act was establishment of monotheism in ancient Persia. Before him, the Persians had worshiped a variety of ancient Iranian gods and practiced the Haoma cult, which involved drinking a celebrated intoxicant purveyed by the priests. The drink stood for Haoma, the god of life, who was believed to permeate the entire universe in liquid form. Zoroaster replaced these cults by worship of Ahura Mazda, the "wise Lord," in later times also called Ormazd. Ahura Mazda became the supreme god of the Persian Empire, which under Darius (circa 500 B.C.) and his successors spread over western Asia. Within a few centuries it had developed a flourishing culture that embraced the whole area from Turfan to Abyssinia, from the Indus to the Aegean Sea.

The god Ahura Mazda was primarily a deity of pure will concerned with shaping the universe along ethical lines. He was the god of truth who overcame lies, the god of purity who eradicated uncleanness. In these definitions we already enounter that fundamental Persian dualism which ran through the entire world of gods and men. Urta and Druj, Truth and Falsehood, are always pitted against one another. As Yasht 49: 3 has it: "There is offered for choice, O wise man, truth for salvation; but for the heretic there is falsehood for his corruption." The godless man is he who prefers falsehood to truth. The real goal of the universe is the complete eradication of falsehood, its conquest by truth. The physical as well as the moral world order was likewise created by Ahura Mazda. He is the creator of the universe, who gave Nature her laws. In the younger Avesta only the creation of pure beings is ascribed to him, while all impurity and evil in nature can be traced to his adversary Ahriman. The world is endangered by the incessant assault of this diabolic figure, but is protected by Ahura Mazda. The latter is regarded as having no physical nature, although at times he is said to consist of fire and is represented as a flame that leaps up out of uncreated light. He does, however, have about him six angelic beings who can be regarded as his various aspects and functions; they possess simultaneously physical and moral significance. These are Vohu Manah, Good Mind; Asha Vahista, Righteousness or Truth; Khshatra Vairya, the Realm of Divine Will; Spenta Armaita, Humility or Piety; Haurvatat, Perfection; Ameretat, Immortality. Later a seventh, Sraosha, Obedience, was added to the company.

These were called collectively Amesha Spentas, the immortal Holy Ones, or the Immortals who bring salvation. Theirs is the task of keeping the world going, so that it "will not rot and will not wither, will not decay and will not pass." The Amesha Spentas may originally have been gods of the Indo-Aryan tribes. Zoroaster, however, recast them in their new roles, personifications of abstract moral ideas and aspects of Ahura Mazda. In the younger Avesta the seventh angelic spirit, Sraosha, originally intended only to emphasize the necessity for obedience, was made into a person and provided with a mythology. He overcomes the demons and smashes the skull of the monster Aeshma Daeva. This struggle is usually accorded a place in Iranian eschatology, since Ahura Mazda can confer Paradise upon the blessed only after the heroic youth Sraosha has defeated this devil.

THE DOCTRINE OF LAST THINGS

Zoroaster's preaching owed its success to the same motif that worked so well for Christ and Mohammed: annunciation of an imminent judgment of the quick and the dead. To be sure, this judgment is presumed to take place upon the death of every believer in Ahura Mazda, for on the morning of the fourth day after death his soul enters the hereafter. He must first cross the great Chinvat Bridge, the Bridge of Parting, which leads from this world to the other. The godless man falls off it and plunges into hell, while the pious man is led by Sraosha safely across into the bliss of heaven. The middle of the bridge is like the blade of a sword: if a pious man wishes to cross, it is turned on its side, and is then fifteen spear-lengths wide. But if the soul of an evildoer wishes to cross, the blade turns so that its razor-sharp edge is upright, and the godless soul plunges into the abyss.

Zoroaster also taught the tenet of a future universal judgment. After nine thousand years the power of Ahriman will at last be broken and the realm of truth and righteousness will be established, for then Sraosha, the spirit of obedience, will triumph. The judgment will be by fire and molten metal; the ancient fiery ordeal will bring the truth to light. As Yasna 57: 9 expresses it: "The trial that you, O Mazda, will hold of blame and merit by the red fire will impress a sign on the souls by molten metal, to the harm of the misbelievers and the profit of the orthodox."

Like the apostles of primitive Christianity and early Islam, Zoroaster viewed the 9,000 years as almost elapsed and the universal catastrophe as therefore impending. But since it did not come, and since the course of the world was in no way changed by Zoroaster's conversions, the Persian religion underwent a modification very similar to what took place in Christian theology during the second century: the anticipation of an immediate judgment faded, and the Last Things were postponed to a distant future. The Saoshyant, the Savior whose coming was already predicted in the older Avesta, and whom Zoroaster initially felt himself to be, was again expected. He will be born in the ninth millennium of the universe. He will be conceived and borne by a virgin who will bathe in Lake Kansava and be fructified by Zoroaster's seed that falls into the lake. With the appearance of the victorious Saoshyant will begin the resurrection of the dead in the flesh. The bones of Gayomart, the First Man, will be awakened to life again; all the dead will regain their bodies, and all men will gather in one place. Each man's behavior in life will be visible upon him, so that the good can be separated from the wicked. The former will go to heaven, the latter to hell, where for three days they will be tormented, while the good look down upon their sufferings from their bliss in Paradise. But these sufferings will last only the three days; then will come the great fire, pouring over the good and wicked alike. All creatures must pass through the stream of fire; but the devout will feel as if they are surrounded by warm milk, while the godless will feel as if they are passing through molten metal. Nevertheless, the fire will purify all, burning away the clinging slag of impurities so that after this purging all, including the wicked—except those who have identified themselves completely with the demons—will enter into the realm of Ahura Mazda. That is the Parsee doctrine of Apocatastasis, the Restoration of All Things.

IRANIAN DUALISM

Thus the longed-for unity can only be achieved at the end of time. All the days of this present eon, however, are filled with a profound struggle between good and evil. This omnipresent dualism, this universal antagonism between good and evil, is conceived metaphysically as well as ethically. A positive and a negative force, a creative and a destructive impulse, confront one another from the very beginning of all things. Sometimes they are termed "Twins" who both derive from an original Father. This myth of the primal Twins preoccupied Iranian speculative thinking from earliest times to the days of dawning Islam. The Twins are also associated with light and darkness. The Prince of Light is Ahura Mazda or Ormazd, the Prince of Darkness is the evil spirit Angra Mainyu or Ahriman. Everything that exists—men, animals, plants—are dualistically split and assigned either to Ormazd or Ahriman.

Just as Ahura Mazda or Ormazd is surrounded by a band of immortal holy ones, the Amesha Spentas, so Ahriman commands an infinite host of devils and demons, the Daevas, also called Druj, from a root that probably means "deceive." The devils are liars by principle. They allege that evil is good. The whole world is peopled by them. All specific evils are attributed to demons. And according to the younger Avesta, this world of devils is constantly growing, since the Persians would consign all negative factors to this camp. The army of the Evil One was composed of their enemies. Greeks and Romans, Turks and Arabs, appear in later writings as the forces of Ahriman.

All the ancient Aryan gods of the original Iranian nature religion were also declared Daevas who belonged to Ahriman's following. Now dwelling in the House of Lies and Death, they try to seduce men into worshiping them. Sacrifices, which Zoroaster abhorred, are their method of entrapping man; when animals are slaughtered for this purpose, the Daevas know that they are being venerated. Behind this idea lay the belief, shared by the ancient Aryans and Semites, that demons feed particularly on the steam rising from sacrifices, and must be mollified by offerings of food and drink. Even in Babylonian cuneiform texts we find statements to the effect that the gods perceive the smell of the offerings and gather like flies above the sacrificial fires.

Zoroaster's religious reform, and his struggle against sacrifices, was connected with his deep respect for animals, and especially with his love for the cow, which at that time was the principal sacrificial victim. For this reason, some scholars have regarded Zoroaster's reform movement as reflecting the influence of the peasant upon the shaping of Persian religion. Zoroaster proclaimed the sanctity of the cow; in his religion the eating of the flesh of cattle is forbidden even more strictly than the eating of pork among the Jews. Moreover, the imagery in which Zoroaster describes the kingdom of god is drawn from peasant life. "To win the cow," is a synonym for heavenly bliss; "to drink sweet milk," for supreme joy; "to enter the promised land of rich pastures," for entry into Paradise. The modesty of means among Zoroaster's followers is evidenced by their hopes of future happiness. To own one cow, let alone two, was in itself a state of paradisiacal bliss. "He who plants grain, plants piety," ordains a chapter of the Vendidad headed "Praise of Agriculture."

The Daevas, to whom cows had been sacrificed, are in all respects the adversaries of the Amesha Spentas. Their negation of the works of the good angels is active rather than passive. Their creations, although destructive, are just as real as those of the Amesha Spentas. Therein lies the profundity of Persian dualism: that the irreconcilable antagonism of the two powers is viewed as an incessant struggle. The good creation of Ahura Mazda has been obstructed and half of it distorted by the penetration of the opposing power. To be sure, Ahura Mazda is the omnipotent, wise and kind Creator, but there are limits to his power. Here we have the problem of the origin of evil, the old problem of theodicy: Ahura Mazda cannot create and cannot will what contradicts his nature. Therefore he cannot be the author of evil, for in that case he would share in the guilt of evil and not be wise and kind. Zoroaster faces up to the alternatives: Either God is omnipotent and the sole Creator of all things, in which case he has also created evil and is not entirely kind, but merciless like Nature, and also not omniscient, assuming that omniscience is identical with the supreme God. On the other hand, if he is all-wise and all-kind, he is not all-powerful, but limited by something outside himself, in which case both physical and moral evil derive from an antagonistic principle. Zoroaster chose the second answer and postponed the solution of the conflict to the distant future, when the good and wise Power would ultimately prevail.

In the Last Days, then, the victory of Ormazd will mean the coming of the kingdom of Light. Hence the Iranian veneration of fire. Borrowing from the forms of ancient Aryan rites, the Zoroastrian priests, who are comparable to the Levites of the Jews, light fires to symbolize the religious ideal of purity. In the Avesta these priests are given the ancient name *athravan*—fire kindlers—which in popular language had come to mean magicians. Under the Sassanids, who kept a sacred fire, *Adhur Gushnasp*, alight in the royal palace as symbol of national unity, the fire cult became a kind of state religion. And since, to outsiders, the fire cult was the most striking aspect of the religion, the Moslems called the Iranians "fire worshipers."

A great role is reserved for man himself in this religious system, for the task of the true worshiper of Mazda consists in preparing for the coming last judgment by helping to bring about the victory, and thus combating evil at every moment. The believer, out of his own free choice and responsibility, becomes an associate of the gods in their work of purification. Zoroaster was the first religious leader to teach a doctrine of rewards or punishments after death, in accordance with moral standards. This amounted to a doctrine of the perfectability of history. Thus his dualism favored individual effort and fostered human energies. Mazdaism was a distinctively activistic religion, directed toward willing and doing. In this respect Zoroaster's religion differed fundamentally from Hindu ways of thinking, to which it was otherwise closely akin. To the Hindus, the negation of life, the subduing of the ego and its dissolution in Nirvana, was the sought-after ideal. Zoroaster, on the other hand, affirmed life in all its paradox; he regarded the dichotomies of life as no tragedy, but as a challenge to bring problems closer to solution by ethical action. The result of such affirmation was a vital ethical code. Men must attempt to live by truth and justice. Although Persian marital customs differed so strongly from our own—marriage between brothers and sisters was not extraordinary, and marriage between father and daughter even occurred—this is no argument against the profundity of Iranian ethics, but only for the relativity of moral systems. This also holds for their peculiar funeral customs.

RITUAL AND FUNERAL CUSTOMS

Parsee ritual was celebrated by a special professional group which had arisen in Media: the Magi (Mobeds). Even before Zoroaster the fire cult had taken central place in the ceremonies of worship, and the religion of the Avesta was a synthesis between the reforms of Zoroaster and the doctrines and practices of the Magi, who pronounced themselves the direct heirs of his first followers. The extant ruins of Iranian fire temples show that the fire chamber in the heart of the building was probably shielded from penetration of the slightest ray of daylight. The sacred fire burning in this room was not to be touched by human hand or tainted by human breath. The priests who would stir up the fire with tongs and shovel were required to wear gloves and a cloth over their mouths, so that they must have looked like modern surgeons. All new fires were kindled from the fire at the sacred altar, were maintained by ritually purified wood, and, once lit in the houses of believers, were not permitted to go out.

The peculiar Iranian funeral customs reflect the close connection between death and the demons. As among the Jews, the Persians believed in *tumah*, ritual uncleanness which arose from corpses. The Parsees believed that Ahriman sent forth the cadaveric demon Nasu in the form of a carrion fly. In order to exorcise the spells of such demons, a four-eyed dog—that is, a dog with two white spots on its forehead—was led into the room. Demons, the theory went, would flee from the dog's gaze. Then the room was consecrated or disinfected by fire; a priest would pronounce the prayers for the dead from the Avesta; and two persons would hold vigil by the body in order to keep the demons away.

The place of burial was the *dakhma,* the funeral tower, which was situated at a distance from cities and was considered unclean. The tower was cylindrical, about twelve feet high. On its roof the naked corpses were laid out in rows. Here they were exposed to the elements and carrion-eating wild life. Vultures therefore swarmed around these towers. The bones, picked clean and dried out by the sun, were stored within the tower. Thus the earth was not contaminated by burials. This strange and possibly prehistoric funeral practice probably comes from the interior of Asia. It is still practiced in some Parsee communities in India. The uninhabited places where devils and demons can work their will are today called "towers of silence."

Zoroaster's religion with its "dualistic monotheism" is, of all the religions on earth, the one most closely resembling the religions founded on the Bible. Like these, it underwent many changes in the course of time. In spite of its universalistic doctrine and its redemptionist character, it had a number of features that were distinctly Persian. Ahura Mazda was the god of Aryans who had promised his followers domination of the earth. The Zoroastrian priests did not undertake direct missionary work; but wherever the power of Persian rule penetrated under the Archaemenids, the religion also advanced. A number of sects developed and spread particularly in the conquered and colonized territories of Syria, Babylonia and Armenia.

ZERVANISM

Zervanism seems to have had its origin in Media, the ancient home of the Parthians, and to have arisen under the dynasty of the Parthian Arsacids (250 B.C. to A.D. 226). The dualism of Ormazd and Ahriman was apparently felt to be too rigid, and an attempt was made to trace the antagonists to a common origin. Both the good and evil powers were therefore referred back to a supreme primal divinity called Zervan, who was beyond good and evil. Zervan had made Ahriman "prince of this world" for nine thousand years. Once that time was over, he would have to struggle with Ormazd for another five thousand years, until at last the representative of goodness and light would triumph. Zervanism was probably never more than an esoteric philosophy which would have been repudiated by orthodox Mazdaists. The true followers of Zoroaster would have none of it for ethical reasons. For them, the dualism of good and evil was central, because it offered man free choice between the alternatives. If that dualism were weakened or rendered innocuous, the underlying morality of Zoroastrianism would be gone; man's ethical self-determination would no longer matter.

CULT OF MITHRA

Mithra proved to be a far more serious rival to Ahura Mazda than Zervan. A deity of light and the sun dating back to the most ancient times in Persia, Mithra-worship had been repressed but not entirely eradicated by Zoroaster's religious reform. His name lives on to this day in the Neo-Persian word for sun, *mihr*. In Babylonia, Mithra merged with the sun god Shamash. In the Sassanid period (A.D. 226–650) Mithra became the central figure of a Hellenistic mystery cult which for a time, under Emperor Aurelian, was raised to the rank of the Roman state religion and even threatened the future of Christianity. Venerated as *sol invictus*—the undefeated sun god—Mithra penetrated far to the West by way of Armenia and Pontus. In the heart of Hellas, however, Mithra remained an alien; the Greeks would have nothing to do with the god of their traditional enemies.

Through the medium of Roman legionaries, to whom the activistic, volitional character of this new religion appealed, the cult of Mithra spread from Asia Minor to Italy and throughout the Roman Empire. The Mithra mysteries fitted naturally into military life, for they had originally been restricted to male associations. Initiation involved tests of courage, the oath to the flag was called *sacramentum,* and the cult of Mithra itself was known as *militia dei.* This exclusively male cult was practiced in underground grottoes and crypts known as Mithræa. Ruins of a great

many of these have been found along the *limes*, the great Roman
line of defense against the Germans, especially in South Germany. Mithra is frequently pictured killing a bull; the motif derives from ancient representations of Hercules which, in their
turn, appeared as far back as the fifth century B.C. In the second
and third centuries A.D. the cult reached its height; Emperor
Commodus (180–192) was himself initiated into the mysteries.
Its decline began with the Emperor Constantine. During the
apostasy under Julian (fourth century) Mithra was once again
officially designated the chief god of the Empire. But with the
full victory of Christianity under Theodosius the Great (395)
imperial protection was retracted, and the fate of the Mithra cult
was sealed, along with other remnants of ancient paganism.

MANICHAEISM

The most influential and widespread of the offshoots of
Zoroastrianism was Manichaeism, named after its founder Mani
(216–277). At times it seemed to be on the point of outstripping
Christianity and becoming the leading world religion. Its doc-
trine was a compound of Mazdaism, Babylonian mythology,
Jewish, Christian and especially Gnostic ideas and dogmas.

There is a story that a man once came to Napoleon and proposed a universal religion to consist of ideas plucked from all the
existing world religions—the best of those ideas, according to the
inventor. This universal religion would be the logical accompaniment to the great conqueror's universal empire. The emperor
listened to the man's proposal, reflected briefly, and then commented: "Your idea for a religion is really excellent. There is
only one little detail missing: You must have yourself crucified
for it."

The historical Mani met both requirements, for he in fact died
a martyr. His eclectic religion had a good deal of vitality and
scored a number of missionary triumphs. Had it not contained
profound ideas, it would not have made such distinguished converts as St. Augustine, whose later polemic writings were to a
considerable degree concerned with refuting Manichaeism.

Manichaeism was to a large extent a "book" religion. Mani

himself was the author of at least seven religious works. For a long time these were known only from quotations, principally by the Arabs; but fragments of the books themselves have now turned up: research expeditions to Turkestan have unearthed them from the sands of Turfan. In addition, sections have been found in Coptic translations of the early fourth century, on papyri deposited in graves in Fayum. These include the *Cephalaia* (chapters), a collection of religious treatises and records of conversations of the master with his disciples.

On the basis of these sources, we are now able to reconstruct the life of Mani. He was born in Babylon, the scion of a noble Parthian family, on April 14, 216, under the last Parthian king, Artabanes V. His father, Patik, belonged to a vegetarian baptismal sect. Even as a boy Mani gave thought to religious questions and studied all the religions of which he had any knowledge. On March 20, 242, the coronation day of Great King Shapur I, he made his first public preachment. The Turfan manuscripts record that Mani then traveled through Iran, Turkestan and probably India with twelve disciples. The Mazdaist Zoroastrian priesthood were incensed against him, but a royal decree granted him and his disciples religious freedom. When his followers began to increase with alarming rapidity, the Magi, the official representatives of the state fire cult, used all their influence to suppress the promulgation of this new doctrine. A solemn disputation was held at the court of Bahram, the new great king. Kartir, the high priest of the Mazdaists, is said to have proposed an ordeal of molten lead to settle the issue. Mani, however, rejected the suggestion, declaring: "That would be an act of Darkness." Thereupon the Sassanid king is said to have ordered that Mani be crucified and his corpse defiled. The death sentence was carried out in Gundeshapur, northeast of Susa, on February 16, 277. Mani's skin was flayed from his body, stuffed with straw and hung at the gate of the city to warn the populace against following his teachings. According to other accounts, he merely died in prison.

Mani was a conscious founder; he called himself the savior (Saoshyant) destined to appear at the world's end. Early in life he understood his mission and regarded himself as the last emissary in a series of revealers of the divine will, the last of the line of prophets and bringers of salvation: Adam, Seth, Noah, Buddha, Zoroaster and Jesus. He was himself, he believed, the last incarnation of Jesus. And just as Mani himself counted Buddha, Zoroaster and Jesus among his predecessors, a few centuries later Mohammed would include Mani among *his* predecessors.

Mani required strict asceticism and celibacy of his close followers, so that they might liberate themselves from the corrupted realm of physical being. His doctrine coincided with basic Zoroastrian views in that he, too, preached a consistent dualism. From Gnosticism he took over the conception of the deathlike sleep of the light-soul in the vessels of matter and its awakening by a succession of divine messengers—he himself being the last of them, for his was the generation of fulfillment. With his unified and rational explanation of the cosmos, Mani provided a Gnostic interpretation of Zervanism, although he expressed himself for the most part in the images and parables of myth. Since he was clearly much concerned with artistic expression, later legend made of him a great musician and painter. Recently discovered collections of Manichaean psalms provide some substantiation of the first part of the legend; Persian-Indian miniature painting, derived from Manichaean manuscript illumination, probably fostered the stories of Mani's artistic gifts.

With his doctrine of the mingling of dark elements and light, Mani provided an explanation for the presence in this world of so much beauty and sublimity alongside of so much ugliness and imperfection. His doctrine that light, or the divine substance, is by its very nature not part of earthly things, but has only been imprisoned by matter, unquestionably represents a profound answer to an age-old human question. This answer was to have a long life, for many dualistic sects in the Byzantine Empire and in the Western world during the Middle Ages had been influenced by Mani. The Christian Church denounced such sects as the Paulicians, Bogomils, and Cathari (Albigenses) as Neo-Manichaeans. The Holy Grail of Arthurian legend was an element out of the mystery cult of the thirteenth-century Albigensians—and thus represented Manichaeism's last gift to the European cultural heritage.

END OF PERSIAN RELIGION

Zervanism, the Mithra cult and Manichaeism were side branches or special developments of the original Ahura Mazda doctrine. We might say that Parseeism, which itself carried on no missionary work, assumed various forms and transmitted a succession of new impulses to other religions. Late and post-biblical Judaism, too, was subjected to various influences from Persia, for Ahura Mazda was the only deity of the ancient world who could be equated with the God of the Bible. The religion of Zoroaster has certain doctrines in common with Judaism: the universal last judgment, apocalypse, and individual reward or punishment. We cannot go so far as to regard the biblical doctrines as Iranian borrowings, since these doctrines appear very early in the history of the Jewish religion. But Zoroastrianism was undoubtedly partly responsible for the form given to certain details. Probably the Satan of late-Judaic religious thought, the Christian "Antichrist," who in some apocalyptic writings bears the name of Armilus, is a version of the Persian prince of demons, Ahriman. Similarly, the demon Asmodai of the Book of Tobias has been identified with the Persian Aeshma Daeva. The new information about the Qumran sect gleaned from the Dead Sea Scrolls has stimulated new interest in the Persian influence upon Judaism between the composition of the Old and the New Testament.

In Persia itself the doctrine of Zoroaster attained a new period of glory under Shapur II, whose long reign extended almost throughout the fourth century. The new Persian state church, with its hierarchically organized priesthood, did not, however, represent pure Zoroastrianism; it was heavily intermixed with elements of Zervanism. The canon of the Avesta fell into the hands of commentators who introduced a number of theological novelties, including some distinctly polytheistic elements. Ahura Mazda became surrounded by many other gods and goddesses, among whom he was *primus inter pares,* first among equals, like Zeus in the pantheon of Greek gods or Odin among the ancient Germans. This reconstructed Zoroastrian religion persisted in Persia until the Arabic invasion of 641. After Islam had become the Persian state religion by force of arms, the old faith survived only in conventicles, secret, underground gatherings. But it was never entirely destroyed. The fire temples in the provinces of Persia continued to exist, and although Orthodox Moslems denounced the Parsees as pagans, small numbers of them practiced their religion down to the end of the eighteenth century. Today there are still some nine thousand members of the sect, now called the Gehr. Around the year 1000 one of these clandestine Parsees, Firdusi, produced the Persian epic *Shah Namah* ("Book of Kings"), one of the major works of world literature, which breathes the whole spirit of the Orient. Its sixty thousand couplets tell the story of the Iranian Empire from its beginnings to the time it fell before the Arab onslaught.

As early as the eighth century there was mass emigration of the Parsees to India to escape the persecutions of Islam. They have remained there to this day, preserving their old customs. The number of Indian Parsees is estimated at no more than 110,000 persons. They are organized like a Hindu caste; a great many of them are influential merchants, industrialists and financiers. The doctrine of *Mazdaznan* was carried to Europe by a German-American named Otto Hanisch (1854–1936); with its emphasis on dietary reform (raw foods) and special breathing technique, it represents a kind of merger of the Persian and Christian religions.

Parseeism owes its survival to the fact that its followers felt themselves to be a chosen people. Neither persecution nor the intrusion of other religions could induce them to abandon the doctrines of their forefathers, although they did accept a number of outside influences.

RELIGIONS IN PRE-COLUMBIAN AMERICA

IT WOULD be impossible to discuss the multitude of religious ideas among the primitive peoples of North America, such as the Sioux and Algonquins, the animistic notions of the Eskimos, or the worship of pueblo tribes in Arizona and New Mexico. We shall confine ourselves to the religions of the great civilizations of pre-Columbian America: the Aztecs of Mexico, the Mayas of what is now Guatemala, and the Inca of Peru. These religions were all extinguished by the Spanish and Portuguese conquistadors of the sixteenth century, who systematically stamped out the highly developed cultures of these peoples. Only the archaeological investigations of recent decades, supplemented by the old monastic chronicles, have enabled scholars to reconstruct with some degree of accuracy a picture of these extinct religions and civilizations.

THE AZTECS

The Aztecs, who were preceded by older civilized peoples such as the Toltecs and Mixtecs, founded their empire, its capital being what is now Mexico City, around 1325. It survived for two hundred years, until its conquest by the Spaniards (1521). When Hernando Cortez and his band appeared in Aztec country, the ruler Montezuma is said to have regarded the coming of the whites as the return of the white savior-god Quetzalcoatl, a deified hero of Toltec times. This hero-god had left his people and gone away to the East, where he had often showed himself in the firmament as the morning star.

Anticipations of salvation and high civilization were curiously mingled with cruelty and cannibalism in Mexican worship. The Spaniards had never seen so well-ordered a country. One of the companions of Cortez related: "Gardens and fields had water-conduits, walled ponds and freshwater pools. The supply of provisions to the capital and exchange of goods was provided for in exemplary fashion by boats on the lagoons and by highroads running in all directions." The marketplace at Chapultepec was such that soldiers who had been in Constantinople and Rome declared that they had never seen so handsome and so large a plaza, with the traffic among the vast crowds of people so well regulated. In some respects manners were more refined than in Europe. But on the same day that Cortez and his captains visited the market square, they were shown a temple and two gigantic idols of hideous aspect. They were allowed to watch a religious ceremony: the ritual burning of three hearts torn from human sacrificial victims. The floor and walls of the temple chamber were black from blood, which gave off a horrid stench. The bodies of the sacrificial victims were carved up, the choicer tidbits being cooked for the priests, and arms and thighs being put aside to be consumed at festivals and banquets. The heads were hung up for display in the temple. What remained was thrown to the predatory beasts kept for the gods. The flesh of very young boys was regarded as a delicacy and served to the king.

The gods, the Mexicans explained, were savage and demanded a great deal, but in return granted the nation health, favorable weather, growth of crops and victory over enemies. The Spanish conquerors were amazed to find these gruesome idols served by nuns from the noblest families and black-clad priests whose costume and bearing reminded them of Dominican monks.

A single festival in 1486 was reputed to have cost more than 60,000 lives, the victims no doubt being prisoners of war. They were thrown into flames in honor of the god of fire. In view of these cannibalistic orgies, the conduct of the conquerors is more understandable, although still far from forgivable. To the Spaniards, the religion of the Aztecs was a ghastly cult in honor of the devil. According to the studies of Willy Krickeberg, the human sacrifices were a re-enactment of divine self-sacrifice at the creation of the world. The Aztecs believed that periodic human sacrifices were needed in order to keep the sun and moon, which the gods had put in motion, from coming to a standstill.

To obtain human material for these sacrifices, "holy wars" were waged whose object was to capture rather than to kill. Prisoners regarded it an honor to be sacrificed to the gods. The sacrifice itself was performed by the priests, who tore the still pulsating heart out of the body in front of the shrine. According to the Spanish accounts, regular cannibal feasts took place in which youths specially fattened for the holy meal were sacrally roasted and eaten. All these practices, which we find revolting, were meant to provide the gods with strength.

The Aztecs' god of war and national god—although there were many other deities—was named Huitzilopochtli ("Southern Hummingbird"). Born several times in supernatural fashion, he watched over the fruitfulness of the fields. He was also called "the terrible god," and his temple was named Tlacatecco ("place where men are slaughtered"). Every year in December a gigantic effigy of him was made of flour, honey and children's blood. Holes were then drilled through it—an act representing the symbolic killing of the god. Then the figure was dismembered, his heart being given to the king to eat, while the rest was consumed by the priests, soldiers, men and boys—but not by women.

The ritual was celebrated by numerous celibate priests who lived in the temple grounds and underwent various penances, such as scourging and the draining of blood from the tongue and ears. A calendar, based on extremely exact observations of the heavens, regulated the celebration of the cult. The year was divided into eighteen periods of twenty days each, with five intercalary days that were regarded as unlucky. The ritual included ball games played at certain times outside the temples; apparently these were scenes from an ancient religious drama representing the course of the sun and intended to influence the same. In some parts of Mexico these religious ball games have continued down to the present day.

The fate of the dead in the hereafter depended not on conduct in life but on manner of death. Sacrificed prisoners and women who died in childbed entered the paradise of the sun god, where they lived on as butterflies or brilliantly colored hummingbirds. Those killed by lightning and drowning, and those who died of dropsy, entered the realm of the wind and rain god on the cloud-capped mountains. All others entered the general land of the dead, the realm of the god Miclantecutli.

Thus animism, nature myth and magical customs and rituals were conjoined, among an agricultural people, with the advanced organizational forms of high civilization. In spite of their cruelty and inhuman religious practices, the Aztecs were highly praised in the accounts of Spanish administrative officials and the early missionaries, not only for their material achievements, but also for their love of truth, their honesty and their sense of justice.

THE MAYAS

The religion of the "Greeks of the Americas," the Mayas of Guatemala, Southern Mexico and Yucatán, has much in common with that of the Aztecs (hieroglyphic writing, rituals, sacral ball games), but it was not so bloody and cruel. Human sacrifice was far rarer; for the most part the Mayan gods were content with offerings of plants and animals. The priests, who practiced soothsaying, astronomy and calendar-reckoning, were trained in special temple schools. The temple fire was entrusted to vestal virgins. The Mayan pantheon resulted from the merging of various tribal cults and systematic elaboration by the priesthood. Corresponding to the Aztec Quetzalcoatl was the sun god Kukulkan, who acted as both fertility god and lawgiver. In addition there were various nature gods and a complex mythology of the elements. The empire of the Mayas, the oldest civilized people of the Americas, had collapsed before the Spanish conquest, and the oldest religious sites already lay in ruins; but the Mayan language is still spoken by one and a half million peasants. Archaeological investigation of their ruined cities is only in its initial stages, but the great development of Mayan artistic styles is already apparent.

THE INCA

The Inca ("People of the Sun") of pre-Columbian Peru were, in comparison to the Aztecs and Mayas, distinctly an imperial people with remarkable political gifts who welded subject nations into a long-lived empire. This empire flourished from about 1150 until the conquest by Pizarro in 1532. At the time the

Spaniards arrived, it extended from southern Columbia to northern Chile. South of Lake Titicaca mighty ruins of Inca times still exist in a fair state of preservation.

Land was collectively owned by the ancient Peruvian village communities. It was tilled on strict collectivistic principles so that the economic organization of the Inca Empire may be considered an example of state socialism. Political organization was strictly monarchic. The reigning Inca was considered the "son of the sun"; he sprang from an aristocracy that dominated the country. The populace was divided into nobles, freemen and slaves. Among the latter were the practitioners of certain skilled crafts, such as the goldsmiths, potters, weavers, road and aqueduct builders.

The priests formed a special caste, as did the virgins of the sun, who served the sun god and lived in convents. From among them the Inca chose his wives; his sister, however, was his principal spouse. The Inca's power as an incarnate god and sacred king was nearly unlimited. He it was who celebrated the rites of the sun cult. The great sanctuary of the sun god Huiracocha was located in Cuzco. In many Inca hymns this god appears as creator of the world, and of civilization. One text runs: "O Huiracocha, lord of the universe, you are now man, now woman. Lord of warmth, lord of fruitfulness. Can soothsaying teach where you are? When you are above, when you are below, when you are all around, by your royal throne and scepter, hear me!"

But such prayers were reserved for the nobility. The common people practiced an extravagant mummy fetishism (*huaca*) which probably stemmed from an ancient cult of the dead. In addition, the common people practiced ancestor worship, sacrifice—including human sacrifice—and worship of a variety of demons.

The bodies of the deceased rulers of the Inca were mummified and worshiped as gods in the great sun temple in Cuzco because of their *huaca,* that is, their power and holiness. The mummies, seated on golden thrones, were installed in the principal temple of the Inca Empire along with the golden image of the sun's disk. The ruins of that temple, Curicaacha ("golden enclosure"), are today in the possession of the Dominican Order.

None of the pre-Columbian religions in the advanced civilizations of the Americas achieved real monotheism. In the Inca Empire the vast mass of the people were subscribers to the sun cult, while the Supreme Being whom the upper crust invoked was vague and indefinite. Such dualities were generic to the realm of the Inca. The masses lived within the framework of a severe socialistic planned economy that greatly restricted individual liberties; but an elite group was exempted from these rigors. Thus the ancient empire of the Inca contended with problems that have become burning topical issues for the whole modern world.

Extinct Religions
Within Europe

THE RELIGIONS OF THE TEUTONS

IN HIS *Philosophy of History* the German philosopher Hegel dismisses the religion of the Teutons in these words: "We know nothing of their religion, because it amounted to little; it was without depth, a state of stupefaction. To be sure, a peculiar Nordic mythology existed, but the religion simply had no depth to it." Hegel could say this because he was unfamiliar with studies in Germanic folklore which were then only beginning. He based his opinion solely on Tacitus' *Germania* instead of the Edda and the sagas.

Aside from archaeological material, most of our sources are of comparatively recent date, since the traditions of the Teutonic tribes were recorded only after their conversion to Christianity. The two Eddas, the skaldic poetry of the Viking period and the family traditions of Icelandic colonists, differ greatly in value. But critical examination of all the remaining evidence, including the runic inscriptions and Roman accounts written between A.D. 100 and 500, furnishes us with a fairly clear picture of the various strands that entered into the religion of the Teutonic peoples. It apparently arose out of a merging of a fertility religion, the cult of the Vanir, which had its home in Scandinavia, with the younger cult of the Aesir (*ass* = beam, stake god); if the derivation is correct, the veneration of wooden idols was characteristic of the latter cult, which was a form of ancestor worship. The transition from animism and a cult of the dead to personal gods must have taken place very early. The primitive stage of Teutonic religious thought is concealed beneath the mythology as we know it.

TEUTONIC GODS AND THEIR CULT

In addition to the ancient fertility god Frey (Icelandic Freyr), the most important of the gods common to all the Teutons were Tiu, Donar and Woden, whom Tacitus equated with Mars, Jupiter and Mercury. The oldest of them was the sky god Tiu (Tyr), who was called Saxnot in Old Saxon; he represented the realm of justice but was also a pure war god among the West and North Teutons.

Donar, a god of thunderstorms and fertility among the South Teutons, was called Thor in the north, and was the favorite god of the Icelandic farmers. The Normans and Varangians, like their Viking forbears, were also devoted to his cult, which survived far into Christian times. The myths represent him as a heavy-drinking, peasant god, a protector who struggled against such menaces as the giants or the Midgard serpent. Thor's weapon was the hammer (the thunderbolt); the crash of thunder meant that Thor was hurling his hammer against the giants. Amulets in the form of tiny hammers or axes were distributed throughout the north of Europe.

The name Woden is etymologically related to the Old English *wod,* meaning mad, furious and also frenzied in the sense of poetic ecstasy. Woden was considered the war god and leader of the Val, those killed in battle; but he was also lord of magic and runic knowledge. Soldiers and skalds paid tribute to him. He first appears in the north in Viking times under the name of Odin, and soon developed far beyond the dimensions of a demon of storms and guide of the dead (originally he had probably been a demon who came to take away the dead) into the All-father and king of the gods. The Nordic Odin usually appears in the ancient documents as a one-eyed old man with a slouched hat and blue mantle, carrying a spear. He rides through the air on the magic eight-footed horse Sleipnir; the ravens Hugin and Munin sit on his shoulders and whisper into his ears what they have seen on their flights over the world.

Loki, Balder, Heimdal and many of the other so-called gods were probably not deities with cults of their own, but rather figures spawned by mythologizing imagination. Among the female goddesses, the northern Teutons held in high esteem Freya, goddess of fertility and love; the bisexual earth goddess Nerthus (who also had a place among the Vanir as Njörd), and the prophetic mother of the gods Frigg, Odin's wife.

The Teutonic tribes seem to have done little toward creating the institution of a priesthood with special training and secret knowledge. Among the Icelanders, for example, ritual sacrifices were performed by the *gode*, the secular leader of a district, whose dignity was hereditary. In Scandinavia the *jarl* similarly performed the functions of a priest. Tacitus mentions both private and public worship among the Germanic tribes.

Originally, acts of worship were performed in sacred groves and at consecrated places; in later times, however, they took place inside living quarters, in feast halls or in a special sanctuary. In Viking times public sacrifices (*blot*) followed by feasts and heavy drinking were the rule; human sacrifice also occurred. The preferred times for festivals were the beginning of spring and fall, and midwinter; in addition, the summer and winter solstices were celebrated. The Yule festival—later Christianized into Christmas—was important in domestic worship, for it was dedicated to the elves (*alfar*), helpful spirits of the dead—deceased ancestors, that is—to whom offerings were made, often in the form of bowls filled with butter. The spring sacrifices were usually associated with solemn processions. Thus the goddess Nerthus, whom Tacitus calls "Mother Earth," was driven about the country in a covered wagon drawn by cows so that the blessing achieved by the festival would be communicated to the entire countryside and bring good fortune. This was called the blessing *til års ok fridar* (for a good year and peace).

Many springs and mountains, meadows and woods, houses and farms were associated in Teutonic folklore with all sorts of spirits, dwarfs, kobolds and giants. Usually these spirits were well disposed toward men, whom they instructed in the magic powers of plants and stones, runes and sayings, and to whom they taught the secrets of oracles, animal voices and the flight of birds.

TEUTONIC BELIEF IN FATE

If we consider the nature of the Teutonic gods, we see that they stand at the head of a magical world governed by fate and closed tightly within the ring of an immutable order. Salvation in the Christian sense was never ascribed to the Teutonic gods. The Aesir, a great family of gods with Odin as their head, resided in Asgard, the human race in Midgard—the inhabited world—and the demons in Utgard, the unfenced wastelands. But life in Asgard resembled life on earth, since all these Teutonic gods were exalted beings in human form possessed of magical powers. They were not regarded as immortal; unlike the parallel gods of Greece, they were subject to growth and decay. Woden sacrifices an eye to the giant Mimir to learn when the time of misfortune will come. Tyr, the war god, sacrifices his right hand in order to fetter the Fenris wolf. The gods know of the fate that awaits them, and they go toward it with composure, prepared for doom. Their feelings, however, are not of pious submission to the unalterable, but of gloomy horror of impending nemesis. The Teutonic apocalypse has a dark, merciless note.

The Icelandic sagas are pervaded with a sense of total subjection of men and gods to their destiny (*wurd*—Anglo-Saxon *wyrd*). Fate is an inescapable power whose intentions cannot be divined. At the foot of the world-tree Yggdrasil, an age-old giant ash, sit the three Norns—resembling the Greek Moirae—Urd (what has been), Verdandi (what is coming to be) and Skuld (what will be), spinning and weaving and ultimately cutting the thread of life of both men and gods. The Teutonic belief in fate was marked by a far deeper pessimism than the sense of tragedy in the brighter Mediterranean world. "Beware of yourself," says Njal in the Icelandic *Saga of Burnt Njal.* "I cannot help myself," Thord replies, "if death is doomed for me. No man can do aught against the decree of the Norns."

Sometimes this fatalistic piety reached the point of total passivity and resignation; but most Teutonic heroes preferred to sell their lives as dearly as possible, even, or rather especially, in the face of certain doom. Thus Hagen Tronje in the *Song of the Nibelungs* goes into the land of the Huns although he is already certain he will die in this expedition. "If anything is mightier than fate, it is man who bears his fate intrepidly," as the poet Emanuel Geibel has expressed it. The Teutonic peoples required such an attitude of the man concerned for his honor, which was more important than life, and for his posthumous fame. To the ancient

Teuton, then, to act ethically did not mean obeying superhuman standards, but acting according to one's individual fate.

"Teutonic heroism—far from being merely dash and bellicosity —is at bottom nothing but dauntlessness in the face of approaching fate and death. Only the man who has withstood this last trial has won the crowning glory of life. There is no other value in life equal to that. 'Property dies, families die, you yourself will die. Only one thing do I know that never dies: the fame of dead men's deeds.' Icelandic sagas have exposed the error of our conception of the eternally pugnacious, ferocious, bloodthirsty Teuton. The very best and bravest men among the heroes of the sagas are patient and restrained to the utmost extreme. They take up their weapons only at the last moment, when no other choice is open to them" (Walter Baetke). But once the honor of the clan had been affronted, the law of the blood-feud forced every member of the clan to avenge the disgrace.

THE MAGIC OF THE RUNES

Teutonic runic magic was closely connected with the belief in fate. The runes, which were scratched into stone, wood, bark and bones, were symbols for sounds, like our present letters of the alphabet; but they served also as conceptual signs and were used for oracular purposes. The rune was a typically Teutonic attempt to control immanent forces by means of a symbol. Runes were spells in writing, and therefore magic acts. Runic letters were tossed like lots. To guess the runes and thus activate the living forces within them, so that their magic became effective, required more than knowledge—it was an art. The rune-master who commanded this art is known to us from Scandinavian inscriptions: he was in the habit of self-assertively stressing his own innate powers. The runes, as an old rune-stone expresses it, were *raginakundo,* sprung from the powers. To partake of the energy of these powers confers power, and men therefore sought to acquire some of it for themselves—that is the significance, as we have seen, of all magical activities. Even the gods owe their superhuman power to their knowledge of the runes. Odin is the god who knows the runes, as can be seen from the much-discussed lines from which it has been wrongly inferred that Christian ideas had invaded the ancient Teutonic sagas of the gods:

> I ween that I hung on the windy tree,
> Hung there for nights full nine;
> With the spear I was wounded, and offered I was
> To Odin, myself to myself.
> On the tree that none may ever know
> What root beneath it runs.
> They gave me neither food nor drink,
> I bent and looked down below . . .

The god sacrificed to himself, on the gallows-tree sprung from a mysterious root, wounded with the spear and given neither food nor drink—certainly this might seem like a pagan reshaping of Christ at Golgotha. But the poem continues:

> I took up the runes, shrieking I took them
> And forthwith down I fell.
> Then began I to thrive and wisdom to get,
> I grew, and well I was.
> Each word led me on to another word,
> Each deed to another deed.

The god who sacrifices himself does not do so for the salvation of man. Concepts like sin and the need for salvation were alien to the Teutonic way of thinking. What is described here is a mystery of initiation into the wisdom of runecraft, the acquisition of knowledge in order to dominate the world. Odin does not invent the runes, he finds them—for they lie at the foot of the world-tree —and takes them from the powers.

Magic powers are active in individuals and the clan as well as in runes. That is the significance of *fylgja,* which is conceived as a spirit charged with force, becoming visible in such manifestations of life as breathing, flushing of the face, gestures. Often this power appears as a distinct shape, sometimes as the figure of an animal. The appearance of the fylgja frequently forewarns of disaster or death; but it may also take the animistic form of a protective spirit or *haminja,* a power bringing good fortune. In the latter case it represents the force indwelling in man that enables him to create a prosperous and happy life for himself. "The healthy, flourishing person shows by his very appearance that he bears within himself vital force or salvation. On the other hand, impending disaster, especially death, makes its imminence known by absence of color and drooping vitality. These outward tokens are by no means restricted to the aged or the wounded; they may be seen in those who seem to be in full possession of their strength. When Brynhild in the Edda learns that Siegfried has been killed, as she demanded, she breaks into prolonged piercing laughter. Her husband Gunnar reprimands her. 'Why are you losing the bright color of life, you source of all mischief. I believe that you are fey'—that is, doomed to die. He could not know that Siegfried's death had undermined her will to live, had severed the roots of her being, and that she would soon choose death on Siegfried's pyre. Her destiny—but her inner destiny—was fulfilled before her outer fate was sealed, and that could be detected in her appearance" (Helmut de Boor).

IDEAS OF DEATH AND THE ULTIMATE END

As the ancient Teutons conceived death, it did not isolate men but brought the dead back to their clans, who buried them in the family funeral mounds where they continued their common life. In Teutonic folk belief, every so often the "wild huntsmen" would break out of these mounds, led by Woden on a white horse, and would go rushing through the air. This happened particularly on the twelve frosty nights of Yuletide. Modern research tends to see the origin of this notion not so much in nature mythology as in an actual ecstatic secret cult, a warlike league of men who imitated the god by going about the country on nocturnal rampages. The medieval cult of St. Nicholas processions seems to have become linked with the legends of the "wild hunt." The gatherings of vigilantes in Bavaria known as the *Haberfeldtreiben*—a custom now slowly dying out—also seem to have some such derivation.

The idea of Valhalla grew out of this conception of the still living dead in the funeral mound. We find Valhalla first described comprehensively in the skaldic poetry of the seventh and eighth centuries. "Val is the collective name for a group of the slain from a single battlefield. Valhalla is the hall in which they dwell together. The clan funeral mound represented a continuance of the farm jointly farmed by a peasant clan. Valhalla, similarly, was based upon the sworn band of warriors whose collective existence persisted beyond death. Initially, Valhalla was not located in the realm of the gods, nor did it shine with that fabulous radiance ascribed to the later Nordic Valhöll. Similarly, the Valkyrs, the 'choosers of the Val,' only later took on the warrior splendor that is so familiar to us. Glorification of the gloomy dwelling of the dead took place only in later Viking times, the seventh and eighth centuries" (H. de Boor).

For the fallen heroes, however, even the idealized hereafter in which Odin's handmaidens, the Valkyrs, dispensed the mead to the slain remained a dread place. "Not joyful was the band. Doomed were they to wend their way to Valhalla," says the Haakon Saga. It is in all cases better to live than to be dead. Thus an Icelandic collection of sayings puts it: "The handless still hies,/ the halt hold the saddle,/ dauntless the deaf man battles./ Blind is better than burned;/ worthless and wan are the dead." The famous outburst of Achilles: "Better a wretched serf in the light than a prince in the realm of the shades," corresponds wholly with the Teutonic feeling about death.

Yet men and gods must die. All are ultimately drawn down into the universal doom which the Völuspa of the Younger Edda describes as the prophesy of the seeress Völve. The final act of the universal drama is precipitated by the killing of the bright and good god of spring, Balder, a passively suffering god whose death is brought about by Loki, the author of all evil. The cunning Loki appears as an ambivalent Luciferian figure, now helper, now foe of the Aesir. He is the begetter of Hel, the goddess of death, of the Midgard serpent and of the Fenris wolf. Loki, this god of mischief, seems almost an alien in the Teutonic pantheon; and for this reason scholars have concluded that he must originally have been a demonic being in some sun cult. In the Scandinavian Balder-Loki myth there seem to be echoes, on the one hand, of Indo-Aryan dualism in its Persian form (Ormazd-Ahriman); on the other hand, the fate of Balder is reminiscent of the dying and resurrected vegetation gods of the Oriental religions (Adonis, Attis, Osiris, Tammuz). The Teutonic salvation myth, variants of which have entered numerous Germanic fairy tales, likewise reflects the eternal natural cycle of death and renewal. Fairy tales have been appropriately called "the ivy-overgrown tree of Germanic mythology."

The myth tells of Balder's dreams of doom, which he recounts to the other Aesir. His mother, Frigg, thereupon decides to ask all beings and things to pledge themselves not to harm Balder. She forgets only the insignificant mistletoe. The Aesir then play at throwing and shooting missiles at the invulnerable Balder. Loki places a twig of mistletoe in the quiver of Balder's blind brother, Hödur. The twig fatally wounds Balder; he is burned on his ship; his wife Nanna dies of sorrow and is placed on the pyre with him. Hel, the goddess of death, promises to return Balder if all creatures weep for him. All do except for the giantess Thökk, into whom Loki has transformed himself. She refuses, saying that Hel ought to keep what she has. Thökk-Loki weeps only "dry tears," and Balder must remain in the realm of the dead. Loki, however, receives his punishment; the gods fetter him to a rock—like Prometheus—with a snake dripping venom upon him. But ultimately he breaks loose and in the final catastrophe of Ragnarok (which means Doom of the Gods, not Twilight of the Gods) he leads the forces of evil. At last he falls in combat with Heimdal. Odin is killed by the Fenris wolf; Thor dies from the poisonous breath of the Midgard serpent which he has slain. At the end of the Volüspa we read: "The sun shines black, in summers to come ill winds blow. Would you know yet more? Great Garn growls before Gnipa cave. The fetters snap, the wolf runs free. I know still more; far do I see. Near draws the doom of the mighty gods." There follows:

> "The sun turns black, earth sinks in the sea,
> The hot stars down from heaven are whirled;
> Fierce flows the steam and the life-feeding flame
> Till fire leaps high about heaven itself."

But the winter of the universe is followed by a new spring; the world is renewed and a new golden age arrives; the purified earth returns to its primal state and the old gods return.

CONVERSION OF THE TEUTONIC PEOPLES

On the whole we may say that the Teutonic myth of universal doom betrays a weary, depressed mood. The people were ripe for the reception of new ideas. Germanic, Christian and Manichaean elements may have intermixed at the close of the pagan era. Christian missionary work among the Germans began on the Rhine in the second century and was completed in Sweden about a thousand years later. Nevertheless, in the region settled by Teutonic tribes, which extended from Iceland to the Black Sea, Christianity was long accepted outwardly but not received inwardly. The missionaries were most successful when they were able to convey to individual Teutons the idea of Christ as *fulltrui*, a god in whom they could have personal trust. But since apostasy of individuals was regarded as shameful treachery to the clan, conversions came about only when whole tribes declared their adherence to Christianity. The Visigoths made a beginning by becoming Aryan Christians at the time of their incursion into the Roman Empire in the fourth century. Their Bishop Wulfilas made the first translation of the Bible into a Teutonic language; a fragment of it in the Codex Argenteus, the most important monument of the Gothic language, was preserved in Upsala. Ostrogoths, Vandals, Burgundians and Lombards followed in accepting Christianity.

Originally, the Teutonic tribes scarcely manifested any profound grasp of the doctrines of the new religion. They misunderstood a great deal. Apparently, very few among them noticed that they were expected to shift to a new conception of reality. Walter Baetke has rightly observed: "It is perverting the relationship of Christianity to the Teutonic religion to regard it as a consummation or perfecting of elements already present in the pagan faith. Christianity did not answer questions that the early Teutons had already posed. . . . Rather, Christianity had first to make them desire salvation in order to bring salvation to them. The Teutonic religion provided no base on which Christian missionaries could build this aspect of their doctrine."

It might in fact be said that, on the contrary, a certain Teutonization of Christianity took place, for Teutonic thought, forms of public worship and ways of life influenced Christian liturgy, art, ecclesiastical customs and even canon law. An instructive example is to be found in the *Heliand*, an Old Saxon version of the Gospels in alliterative verse written about 830 by an unknown cleric. In the poem the personality of Christ is adapted to Germanic ideas of sacred kingship. Christ is envisaged as the leader of a heavenly band, the mighty lord of a loyal following who wishes to lead warriors to Gethsemane rather than Valhalla. The Germanic peoples felt little sympathy for the passive, suffering Christ. When such a Christ was presented to them, they lapsed frequently into paganism. We know from the letters of Boniface (680?–755), the Anglo-Saxon missionary and organizer of the Frankish church, that chieftains who had been forcibly baptized along with their followers threw off the yoke of Christianity as soon as the Frankish kings left the country. The history of the conversion of the Saxons under Charlemagne presents a similar phenomenon.

The ultimate acceptance of Christianity was usually the result of political prudence rather than genuine conversion. It testifies to the wisdom of the Church that the missionary monks made many a concession to the tribal customs and the established rites of the Germanic tribes. At Geismar in Hesse Boniface gravely offended the Germans by cutting down Donar's oak; Charlemagne similarly toppled the Irminsul. But later on such mistakes were avoided and the Christians attempted to preserve as much pagan ritual as possible, while reinterpreting it in a Christian sense. The result is that to this day a good many pagan customs and ideas dating back to the Teutonic past have been retained, especially in German popular beliefs.

After numerous relapses, all branches of the Teutonic people adapted spiritually to the conceptions of the Christian church. They passed from belief in self-salvation or the possibility of influencing fate by magic to faith in the salvation of sinful man through the Savior Jesus Christ.

THE RELIGION OF THE CELTS AND SLAVS

THE CELTS, a people of the Indo-European linguistic family, were closely akin to the Teutons in appearance, vocabulary and in certain religious practices. Our information about the Celts of antiquity is derived from Greek and Roman writers, inscriptions on monuments and coins, and myths found in the oldest literature of Ireland and Wales.

Around 600 B.C. the Celts, who had been forced across the Rhine by the Germanic tribes, represented a considerable power in Western and Central Europe. In the fifth century they began their great migrations as far as Asia Minor. Simultaneously they spread westward to the southern tip of Portugal, where they mingled with the native population, so that nowadays we speak of Celto-Iberian tribes. In the long run, however, Celtic institutions and manners survived only in Gaul and in the British Isles—chiefly in Ireland, Wales, Scotland and the Isle of Man. Ireland and Wales have remained the principal centers of the surviving Celtic language and culture; on the Continent Caesar's Gallic War resulted in a rapid Latinization of the Celts.

A large number of the names of Celtic gods have come down to us in inscriptions, but the gods themselves are either not very distinct or overlaid with Latin elements. A trinity of war gods appears to have been native to Gaul: Teutates (the name may be connected with Teuton), Esus and Tarnis. These appear frequently in inscriptions. There is evidence that a god by the name of Lug was worshiped throughout Celtic territory; he gave his name to such cities as Lyons and Leyden (Lat. Lugdunum). Local female deities also occur in strikingly large numbers; many of these were called Mother or Matron. Worship of Epona, a horse goddess, extended into many parts of the Roman Empire.

Celtic religious rites were apparently well developed at the time of the first Celtic contact with the Romans. There was a highly organized caste of soothsaying priests and medicine men called druids. The name seems to have meant "sage" or "he who perceives sharply." According to Caesar, the druids came from Brittany and formed a separate priestly elite within the population, trained in special schools and organized as a kind of ecclesiastical order which had its headquarters in Carnutum [Chartres] on the Loire. There were also female druids with the gift of soothsaying.

Sacrifices were performed by the druids in the open air, usually in sacred groves, at holy trees (very often oaks) or holy springs. In late Celtic times on the mainland, sanctuaries were built in imitation of Roman temples, but such buildings were unknown in Ireland, which remained pagan until the fifth century. According to Roman accounts, human sacrifice was common in Celtic ritual. Caesar remarks that in illness or danger, Celts would offer or promise a human sacrifice since "the majesty of the gods, they say, cannot be assuaged unless human life is offered for human life." Pliny even asserts that the Celts practiced sacral cannibalism. If it is true that human flesh was sacramentally eaten, that would explain the strict measures the Roman took to stamp out druidism, for there were only two religions Rome persecuted: Christianity and the religion of the Celts.

We are ill informed on the theology of the Celts because, according to Caesar, the druids refused to permit their sacred traditions to be committed to writing. We do know that they worshiped numerous local protective gods and believed that the land was peopled with a great variety of nature spirits. Magical powers were attributed to the druids—for example, the art of rainmaking—and knowledge of spells and exorcisms. To some extent the druids remind us of the shamans of Asia and the Arctic regions. Tree cults were widespread among the Celts, as among the Germans. In later times worship of original Celtic nature gods seems to have been superseded by veneration of elves, fairies, dwarfs, sacred springs, oaks and stones. Until the late Middle Ages the imagination of the Irish was obsessed with fairies, nixies and dancing elves.

The Celts seem to have believed strongly in the immortality of the soul and in its perpetual reincarnation in new bodies. These

beliefs have entered many Welsh legends. In contradistinction
to the Teutons, the Celts developed a naive, sensual optimism,
rather than a foreboding sense of the doom of gods and men.
Death to the Celts was "the central event of a long life," as the
Greek satirist Lucian put it. For that reason the Celtic Gauls had
no fear of death; they found even suicide alluring as a mode of
passing to a better life.

The realm of the dead was known as the Land of the Blessed,
situated on an island in the remote west. Sometimes this Celtic
Elysium was located in a land under water. The Celts had no
counterpart conception of hell. Many of the ancient beliefs lin-
ger on in the legends and heroic epics of Wales—such as the description of the fairy isle of Avalon in the legend of King Arthur.
The concept of King Arthur's round table and the legends of
Tristan, Parcifal and the Holy Grail are partly based on Celtic
traditions as handed down by the bards. Not for nothing did the
Celts in Ireland venerate a special god (Ogmios) of eloquence
and poetry. The poetic gifts of the Celts persisted in Wales, Scotland and Ireland throughout the Middle Ages. The legendary
Scottish king Finn (Fingal) and the blind singer of ancient days
Ossian are among the more notable of the legendary bards.
When monasticism became established in Ireland after its conversion by St. Patrick (died circa 460), the monks preserved a
great deal of the pagan poetic traditions.

THE SLAVS

Like the Celts in the West, the Slavs in the East also belonged
to the great family of Indo-European-speaking peoples. Their
original home lay between the Vistula and the Dnieper. The
Eastern Slavs (Russians, Ukranians, Ruthenians) are usually
distinguished from the Western Slavs (Czechs, Slovaks, Poles,
Sorbs, Kashubes) and South or Balkan Slavs (Slovenes, Croats,
Serbs, Bulgars). The early history of the Slavs is shrouded in
obscurity. In the course of the great migrations of the peoples
they began moving westward and southward, and around the
year 600 reached the Elbe-Saale line in the West and crossed
the middle and lower Danube in the south.

The Slavs who settled along the Dnieper, as well as those of the Oder, developed from an original animism to the worship of personal gods; but all such Slavic gods were connected with agriculture. The Greek Christian Procopius of Caesarea is our oldest source on the South Slavs. In his *Gothic War*, written around 550, he states that they believed in a kind of supreme deity. On the whole, written documents on Slavic religion are sparse. Certain details are mentioned by Latin writers and German chroniclers, and some folk traditions have come down to us. But none of the evidence goes back to a period in which the religion was still alive.

The chief god of the Eastern Slavs, who was worshiped as a deity of thunder and storms, was named Perun. The Lithuanian variant of this name was Perkunas, meaning "god of the oak." A sacred fire was kept burning for this god in Novgorod, and a wooden statue of him with silver head and gold moustache was erected in his sanctuary at Kiev. This temple was destroyed by St. Vladimir in 988. Another Slavic god was Svarog, meaning "crackler"; he was connected with fire worship. His son Dazbog ("god of gifts") was a sun deity and the center of a fertility cult. In the Russian epic *The Song of Igor* (1177), the Russians are metaphorically called his grandchildren.

The Slavs of the island of Rügen and the coast of Pomerania had a god of war and harvests named Svantevit (*svant* = holy), who was depicted with four heads. His wooden temple in Arcona on Rügen held rich treasures which were pillaged in 1168 by Valdemar, King of the Danes. Because he was a fertility god, a grand and joyous festival was held in his honor after each year's harvest. He was famous also for his oracles and his aid in warfare.

The Slavs had four other temples near Stettin, one of which was dedicated to the three-headed god Triglav. These multiheaded gods of theirs were remarked upon by all the German chroniclers. The temple of Svantevit in Arcona and of Triglav in Stettin had sacred horses which pronounced oracles. Common to all the Slavic languages are the words *bogu*, god, and *besu*, demon. Hence, place names ending in -bog, like Jüterbog, always indicate the sites of Slavic worship. They seem to have had no female deities—at least, no names of such occur among the Slavs. Indications of henotheism—the belief in a single supreme god whose existence does not, however, preclude the possibility of others—are clearly evident among a number of Slavic tribes.

One of the notable characteristics of Slavic religion was a highly developed demonology—which persisted in popular beliefs down to almost the present time. Vampires—bloodsucking revenants, originally in the form of birds—werewolves, people under evil spells, ghosts and nightmares are typically Slavic. Nature is also inhabited by friendly demons such as the Russian *domovoy*, which protect home and barn, or the *vili*, elflike female beings sprung from dew and rain in which the souls of deceased young girls live on.

The ancient Prussians, though Slavs, had a different set of gods. Peter von Dasburg, a monastic chronicler, wrote of the Prussians in 1326: "In their idolatry they worship all creatures as God, namely the sun, moon, stars, birds and all kinds of four-footed beasts, even toads." The earliest credible account of Prussian religious beliefs comes from Johannes Silvanus, otherwise known as Jerome of Prague, who speaks of their worship of fire. The Lithuanians also had a goddess of fire, and the Letts a "fire mother."

Ethical elements were rare in Slavic religion; they appear to have been almost entirely absent in the beliefs of the Prussians and the other Baltic tribes, for whom the gods were elevated natural forces rather than personalities. The Baltic religions were founded on the *do ut des* ("I give so that you may give") principle. When St. Adalbert of Prague came to the Prussians preaching the tidings of the new God, they banished him from their country "because due to such strangers our soil does not yield, the trees bear no fruit, no new cattle are born and the old ones die." The first missionaries, Adalbert of Prague (997) and Brun of Querfurt (1001) were ultimately martyred by the Prussians. For centuries, hatred of Christianity continued to be deeply rooted among them, partly because of the murderous policies of the Order of Teutonic Knights, which Germanized and forcibly Christianized the Prussians between 1251 and 1283. The conversion remained superficial—pagan domestic cults flourished beneath a veneer of Christianity, and a dual faith prevailed longer than the state erected by the Teutonic Order. As late as 1880 an old Latvian woman was heard to declare: "They can say what they like, but since we started sacrificing cocks to Usin, horses and cattle have been thriftier." Usin was the horse god whose worship was celebrated on St. George's Day, April 25. By now, however, little of the original elements are left in modern Slavic superstition.

In general, the Christianization of the Slavs was a slow and difficult process. It began in the eighth century among the Slovenes of the Bavarian Alps. The Croats of the Dalmatian coast did not receive missionaries until the beginning of the ninth century. The tenth century saw some progress among Slavs further to the east. Since the Christianization was undertaken from the Frankish Church in the West and the Byzantine Church in the East, there ensued a denominational split among the Slavs which continues down to the present time. The majority of the Latinized West Slavs look to Rome, the East and South Slavs to the Greek or Russian Orthodox Churches. In its missionary work among the Slavs, the Catholic Church often followed the principle of *compelle intrare;* the pagans were "compelled to enter in" by the sword. Inevitably, there were many relapses.

The Christianization of Russia began around the middle of the ninth century. The Greek Orthodox Church was introduced by Grand Duke Vladimir, who became a convert after his marriage to a Byzantine princess. A Russian chronicle gives a vivid account of the mass baptism at Kiev in 988:

Vladimir hastened to his capital to illuminate the people with the light of baptism. In preparation for the celebration, the idols were destroyed, some being broken to pieces and others burned. Perun, the most important of them, was tied by his tail, beaten with clubs and then thrown into the Dnieper. The astonished people did not dare to defend their idols, but they shed tears for Perun, whom they regarded as the last prop of their superstition. Therefore Vladimir ordered it to be explained in the city next day that all Russians, courtiers and slaves, poor and rich, must come to be baptized. The people, who had thus been robbed of the former objects of their worship, poured in great crowds down to the bank of the Dnieper because they thought that the new faith must be wise and holy, since even the Grand Duke and the boyars preferred it to the faith of their forefathers.

Then Vladimir appeared with a group of Greek priests, and at a special signal the crowd entered the river. Grown folk entered up to their chests or their necks; fathers and mothers held their small children in their arms. The priests read baptismal prayers and sang the praises of the Almighty. When the ceremony of baptism was over and the priests had given all the citizens of Kiev their baptismal names, Vladimir, in the joy and rapture of his heart, raised his eyes to heaven and spoke aloud the following prayer: 'Creator of heaven and earth, grant that they recognize Thee, the true God. Strengthen them in Thy true faith. Aid me in the temptations of the Evil One, so that I may worthily praise Thy name.' . . . On this great day, heaven and earth rejoiced.

On that day the lands of Russia became a province of the Church of Byzantium; but it was not until nearly the end of the twelfth century that Russia could be regarded as really Christianized.

THE RELIGION OF THE GREEKS

HISTORICAL INTRODUCTION

THE GREEK religion, like the beliefs of Romans and Teutons, was polytheistic. Zeus could be worshiped along with Apollo, as Odin along with Thor. In all these religions, there are tales of struggles among the gods. Mythology often embodies historical events of early times. When Kronos, later Chronos (Time), emasculates Uranos (Sky) and devours his children, only to be in turn overthrown by Zeus, modern scholars conclude that the Olympian religion established itself only by successively overcoming the followers of older chthonic deities, as the underworld gods are called. We unfortunately know nothing precise about these events, which must have taken place between 2000 and 1600 B.C.

About the same time that Israelites emigrated from Egypt to Canaan, Ionians, Achaeans and Dorians poured into Greece. The Ionians (the Javan of the Old Testament) came first, followed in the century between 1500 and 1400 B.C. by the Achaeans; last of all came the Dorians, around the twelfth century B.C. The conquerors found a vigorous culture flourishing in Mycenae and other places in Greece; but how many of the aboriginal religious ideas they incorporated into their own religion remains a matter of conjecture. They were even more strongly influenced by Crete. The origin of this island culture, called "Minoan" after the legendary King Minos, has not yet been explained. As for the interrelationships between Greece and Crete, the subject seems more complex than ever since the discovery in 1952 that the rulers of Crete kept their accounts in an archaic form of Greek.

Greek history can be divided into six major periods:

1. The Cretan-Mycenaean Period, which closed with the wave of Dorian invaders about 1200 B.C. This pre-Hellenic world can be reconstructed only from archaeological finds and, latterly, from the painful decipherment of the Cretan "Linear B" script.

Double axes and sacred horns were favorite symbols. Economically and culturally, the society was highly developed and obviously influenced by Egypt and Asia Minor.

2. The Geometric Period (circa 1025–700 B.C.), so called after the prevalence of geometric motifs in the art, was characterized by the polis system of small independent city-states originally ruled by kings, later by a land-owning aristocracy. During the ninth to eighth centuries the great epics of Homer and Hesiod were written. Homer's story of the conquest of Troy testifies to the expansion of the Ionians along the Aegean coast of Asia Minor.

3. The Archaic (from Greek *arche*, "beginning") Period (circa 700–500) was an age of political and economic expansion. Many Greek cities founded colonies on the Black Sea, in Southern Italy and on Sicily. Athens became a democracy with a vigorous political life concentrated in a popular assembly and a Council of Five Hundred.

4. The Classical Period (circa 500–323 B.C., the year of Alexander the Great's death) was the era of Greece's supreme glory in art, literature and philosophy. Under the leadership of Athens, the Greek states made a successful stand against the power of Persia in a number of wars.

5. The Hellenistic Period (323–31 B.C.) was the time of extensive interchange between Greek and Oriental culture, the consequence of Alexander the Great's conquests. An eclectic culture known as Hellenism arose.

6. The Roman Period (from 31 B.C.). Greece, which had been a Roman province since 146 B.C., lost her independence completely. However, her intellectual and artistic influence remained so important for centuries afterward that we may speak of an organic Hellenistic-Roman culture.

THE WORLD OF THE GREEK GODS

The Greeks regarded their gods in a double light: as supreme embodiments of human potentialities, and as powers dwelling afar off in the sky and dominating the cosmos. The convention that the gods dwelt on Olympus, a mountain in Thessaly whose peak was usually wrapped in clouds, symbolized both aspects.

In matriarchal Crete, female deities had prevailed, and there is evidence for prehistoric matriarchies on the Greek mainland. But in historical times Zeus, the sky god, father of men and gods, wielded the scepter. As guardian of law and justice, Zeus Panhellenios was guarantor of the moral order and master of destiny. As Homer presents Zeus, he is the only god who never directly communicates with men; he always uses emissaries. As in most polytheistic religions, there was a tendency in Greek belief toward henotheism, so that Zeus was exalted at the expense of the other gods. In part, Zeus absorbed other deities into himself; they lived on in his epithets, such as Zeus Xenios or Chthonios; in part the word *theos* (god) referred only to Zeus.

As the god from whom the kings of the earth were descended, the whole ordering of nature rested in his hand. Zeus knew present and future, watched over the sacredness of oaths, over the rights of guests, fugitives and supplicants, protected home, family and the state. The Olympian Games, celebrated every four years, were his principal festival. They were attended by Greeks from all cities and tribes. Initiated in 776 B.C., they continued for more than a thousand years, until they were abolished in the first year of the 293rd Olympiad (A.D. 393) by the Christian emperor Theodosius the Great. While the games were in progress, sacred peace prevailed throughout Greece.

Olympia boasted many great temples. The Temple of Zeus, some sixty feet in height, was completed about 460 B.C. and contained the great gold-and-ivory statue of the god created by Phidias. Hera, wife of Zeus, had a statue of her own in one of the oldest temples at Olympia, and special games for girls were dedicated to her.

The more mysterious side of Zeus as a god of nature and oracles was linked to Dodona in northern Greece, where he was venerated in a sacred oak grove whose rustling leaves yielded oracular pronouncements. Elements of an ancient fertility cult can be detected in Cretan Zeus, who was venerated in the form of a bull—symbol of fruitfulness. For Zeus was said to have assumed the form of a bull in order to carry across the sea to Crete the Phoenician princess Europa, from whom the continent takes its name. The story of the rape of the beautiful youth Ganymede, a king's son who was raised to Olympus and became cupbearer to the gods, also suggests a connection between Zeus and a dying and resurrected fertility god.

It would seem, then, that Zeus was the quintessence of divinity and omnipotence. But Homer knew of a dark and incomprehensible power that was stronger even than Zeus. This was Moira, Destiny, whose unknown will even Zeus must probe when—according to the Iliad—he throws two lots into the golden scales of Destiny which are to decide the death of Achilles or Hector, which meant, in effect, victory for the Trojans or the Greeks. In Homer the borderline between the abstract and personified figure of Moira can scarcely be drawn; Hesiod, however, gives names to the three Fates: Clotho, the Spinner; Lachesis, Assigner of Lots; and Atropos, the Inflexible. These are the "Daughters of Night," who assign good or evil to mortal men.

In the later poets and philosophers, Zeus is consciously portrayed as the embodiment of the universe. Thus the great tragedian Aeschylus (525–456) proclaims:

> Zeus is the air, Zeus the earth and sky,
> Zeus is the world, and what is above it, is Zeus.
> (Fragment 170)

Or:

> Zeus! So I cry
> when he wills,
> to the unknown, unnamed god.
> Were I to lay all upon the scales,
> It would not weigh so much as Zeus.
> (Agamemnon V, 160 f.)

A god comparable in importance to Zeus was Apollo, who was worshiped with intense religious feeling. Originally from Asia Minor, he was a fearsome and cruel god, and still retains that character in Homer; but the Greek spirit soon reshaped him. The site of his principal cult was Delphi, where he became established after expelling the cult of an older chthonic serpent divinity. Actually, he was a god of purity, as his epithets Phoebus and Soter indicate. His oracle in Delphi became the connecting link between the city-states of Greece. Apollo, too, absorbed a number of other deities; that is apparent from the more than two hundred names under which he was worshiped. As a bright and beautiful god, the embodiment of measure, music and harmony, he was fondly venerated throughout Greece and Asia Minor. He was a god of healing and atonement, and his son Aesculapius became the god of physicians. Apollo, moreover, was the god of striplings, who dedicated their long hair to him when they reached their majority. He himself was always depicted as a youth bearing his symbols, the bow, the lyre and the laurel.

The Pythian Games were celebrated every four years at Delphi. There, at the most important site for the worship of Apollo, a priesthood developed which possessed almost the authority of a church. Delphi was the only spot in Greece that boasted such a sacral corporation. In the interior of the Temple of Apollo rested the Omphalos (navel-stone), which was regarded as the midpoint of the world. The Pythia, the priestess of Apollo, sat on a tripod set over a crack in the earth and uttered her prophesies in a trance. From her pronouncements, the priests deduced the replies to the questions that had been posed to the "knowing god." Delphic Apollo was consulted on political questions, on the founding of colonies, and also on matters of personal life. When cities were visited by plague, war or crop failures, the oracle prescribed the necessary acts of expiation. From the beginning of the seventh century, the fundamental commandments of morality were disseminated among the people by way of the Delphic oracle. Delphi established the concept of *dike*, right and justice. The most famous of the Delphic sayings, however, was the *Gnothi seauton*, Know thyself, which really means: Consider that you are only a man; be conscious of your powerlessness and do not get above yourself. "God loves to cast down everything that towers too high," says Herodotus. Complete human happiness violates the cosmic order, which prescribes a certain limit even for happiness.

But to return to the Olympic pantheon: The sky god Zeus united with the earth goddess Gaia in a sacred marriage (*hieros gamos*). Hera, his subsequent wife, was a local vegetation goddess of the Argos district whom Zeus subjugated as his Greek tribes overpowered the aboriginal population. Hera became the patroness of women, marriage and the home.

Athena was originally associated with a fetish on the Acropolis of Athens, the *palladion* that protected the city. Despite her primary role as the patroness of Athens, she was worshiped throughout Greece in temples of her own. Pallas Athene, as daughter of Zeus, displays masculine traits, assumes part of her father's powers over thunder and lightning, and is always closely associated with him. Mythology made her the personification of reason, who sprang in full armor and the strength of youth from Zeus's head. Born without a mother, she remained always virginal, and was venerated in her own city as "divine maiden," exalted above all the pangs and joys of motherhood. The spear and raised shield were her proper weapons; she was both goddess of heroic battle and patron of the arts, the sciences and the crafts. Annually, in July, the Panathenaea were celebrated with musical and gymnastic contests. While Homeric songs were recited, a splendid new robe for the image of the goddess on the Acropolis was carried through the city. On the frieze of her temple, the Parthenon, the sculptor Phidias and his school immortalized this great Athenian festival in one of the most beautiful works of art the world has seen. Her statue of gold and ivory in the interior of the temple, already famous in classical times, was made by the same artist; unfortunately, it was subsequently destroyed, as was the bronze statue of Athena Promachos, which sailors were wont to hail from afar as the sign of Athens. At the conclusion of her festival, many cattle were sacrificed, and the Panathenaea ended in a great popular feast.

Poseidon, depicted in Homer as the brother of Zeus and god of the sea, was probably a pre-Greek god, originally the spouse of the goddess of earth. Zeus had to share his power with Poseidon and his other brother, Hades, prince of the underworld. Poseidon's storms shake the continents; his trident shatters the rocks. Poseidon "the earth-shaker," with his palace in the depths of the sea, is always described as a wild and resentful god, demonic and unpredictable as the sea itself. He was worshiped especially on islands and in coastal areas—his temple at Cape Sounion on the coast of Attica illustrates to this day the reverence that was felt for him. One of the principal sites of his cult was on the Isthmus of Corinth, where in his honor the Isthmian Games were annually celebrated with chariot races. Whether the sea was his original element is uncertain; in Arcadia, the most inaccessible district of Greece, he was worshiped in the form of a horse. His connection with the winged horse Pegasus is fundamentally unclear, although Pegasus was regarded as a scion of Poseidon. Pegasus as the symbol of poetic imagination is a late concept, unknown to the Greeks.

Zeus's brother Hades, the god who ruled over the shades, is called by Homer "the underground Zeus." But there are only isolated traces of any real Hades cult. Black sheep were sacrificed to this merciless and inexorable god—the sacrifice being performed with averted head. To invoke Hades, it was necessary to strike the ground with both hands.

The age-old cult of Hermes, son of Zeus and messenger of the gods, was practiced throughout Greece. Hermes was the "guide of souls" (*psychopompos*) who conducted human souls to Hades. As god of dreams and sleep, he touched the eyes of slumbering men to waken them. Inventor of the shepherd's pipe and the lyre, Hermes led the dance of nymphs and Charites (goddesses of grace). Nevertheless, there was something chill and mysterious about his nature. Swift and fugitive, he suddenly would appear at the side of men as the "god who is met unexpectedly." As god of roads, he was the protector of all travelers, the guardian of merchants, but also the patron of thieves and scoundrels. Many realms belonged to him, for he was simultaneously a fertility god and a pastoral god; the phallus placed in the center of a heap of stones at crossroads was sacred to him. Everywhere in the squares and streets of Greece "herms" were erected: stone pillars with the head of Hermes and prominent phallus as symbol of the secret force of life. Such herms were also placed at all the entrances to wrestlers' schools and other public buildings.

A number of other gods must be listed: Ares is familiar as the god of raw strength, who represented the savage tumult of war. Artemis, the goddess of the hunt, went about with a retinue of nymphs; she was the virginal twin sister of Apollo and was also venerated as a goddess of night and the moon. In Ephesus, where her worship took a special form, the Apostle Paul had a famous encounter with her. Then there was Aphrodite, the goddess of beauty and love, whom myth reported rose out of the sea near Cyprus (the "foam-born goddess"). In Corinth, at least, her cult included sacred prostitution, which suggests Oriental origins and a relationship to the Babylonian cult of Ishtar. Her husband was considered to be the smith Hephaestus, her son Eros, the god of love. Hestia was goddess of the hearth and of fire, Pluto the god of the underground of wealth, especially such wealth as came from the interior of the earth. Sacrifices were offered to Hestia, but Pluto never commanded a special cult of his own. Among the minor deities were the shepherd-god Pan, who played the flute; the wind god, Aeolus; the goddess of dawn, Eos; the Spartan moon goddess, Helena; and many others.

The Homeric Greek felt a kinship with his gods, for he believed that his family was descended from them. Moreover, he did not differ from them. The gods of Homer, as was long ago remarked by Aristotle, were nothing but "imperishable men." Ethically, too, they were not superior to men; they were only far more powerful. The gods loved and hated, rejoiced and suffered like men. Their actions were often highly arbitrary, so that they could not be trusted. These gods were not "otherness incarnate," nor did they live in a realm beyond the world. Their will, too, was restricted by the eternal cosmic order. Homeric gods possessed no absolute omnipotence.

The fundamental character of Homeric piety was life-affirming; for all that the perishability of existence was fully acknowledged, life was regarded as the highest good. Achilles in the *Odyssey* expressed that affirmation of life in the famous lines: "I would rather be above ground, the servant of some man of meager means, than ruler over all those dead and gone."

THE MYSTERIES AND THEIR GODS

The mystery cults were always practiced by relatively small groups of initiates who were isolated from the mainstream of the popular religion. For the most part, the mysteries came from Asia Minor or from northern Thrace. Such was the case with the cult of Dionysus, which came to Greece around 600 B.C. A Thracian god, Dionysus became linked in Greece with the cult of the wine god Bacchus. In intoxicated ecstasies, amid frenzied music and wild dances, his worshipers paraded in hordes over the country, threw themselves upon bulls, which were regarded as unknown gods, and rent them alive, eating the still warm and quivering flesh in the belief that they were eating the god himself and thus uniting with him. The orgiastic character of Dionysian worship and its sacramental cult of mystical ecstasy was tempered under the Greek influences of Delphi; but the wildness persisted throughout the whole history of Greek religion. Friedrich Nietzsche attributed great importance to the Dionysian element in Greek culture, but in fact it comported no more with the Greek character than pessimism. The Greeks actually changed the nature of this alien cult by making Dionysus a native vegetation god and providing him with demonic servants, the goat-tailed satyrs and the wild women known as maenads. The god of ecstasies became lord of the vintage and the festivities connected with it: rustic amusements and masquerades. This explains the relationship of Dionysus to the drama, which was rooted in such popular customs. In this way the un-Greek aspects of the god were softened and his worship was reshaped in the Hellenic spirit.

Linked with the worship of Dionysus was the Orphic cult, named after the Thracian singer Orpheus who, according to the legend, was torn to pieces by the maenads in their holy madness. Only his head remained unharmed; it floated across the sea to Lesbos, where it was buried and became the source of Orphic oracles. The name of Orpheus became identified with mythological, theological and cosmological literature dealing with the path of salvation and redemption. The principal myth of the Orphic cult was the legend of Zagreus, son of Zeus and Persephone, who was guarded by the Cretans but lured away by the Titans. He fled in various guises, the last being that of a bull, but the Titans caught him at last, tore him to pieces and ate him raw. Wrathful Zeus killed the Titans with his thunderbolts and created men out of their bodies. Consequently, man consists of two parts: one titanic and earthly, the other Dionysian and divine. By asceticism and purifications the soul, man's Dionysian part, can be liberated and return to its heavenly origins. This is the Orphic myth which —along with Plato—held that the soul was imprisoned in the body and passed through a cycle of rebirths. Out of this dualism, doctrines of transmigration developed: the soul had to voyage through various bodies of both animals and men before it was purified at last and could enter into the godhead.

The mystic current in Greek religion found its fullest expression in the Eleusinian Mysteries, the most famous of the mystery cults of antiquity, which lasted down to the fourth century A.D. Eleusis was a small city near Athens, in the innermost corner of the Bay of Salamis. The celebration of the Mysteries ultimately reached the status of a national cult, and nine days every September were set aside for special rites. The myth of the cult, which we know from the Homeric hymns, ran as follows: The underworld god, Pluto or Hades, had abducted Persephone or Core (personification of the sowing), and her mother Demeter wandered about in despair, seeking her daughter. She was so inconsolable that all growth in nature ceased. In the guise of an old woman she came to Eleusis where, unrecognized, she was employed by the king and his wife as a nurse for their little son. When secretly attempting to confer immortality upon the child by anointing him with ambrosia and blowing her divine breath into him, she is surprised by the queen. Thereupon she confesses her identity and orders the building of a great temple. But Persephone has not yet been found, and no seed sprouts. At last Hades permits the release of Persephone on condition that she spend two-thirds of the year with him.

The myth in the form we know it today is obscure and composed of various strata. The story of the child, which plays a great part in the rites of the mysteries, probably derives from the myth of Bacchus. The key element of the mystery was probably the dramatic presentation of Demeter's sorrow over the death of her daughter and her efforts to restore her to life. From this the communicant drew a consoling faith in a better life after death. The hymn to Demeter ascribed to Homer therefore closes with the words: "Blessed the man who has witnessed these holy ceremonies, but the uninitiate who has not partaken of these sacred acts will not have the same lot after death in the darkness of Hades." Demeter, goddess of the blessings yielded by the earth—her name means "earth mother"—is the archetype of the *mater dolorosa*, at once suffering and gracious. The cult of Demeter was an agrarian religion with major emphasis upon femininity, in contrast to the Olympian religion and the austere masculine character of Homeric piety. The chthonic cult was rooted in belief in the soil as mother. Birth, growth and death, that is, return to the maternal womb of earth, were the fundamental problems in this early religious philosophy. What conferred greatness and lasting qualities upon this cult of the corn goddess Demeter was not the sexual symbolism, but the promise to its participants that a happy life in the hereafter awaited them. In other respects Greek religion was very much of this world; the hope of the hereafter expressed in the mystery cult of Demeter was the great exception. Only Christianity was able to vie with and ultimately to supplant the Eleusinian Mysteries.

ORGANIZATION OF WORSHIP AND THE POLIS

The Greeks always strongly stressed the national character of their worship. In foreign countries, for example in Egyptian Naucratis, they set up temples dedicated to "all the gods of the Greeks." To be Greek was to acknowledge Zeus as the great god of the sky. The same was true for the other gods. Poseidon was associated throughout the Greek world with water, the sea and horses; Artemis was venerated everywhere as a goddess of nature and the hunt; and Athena was universally considered both the virginal protector of cities and the patron of arts and sciences. So, too, everywhere in the Greek world, the grain and the fields were dedicated to the mysterious earth mother Demeter, although her mystery cults assumed many different forms.

Along with these common elements, however, we must also take note of local and historically conditioned divergencies. The rituals of Athena differed in Athens from the Athena rituals of Sparta; the Spartan Artemis had traits unlike the Artemis of Ephesus; the Apollo of the Delphic Oracle had little in common with his namesake in Arcadia or Delos. There was no standardization in this matter. Neither was there a fixed pattern of worship. Even within one and the same city, people of different districts might worship deities who, though bearing the same name, were credited with quite different functions and differing natures. In Athens, for example, the city goddess Athena Polias was venerated along with the goddess of victory, Athena Nike, and the goddess of health, Athena Hygieia. Each Athena had a temple of her own, and special feasts and rites. On the other hand, the patroness of the city of Athens was also worshiped in the rival city of Sparta. An even more glaring case of disparate identities under the same name is that of Olympian Zeus, who bore scarcely any resemblance to the similarly named oracular god of Dodona, where, moreover, he was worshiped by priest-sorcerers in a manner analogous to the rites of primitives in the African jungle.

Neither was there any consistent dogma which governed the practice of religion within the Hellenic world. Yet Greek worship was everywhere a state institution. The Greek city-states, much as they differed in political organization, all built temples and supported public worship. The priests were officials rather than doctrinal preachers. They were responsible for the upkeep of the temple and the offering of sacrifices, and were selected by the state or the popular assembly either by lot or election. In other words, they were civil servants. Even the few hereditary priesthoods in some of the mystery cults were answerable to the government.

Greek temples differed from those of all the surrounding peoples both architecturally and functionally. The house of the god was divided into three or four parts. The rite of sacrifice always took place outside, so that the ordinary Greek citizen scarcely ever saw the inside of a temple. Such practices were unknown in the Orient. The beauties of the temple were primarily intended for the gods, not for the believers.

State intervention in the sphere of private religion occurred only in exceptional cases. But the gods themselves might act on their own behalf. The life of man demonstrated how inconstant is fortune, so that according to Herodotus all human things move in a circle and man himself can never be continuously happy. To explain this, the Greeks often referred to the ancient doctrine of hubris, human presumption, which would be punished by Nemesis, the vengeance of the gods. The highest virtue to the Greek was therefore *sophrosyne*, prudent moderation. *Medén agán*, not too much, guard yourself against all excess, was inscribed upon the temple of Apollo in Delphi. In general, however, Greek worship accompanied man's daily life without ever dominating it.

The Christian believer is called upon to practice his religion soberly. To the Greeks, the predominant expression of religion was joy. The language they used in referring to it reveals the close link between divine worship and festivity. Public worship was referred to as a "cessation of daily labors." The expression "without worship" meant simultaneously "without festivity." Even the Greek word for offering is synonymous with festival, so that the same word may mean a religious sacrifice, a wedding or the celebration of some other festive occasion. Another element that gave a joyous tone to Greek religion was its remarkable polytheistic tolerance. Greek travelers were willing to venerate any of the gods of the peoples they encountered, and a good many of these were adopted into their own cults. When Jason arrived in Colchis with his band of Argonauts, he poured sweet wine from golden cups as an offering to the gods of the country. And a classical gloss on this verse in the poet Apollonius of Rhodes explicitly states: "He who enters a foreign land sacrifices to the gods worshiped in that land."

THE CULT OF HEROES

The religion of the Greek polis in the narrower sense centered partly around the deities of the city, partly around the local heroes, the strong men who had once lived on earth and who after their death became protectors of posterity. Originally, the heroes were the forefathers of the most prominent families of the city, whose bones were buried within the city walls. The more such graves of heroes a city had, the happier it was. When a city was conquered, therefore, the enemies would carry away these sacred bones. Ingenious measures were taken to secure the safety of the remains. The ashes of Solon, for example, were scattered over the whole island of Salamis, so that they could not fall into enemy hands. Such a measure had its disadvantages, since the cult of the heroes was associated with the graves. The foremost clans took charge of the rituals of the cult, which reinforced their positions of power in the city. Since the common people had no genealogies and no ancestor cult, it followed in the opinion of the nobles that they had no gods. Consequently, their only chance to obtain gods was to attach themselves to the cults of the noble families. The introduction of democracy changed this situation, for then the cult of heroes became nationalized and thus accessible to all citizens.

The rites of hero worship involved the slaughter of a bull at the grave. The blood was allowed to run into a pit that was connected with the grave by a pipe, so that the ashes of the dead hero would be moistened with blood. Religious duties were mandatory for each citizen. Socrates was condemned to death because he had not fulfilled the obligations of the cult, although he pleaded to the court that he was by no means an atheist, but on the contrary felt profound veneration for the gods.

The Greeks believed that the semidivine heroes had also taken part in the Persian Wars. There were innumerable tales connected with individual Hellenic heroes. For example, the Attic national hero Theseus, who in ancient times had killed the Cretan Minotaur and thus released his city from shameful tribute, came to the aid of Athens a second time at the Battle of Marathon (490 B.C.). The welfare of a region depended on the mysterious blessings conferred by its heroes. The most famous of these, venerated almost as a god by Greeks everywhere, was Heracles. The myths of his exuberant masculinity, elaborated especially by the Dorian tribes, and his twelve labors, were told and retold in classical literature and art. Almost equally famous was Jason who with his band of chosen companions, the Argonauts, sailed the *Argo* to Colchis and there secured the aid of the sorceress Medea in stealing the Golden Fleece. Looming large among the heroes of the Trojan War is Achilles, son of Peleus and the sea goddess Thetis. The story of the slaying of Achilles by Hector's brother Paris, whose arrow is guided by Apollo to Achilles' only vulnerable spot—his heel—is a post-Homeric elaboration that closely parallels the Siegfried legend.

THE CLASSICAL ENLIGHTENMENT

The classical era had its own enlightenment, that is to say a movement to re-examine religion and pare away excrescences of myths and a surplus of anthropomorphized gods. In our account we have mentioned only the more important deities; but there was a great multiplicity of them. As early as 500 B.C. the philosopher Xenophanes criticized many of the old myths for their immorality. Zeus, for instance, was credited with so many amorous adventures with women and boys that he could scarcely serve as a moral exemplar. Xenophanes even protested against the very principle of polytheism. He maintained that there could

PLATE I   *Fetishes* are artifacts believed to be imbued with magic. Lifeless things and animals are venerated because they are believed to possess special powers. The fetish mask of the Beri-Beri, above left, serves to fend off misfortune. Above right: A Tibetan mask with a *Dorma* made of butter. Below: In the brightly painted fetish hut of Dahomey are buried the bones of deceased members of the family. The high priest converts these into fetishes by a complicated ceremony.

Laenderpress

Bavaria

PLATE II *Cult of the Dead.* Above left: The Dajaks preserve the skulls of their dead in the belief that the wisdom of the ancestors will pass to the descendants. Right: At the funeral feasts of the Aymara, cakes in human form are placed on the graves. It is believed that the dead return in time to their families. Below: The body of a poor Toradja woman lies ready for burial. Her daughter brings food to her and watches by her.

Laenderpress

PLATE III *Ancestor Worship.* Above left: The Libolos believe that the souls of the dead have found eternal peace in these wooden figures. Above center and right: Totem poles of the Maori and of the Indians. The poles often indicate the clan membership of the family. Below left: A Buddhist woman prays before the ancestor altar for her forefathers, whose names are inscribed on the tablets. Sticks of incense are burned in the bowl. A wooden cymbal in the shape of a fish is beaten as a sign of atonement. Below right: Stone pillars in front of the house are considered resting places for the souls of ancestors. Their descendants, when faced with important decisions, meditate in front of these pillars in the hope that the wisdom of the ancestors will be conveyed to them.

PLATE IV *Cult of the Dead among the Egyptians.*
Above: Among the grave-goods in a pyramid was
found an effigy of rowboat with crew intended to carry
the deceased through the realm of the dead. Center:
The mummy at the entrance to the tomb. Beside him
are the god Anubis and the dead man's wife and
daughter. Below: A deeply moving lament for the
dead. The mourners' arms are raised, beseeching the
redeeming power, which remains invisible.

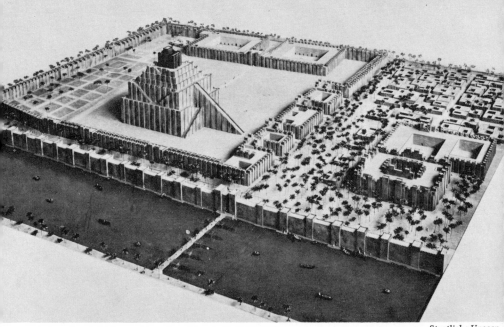

Staatliche Unseen

PLATE V *Babylonia*. Within the Sacred Ground of the Temple of Marduk in Babylon, above, is the Temple of the Epiphany of Esangila, where stood the pure gold statue of Marduk and the ziggurat with the tower of the deity. Below left: Brick relief on the Ishtar Gate in Babylon. The bulls of the god Adad and the wise dragon of Marduk are represented in order to invoke the gods themselves as guardians of the city. Below right: The stele on which is inscribed the Laws of Hammurabi. The king is shown receiving orders from the sun god. The text of the Laws is below the relief.

Archiv für Kunst und Geschichte   *Kunstarchiv Arntz*

Hirmer

PLATE VI *Egypt*. Above left: The god Ptah
and King Sesostris, 2000-1788 B.C. Sesostris receives divine powers from Ptah. Above right:
Ranofer, high priest of Memphis. Rectangular
props attached to the sculptured body are reminiscent of pillar-statues. Below: Pyramid of
Chephren looming above a whole area of tombs.
The gigantic structure was meant to immortalize
the sacred power of the king.

Foto Marburg

Hirmer

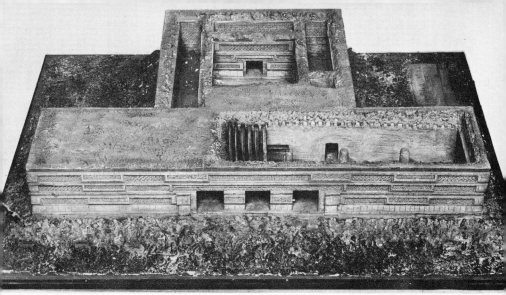

PLATE VII   *Mexico*. Above: Model of the many pillared palace in Mitla, famous for the artistry of its carvings. Center: Primeval anxiety, a sense of the transitoriness of life, is expressed by this mask, whose face consists of two halves. One side shows a living man; the other, a corpse. The mask expresses the fundamental attitude of ancient America. Below: Pyramid of Chichén Itzá. The god descends the 367 steps from heaven to earth. Only priests and rulers were permitted to the sanctuary on the topmost terrace.

a

PLATE VIII *Pre-Columbian*. The gods of the Central American Indians of pre-Columbian times demanded human sacrifices. The priest cut the human heart, top left, as an offering to the god. At a sacrificial feast, top right, the priest pulled the heart-skin of the sacrificed victim over his own head, thus to present it to the god. Below: A stone table from a temple of the great sun god Quetzalcoatl, depicted as a feathered bird atop the tree of life.

Irmgard Groth Kimball

Irmgard Groth Kimball

Ullstein

only be one immutable divine power. Nevertheless, the general concept of "divinity" was more and more losing its force, and was equated with providence or destiny. The Ionian natural philosophers, Hippocrates the physician and Heraclitus, the blind man of Ephesus (circa 500 B.C.), also took issue with the excesses of religion. From Heraclitus' *On Nature* comes the following fragment: "They purify themselves by staining themselves with other blood, as if one stepped into mud to wash off mud. But a man would be thought mad if one of his fellow men saw him do that. Also, they talk to statues as one might talk with houses, in ignorance of the nature of gods and heroes."

The greatest challenge to the concepts of religion came from the Sophists, who wandered from city to city, giving instruction in all branches of knowledge. They acted as the spokesmen of philosophical radicalism and represented everything as relative. Protagoras declaring that man was the measure of all things was voicing this selfsame spirit. Such a view sapped the substance of all moral and religious standards.

Socrates (469–399) attacked these Sophists, although he seemed outwardly one of them. His aim was to demonstrate that the doctrines of the Sophists were corrupting and empty of content, and that it was essential to establish ethical behavior as the supreme standard for the conduct of life. He believed that men possessed a daimon, an inner voice that told them what their moral duties were. The Socratian daimon has frequently been equated with what we would call conscience. There was no place for Orphic-Dionysian mysticism in Socrates's thought. His religious independence consisted in an ethically founded trust in God; he bade men practice self-examination and seek self-knowledge so that, ultimately relying upon God, each man could stand on his own feet and become an individual. Dispensing such doctrines, he became a leader of Athenian youth. His association with such wild young blades as Alcibiades and Charmides aroused suspicion among the conservative citizens. He was accused of corrupting the youth and neglecting religious duties. By a small majority, he was condemned to death, and with utmost composure drained the cup of poison, certain that he had always walked in the ways of the deity.

The teachings of Socrates were preserved for posterity chiefly

by his greatest disciple, Plato (427–347)—who, however, soon
constructed his own philosophical system on the basis of Socratian influences. The best known element in the Platonic system
is his doctrine of ideas, which holds that ideas exist eternally.
Reality is not what we perceive with the senses, but the ideas
behind things. Truth can be a great many different things at different times, but the idea of truth is always the same. The Platonic doctrine of ideas distinguishes strictly between the material
world and the world of ideas; the two are opposed to one another.
Thus Plato brought into Greek thought the dualism that persisted
into the Hellenistic Age and exerted a particularly strong influence upon Gnosticism. Highest of the ideas is the idea of the
good, which might be called Plato's concept of God. In the writings of his old age, the *Critias* and the *Timaeus,* the ideas are
represented as actually gods.

The significance of Plato within the context of religious history
is his criticism of the Greek myths. In his last work, *The Laws,*
Plato expressed his own religion in these terms: "There are gods.
They are concerned about us. But neither by sacrifices nor
prayers may they be persuaded to do anything contrary to
justice."

Plato himself was tolerant toward the popular religion, which
he thought was of value for the preservation of the state. This cannot be said for the philosophies that had their origin in Platonism.
We cannot, however, go into a discussion of stoicism, neoplatonism or epicureanism, and must limit ourselves to the following
remarks on the classical enlightenment:

Philosophical criticism had undermined traditional religion
and promoted individualism. The mysteries and local cults prof-
ited by this situation. The classical enlightenment took the form
of rationalistic religious criticism, arguing that Zeus, Athena,
Apollo and the other gods had never existed except in the form
of lifeless statues. Thus Herodotus could declare that Homer and
Hesiod had given the Greeks their gods. And the philosopher
Euhemerus attempted to demonstrate rationalistically that the
Greek gods had only been men of distinction. Nevertheless, their
reality was strongly felt, because they actually embodied forces
and attributes of human life. Deification in myth took place because the Greeks thought figuratively. The road from many beau-

tiful individuals to the abstract concept of beauty went by way of the concrete image of beauty, Aphrodite. Gods are more than dressed-up concepts. Men prayed to Aphrodite; it would be absurd to pray to a mere concept.

The gods of polytheism display the great and variegated potentialities of humanness; but they display also the inner dichotomy and contradictions inherent in man. That is why Greek tragedy proved to be the last word of classical mythology, unveiling the dark side of myth. And that is why Jakob Burckhardt and Friedrich Nietzsche, who fixed their eyes chiefly on nemesis, the force of destiny which ruled even the gods, spoke of the secret sorrow within the beauty of Greek images of the gods, and of the sadness in their gaze. In discovering the tragic and hapless elements in Greek thinking, these philosophers corrected the excessively optimistic view of the Greeks held by Winckelmann and his age. Hegel, too, had made this discovery; in his *Aesthetics* he perceptively says that the gaiety of pleasure among the Greeks was always associated "with a quiet touch of sadness, that smile amid tears in which neither a true smile nor true tears develop."

THE RELIGION OF THE ROMANS

THE ROMAN religion, too, was a composite of numerous elements. Its underlying strain of magic survived in worship and ritual through the period of Roman kingship (six kings down to Tarquinius Superbus), the aristocratic republic (from 510 B.C. on) until well into the Empire (from 27 B.C. on). The Italian peninsula had been the home, from very ancient times, of agricultural tribes such as the Latins, the aboriginal inhabitants of Latium, who spoke an Indo-European language, and tribes such as the Etruscans in Central Italy, possibly immigrants from Asia Minor, whose language is still a riddle.

The Etruscan religion probably exerted a powerful influence upon the Roman—especially its highly developed cult of the dead and its concern with the hereafter. Etruscan necropolises have been discovered, whole cities of the dead with impressive mural painting. From the Etruscans also came the Roman practice of soothsaying, wherein the augurs divined the will of the gods by observing the flight of birds. Another Etruscan institution was the corps of special priests (*haruspices*) who examined the intestines or liver of animals for omens. This practice, too, was inherited by the Romans. Young Etruscan priests were instructed in their art by the use of models; the well-known bronze liver of Piacenza (its roundness representing the universe) is divided into thirty-six areas; each subject to the will of particular deities. From the position of the intestines of slaughtered animals, it was believed the future could be read, and thus unpredictable fate could be predicted after all.

Adjacent to Tuscany in the south was Latium, inhabited by a number of related tribes: Latins, Sabines, Umbrians and so on, some of whom lived in cities. The most important of these cities was Rome. The tribes had cults of their own, the chief of them being that of Jupiter Latiaris on the Alban Hills. When Rome assumed the political leadership of Latium, she also took over this cult, which was celebrated down to the fourth century A.D. In addition, the moon goddess Diana was venerated by all Latins. Her greatest sanctuary was situated in a grove in Aricia on Lake Nemi, which was long regarded as the sanctuary of all the tribes, and which likewise survived until late in imperial times. Finally, from the eighth century B.C. on there were increasing numbers of Greek colonists in southern Italy. The imposing remains of their temples commemorate their presence there to this day.

The ancient Roman religion is a perfect example of a pure folk religion, built up from elements of family and state cults. The Romans were not a creative people in this field; they borrowed almost all their deities from outside. If we consider Roman religious history in terms of this assimilation of foreign elements, we can divide it into three major periods. Foreign gods flowed into the Roman consciousness in three great waves: the Etruscan wave of the eighth, the Greek wave of the sixth and the Hellenistic-Oriental wave of the third century B.C. It has therefore been commented (F. Altheim) that syncretism marked the very beginning as well as the end of Roman religious history, for what we now regard as the religion of the ancient Romans was already a fusion of Etruscan and Latin elements.

THE ROMAN PANTHEON

The oldest supreme triad of the gods of Rome were Jupiter, Mars and Quirinus. Each of these gods had a priest especially in charge of his cult; these priests were called *flamen dialis, flamen martialis* and *flamen quirinalis*. They ranked directly beneath the *rex sacrorum*, whose sacred functions they took over after the institution of the republic. Jupiter, whose name may be a rendering of *Zeus pater*, was a typical Indo-European deity. He was the god of light, which was why the day of the full moon was sacred to him: on that day the sky is light even after sunset. His priest would celebrate the day of the full moon by sacrificing a white sheep to Jupiter at the citadel on the Capitoline Hill. Here, too, was situated the Auguraculum, an open space where the augurs —also servants of Jupiter—read his will from the flight of birds and other signs in and against the sky. A great temple to Jupiter Optimus Maximus (Jupiter, Best and Greatest) was built on the southern end of the Capitol and dedicated in 509 B.C. On this site there had formerly stood a temple to the god Jupiter Feretrius, who struck the guilty with thunderbolts; his priests were the *Fetiales,* who presided over the sanctity of treaties. An age-old fetish was preserved in this temple, a belemnite or thunderstone, from which the god took the name Jupiter Lapis. Beside this stone treaties were solemnized, a sacrificial pig being killed with a thunderstone. The meaning of the ritual act was: Just as this stone kills the animal, so Jupiter will slay the Roman people if they do not fulfil their obligations. Evidently ethical and political ideas were connected with Jupiter from the very oldest times.

Jupiter Optimus Maximus was the "expression of the Romans' faith, to which they remained loyal until they broke entirely with the religion of their forefathers. The nation trembled before Jupiter more than the worshipers of Assur and Marduk had ever trembled before these dread deities. Even a foreigner like Antiochus Epiphanes erected a temple to Jupiter in his capital and made valiant efforts to spread this worship. Only the Jewish people made the same claim of supremacy for their deity, and withstood the pressure of Antiochus and the Romans. But their resistance was overcome, and under Hadrian a temple of the Capitoline god rose above the ruins of the temple at Jerusalem, until at last Christianity drove Jupiter Optimus Maximus out of his Capitol forever" (Söderblom).

Like Jupiter, Mars was also a deity common to Italy. He was the war god and the defender of the people, the city and the crops. The old Roman year began with his month, March. Outside the walls of the city, an altar was erected to him on the Field of Mars. Here, every fifth year, the citizenry participated in a purifying ceremony. Sacred processions to purify the fields were also held by peasants in his name. At the festivals of Mars, horses, weapons and trumpets were purified. The god himself was venerated at the altar in the form of a lance. His priesthood consisted, in addition to the *flamen martialis,* of the Salians (Leapers), who performed magical dances in full armor. These dances were meant to symbolize the defeat of enemy armies and the victory of the Romans. Horse races were also held several times a year in honor of Mars.

Little is known about the third Roman god, Quirinus, who perhaps belonged originally to the Sabines. He seems to have been similar in character to Mars, and soon merged completely with the god of war.

The other ancient Roman deities watched over hearth and fields, and thus reflected the agrarian character of early Roman people. Such were the goddesses Tellus and Ceres, the first the goddess of the soil, the other the patroness of crops, who also had some attributes of a goddess of death. In the spring (April 15), at the time of sowing, a cow in calf was sacrificed to Tellus; a few days later, on April 19, the Cerealia were celebrated in honor of Ceres. Flora was the patroness of flowers, Pomona of fruit trees; Consus and Ops watched over the harvest. In fact, every aspect of agriculture had its special deity; we know the names from the *Indigitamenta,* a list of the formulas used to invoke the deities worshiped in oldest Roman times.

Faunus was the god of herds and guardian of game; his priests, the Luperci, celebrated the festival of their god—whose chief function was to protect herds from wolves—on February 15 in the Lupercalia, where Faunus had his sanctuary in a sacred grotto at the foot of the Palatine. The rites consisted of processions in which the priests struck all participants with lashes cut from the skin of a buck sacrificed to Faunus. This was presumably supposed to convey supernatural physical strength.

In addition to these nature deities there were others such as Saturn (Chronos), probably an Etruscan god of fertility, whose festival on December 17—the Saturnalia—was celebrated with a buffoon king. The Saturnalia were a kind of Roman carnival. There was also the water god Neptune (Poseidon), whose day was June 25, and the fire god Vulcan (Hephaestus), with a festival on August 25. The Romans hardly bothered to tamper with the Greek character of these gods.

Far more typical of the authentic Roman spirit were the hearth and family gods. Foremost of these was Janus, god of the door, with two faces; originally, as his name indicates, he was the door itself, to which primitive belief ascribed secret powers. Later he became the god of everything in its beginnings, and so the god of the beginning of the year—January. In wartime his temple was opened; in peace it was kept closed.

Vesta was the goddess of the hearth and the hearth fire. All family festivals were celebrated at the hearth; oaths and vows were taken in the presence of flame, purest of the elements. Since the state was conceived of as an extended family, Janus and Vesta ultimately became state deities. The priest of Janus was accorded the highest rank in the priesthood; the priestesses of Vesta were the six Vestal Virgins who maintained the hearth fire of the state, and likewise held high rank.

Among the domestic gods, the Penates were deities of the stores; the Lares safeguarded the fields. In domestic worship, in addition to Lares and Penates ancestral gods known as Manes were worshiped; these were originally underworld deities (*di manes*). Offerings were made to the dead who had joined the Manes, in order to placate their ghosts. An annual festival, the Parentalia, was celebrated for them on February 15.

Finally, the Genius (begetter) was venerated as a tutelary spirit. Originally he was the embodiment of the powers of generation. Every man had his Genius and every woman her Juno—corresponding somewhat to the Greek daimon. Later the Genius of the Roman people as a whole was worshiped, since every people was credited with its own tutelary deity.

One curious group of ancient Roman deities consisted of bloodless conceptual gods, personifications of abstract ideas, such as Fides (Faithfulness), Salus (Welfare of the state), Concordia (Harmony), Quies (Tranquillity), Clementia (Clemency). The malarial fevers of the marshy districts around Rome even resulted in the veneration of a goddess of fever, Febris. All these deities, especially Fides, were worshiped with rather modest rites in early Rome, but during the imperial period their cults underwent wild exaggeration, when the gods were viewed as embodiments of the virtues of the rulers.

CHARACTER AND ORGANIZATION

Unlike the strongly individualized Greek gods, the Roman deities were only feebly personified. More spirits than gods, they were nevertheless numina, endowed with specific forces and issuing from potent realms of being. Ancient Roman religion also had no real myths, no genealogies of the gods, no cosmogonies, and no developed conceptions of life after death. When Greek influence reached its apogee in the period of the republic, the Greek myths began to appeal to the Romans, and the individualized Greek gods were equated with the native Roman gods. Previously, Roman religion had had a rather legal and formalistic character in which household and governmental functions dominated. With good reason Hegel speaks of the Romans' "religion of utility": "Roman religion was wholly prosaic, its aims limited and utilitarian." As an example, Hegel points out that the Romans even had a goddess Moneta, who was worshiped as the deity of coinage. "What a far cry between these prosaic ideas and the beauty of the spiritual powers and divinities of the Greeks."

The relationship of men to the gods was defined in legal terms, and the language of worship itself was permeated with juridical ideas. Practice of the cult was considered a legal act, so that a great deal was made of carrying out all ceremonies according to prescription. To this extent, Rome with her ideal of ceremonial exactitude provides the perfect example of a religion of outward observances. The priests were state officials, partly specialists in, partly representatives of, their gods. They were divided into individual priests and colleges of priests. The highest of the individual priests was, in the days of Roman kingship, the king himself. As we have said, his dignity survived into republican times in the office of *rex sacrorum.* In household worship, the paterfamilias corresponded to the *rex sacrorum;* the father led the family in all its religious acts. The three high gods had their *flamines,* whose duty it was to blow up (*flare*) the sacred fire. The *flamen dialis* was especially subject to purity restrictions and taboos. He was not allowed to touch anything unclean, to attend funerals, to hear lamentations. Wherever he appeared, work had to cease.

Some of the colleges of priests were directly in charge of worship of the gods. Among these were the already mentioned Luperci of Faunus, the brotherhood of priests of Mars known as the Fratres Arvales, and the Salii, who performed mimic war dances in their red soldier's cloaks. Among the colleges of priestly specialists were the augurs, the experts on the flight of birds; the haruspices, who specialized in examining entrails; and the fetiales, who supervised all treaties dealing with war and peace. Overall supervision of religious matters was entrusted to a pontifical college, the head of which was the *pontifex maximus.* Among his obligations were the preservation of all religious traditions, especially those having to do with public worship and regulation of the calendar. The title was subsequently transferred to the Roman pope. Membership in the pontifical college was made up of the priests, the *rex sacrorum,* the *flamines,* and the Vestals. Later the whole system degenerated; priestly offices ceased to be conferred upon the worthiest candidates and instead were sold to the wealthiest. Thus the whole institution lost its original meaning.

DEVELOPMENT

From the sixth century B.C. onward, the intellectual and geographical horizon of the Romans steadily broadened. Their gods' interests and sphere of action followed suit. Many foreign gods were adopted by Rome; a constant process of assimilation went forward. The gods of conquered countries were literally called to Rome by *evocatio;* they were given permanent temples of their own in the Eternal City. This was more than a sign of the Romans' unusual tolerance; it was deliberate religious politics. The native deities, the *di indigetes,* were joined by a large troupe of foreign gods, the *di novensides,* whom the Romans soon regarded as their own. In place of the old trinity of Jupiter, Mars and Quirinus, the sixth century brought in the new triad of Jupiter, Juno regina and Minerva. The Tarquins erected a great new temple on the Alban Hills to Jupiter Latiaris, protector of the Latin League.

One highly important development in Roman religion was the introduction of the Sibylline Books, a collection of oracular sayings connected with the cult of Apollo. These originated among the Greeks in Cumae, the southern Italian Delphi. In 509 they were transferred to the crypt of the Temple of Jupiter on the Capitol, where a fifteen-member college of priests was charged with the duty of interpreting them.

This innovation coincided with the introduction of the Greek gods into Rome. The first Greek deities to be worshiped publicly were such demigods or heroes as Heracles (Hercules) and the twins Castor and Pollux, for whom a temple was built in the heart of the city. In 431 b.c. Apollo received a sanctuary of his own in Rome, and was venerated as tutelary god of the plebs. Artemis became merged with the old goddess of the Latin League, Diana, and Aesclepius of Epidaurus was brought in as the god of healing; the snake, which was sacred to him, was carried to Rome in solemn procession. In 217 b.c. the Greek twelve gods of Olympus were officially absorbed into the Roman state religion, and a scheme of identities with the native gods were formally established: Zeus-Jupiter, Hera-Juno, Poseidon-Neptune, Athena-Minerva, Ares-Mars, Aphrodite-Venus, Apollon-Apollo, Artemis-Diana, Hephaestus-Vulcan, Hesta-Vesta, Hermes-Mercury, Demeter-Ceres. These Latinized gods were represented by gilded statues in the Roman Forum, like those they already had on the Agora in Athens. Thus the ancient Roman deities acquired personalities, and mythology took root in a Rome hitherto barren of myths.

During this period, however, Rome had also produced a few new gods of her own—for example the Dius Fidus, an aspect of Jupiter, to whom a temple on the Quirinal was erected in 466. A temple for the goddess Fides followed about a hundred years later. Juno acquired increasing importance as the goddess of fertility and childbed; she was worshiped as Juno regina and by many other names. The goddess Fortuna enjoyed a similar rise in favor after she had merged with Tyche, the Greek goddess of fate. Processions and public entertainments for the gods, which also served the human craving for spectacle, at first struck the Romans as scandalous innovations, for the offices of religion had hitherto been performed by the professional priesthood. But in 105 b.c. popular election of the major priestly colleges was introduced. The inevitable consequence was the intrusion of political passions into the sphere of religion.

From the end of the third century b.c. on Oriental deities began penetrating Rome. By the time of Christ's birth, the cults of these gods were strongly entrenched in Roman religious life. Probably the most important date in the history of Roman religious eclecticism was 204 b.c., when the second Punic War, though drawing to a close, had left Rome utterly exhausted. On orders from the Sibyl, the cult of the Great Mother, Magna Mater, was introduced: at the expense of the state, the sacred black stone of the Phrygian Cybele was brought from Pessinus, a city in Galatia on the borders of Roman Phrygia, to Rome. In 191 B.C. a temple on the Palatine was erected to this mother of the gods from Asia Minor. Cybele was worshiped under the name of Magna Mater Deum Idaea. From then on, foreign deities were taken into the official state religion in ever increasing numbers. But the cult of Cybele, which was especially favored by women, continued to take precedence over the other mystery cults, even in the provinces. In 1955, in fact, a temple to the Great Mother was excavated at Neuss on the Rhine; it contained a blood pit for the baptism in blood which was required of initiates.

As the days of the republic drew to a close, a general religious degeneration began. Greek critical attitudes toward religion, to which such Romans as Cicero subscribed, contributed to a breakdown of popular faith in the old gods. The temples decayed, the rites were neglected. Popular election to the pontifical colleges also made for religious confusion because persons ignorant of the ceremonies and of the methods for calculating the sacral calendar took office as priests. The emperor Augustus attempted to check the spreading dissolution and to renew the old religion by assuming some of the important offices himself, including that of Pontifex Maximus (in 12 B.C.). Augustus rebuilt old temples, and the literature of his time (Virgil, Horace, Propertius, Ovid) reflected the newly awakened interest in religion. Augustus himself was venerated as Soter (universal savior). Like Julius Caesar before him, he was declared *divus* (divine); and a temple was erected to him after his death. The Roman cult of the emperors developed out of the old worship of the Genius mingled with the Oriental idea of the god-king—which had come from the Greek colonies of Asia Minor by way of Greece proper into the Roman Empire. Sacrifices were offered to the Genius before images of the emperors. The new cult helped to bolster the spiritual and political unity of the Empire. It was meant to do just that. For the same reason Jupiter Optimus Maximus was declared the supreme god, and the principal gods of all the peoples of the Empire were equated with him. In all provincial capitals imitations of the Roman Capitol were built. The cult of the emperors has been called a "masterpiece of statecraft." "Even if it lacked real religious content, it shows what force was contained in a good organization" (M. P. Nilsson).

Under the Empire, the trend toward the adoption of foreign gods gained even greater strength. New Oriental cults were introduced—the cults of Isis, Serapis, Adonis, Atagatis of Hierapolis, and so on. Under Caligula the worship of Isis, which had come from Egypt around 160 B.C., was adopted as a state cult and a temple to Isis was built on the Field of Mars (A.D. 58). The Persian sun cult of Mithra became the favorite religion of the Roman legionaries. Caracalla (211–217) accorded equal rights to all the gods of the Empire. Under Emperors Elagabalus and Aurelian, the height of Orientalization was reached in the state cult of Sol invictus (i.e. Mithra), for whom a gigantic temple was built on the Field of Mars. This god's festival was celebrated on December 25!

Nevertheless, the success of the Oriental cults was largely a token of the process of dissolution of ancient Roman religion. This religion had once served as a school for ethics, morality and valor. But for the Romans' strong sense of duty to the gods, the Imperial Romanum could never have arisen. But now that each Roman could choose among so many religions and cults, he paid for his personal freedom by spiritual uncertainty about the highest things. Tradition seemed shattered, and the sceptical, rationalistic criticism of myths and religion propagated by such philosophers as Cicero, Seneca and Epictetus helped to snuff out the flame of old Roman piety. A tendency toward multifarious superstitions spread throughout the Empire.

In conjunction with the foreign mystery cults, however, there also developed a longing for an answer to the profoundest questions of life—such matters as sin and redemption, death and a new life after death, and what transformations the soul must undergo. Apparently the answers of the secret cults, of the Hermetics (named after Hermes Trismegistus, the god in the guise of sage and lawgiver) and the Gnostics did not go far enough. In any case the universalistic message of Christianity, the message of brotherly love and the help of God for the poor and heavily laden, exerted a more lasting effect upon the souls of men. The Christian view of history regards this denouement not as sheer chance, but part of the scheme laid down in Gal. 4: 4: "When the time had fully come, God sent forth his son . . ."

The Great Religions
of the East

INDIAN WORLD-VIEW

WHEN we speak of the great religions of the East, we think of those religions that have sprung from the soil of India, China, Tibet and Japan. They have been called "religions of eternal cosmic law," because they proceed from immutable laws of being. They manage entirely without notions of a personal God, or predicate a completely different view of salvation and loss of salvation than do the religions based upon the Bible. Undoubtedly, geographic and geophysical factors are partly accountable for the fact that life in India and the Far East has a different rhythm from life in the West, and that thinking is circular rather than linear. Because of the consciousness of vast stretches of time, moreover, historical consciousness is only feebly developed.

India, in particular, is a country in which from time immemorial men have had less interest in their own history than in the solution of the eternal riddles of life. The magnificent contrasts of the country, its great climatic range and tropical abundance, seem to have developed a tendency to abstraction and speculative cosmological thinking that is alien to Europeans. Hegel spoke of the "conceptless idealism of imagination" among the Indians, of the "dreams of the unrestricted spirit itself." Perhaps it takes the floral brilliance of India, the heavy perfume of exotic blossoms and the vastness of the jungles to make men so weary of life, to bring them to that sublime melancholy of the Buddha in which they wish to be rid of the world and all its sufferings, including their own selves. The Occidental can direct his will at various objects; but as a rule he cannot grasp extinction of the will, the individual's indifference to his own person. Confronted with such a phenomenon, he is only staggered by the endless possibilities of that strange creature known as man. But Buddhism was only a religious reform movement, and today has almost entirely vanished from the Indian subcontinent. The true native religion of India is Hinduism.

HINDUISM

THE WORD Hinduism is derived from Hindostan, the Persian name given by Mohammedan invaders to the country watered by the great Indus River. The term Brahminism, a common synonym, comes from the Hindu priestly caste of Brahmins, not from the god Brahma. By Hinduism or Brahminism we mean both the faith and the way of life that has, since ancient times, dominated the thinking and feeling of all those Indians (about 66 per cent) who have resisted the inroads of the foreign religions (Islam, Parseeism, Christianity); or the sects (Buddhism, Jainism, Sikhism) that have proliferated within the country. According to the latest figures, there are estimated to be 366.5 million Hindus in India proper; in addition, there are some 11 million in Pakistan and a few million in Nepal, Kashmir, Ceylon, Indonesia and so on.

THE VEDA

Hinduism is based on the Veda (Knowledge), which represents the early stage of Indian religion. It was essentially a sacrificial religion with a multiplicity of gods and a pluralistic cosmology. The greater part of the Vedic literature was composed in Sanskrit, which is considered the ecclesiastical language of cultivated Indians. Treated by grammarians as early as the fifth century B.C., Sanskrit is the language of the classical religious texts of India which date from between 1500 and 800 B.C.

The Veda consists of four collections of texts:

1. Rigveda (Knowledge of Hymns): ten books consisting of 1,028 songs, usually of four lines of verse. With verbose eloquence the gods, especially the proud king of the gods, Indra, are invited to partake of the sacrificial meals. These hymns reveal a good

deal about early social conditions among the Aryan tribes who immigrated into India around 1800 B.C.

2. Samaveda (Chants) presents the major melodies with which the singing priests (*udgatar*) accompanied the sacrifices.

3. Yajurveda (Science of sacrificial formulas) is a compendium of the formulas and prayers, composed partly in prose, partly in verse, that the priest must murmur as he makes sacrifice. Thus the Yajurveda is a kind of liturgical book.

4. Atharvaveda (Veda of spells) contains the exorcisms and spells Brahmins must know for various situations. This voluminous collection (731 hymns with 6,000 verses) is of later date than the other three Vedas.

Other, usually later texts, were subsequently received into the corpus of religious scriptures. These were the Brahmanas, general doctrinal texts for the priesthood. This essentially exegetic and theological literature deals chiefly with the ritual of sacrifice. The more philosophical Upanishads ("confidential sessions") contain esoteric wisdom, often of great profundity, for disciples and priests in training. They have had a profound influence upon some Western philosophers (Schelling, Schopenhauer). The Indians usually refer to them as the Vedanta (Conclusion of the Vedas) since they embody final thoughts on the Veda texts.

The mystical piety of the Upanishads shifts the emphasis from knowledge of sacrificial techniques and their meaning to salvation through the liberating knowledge conferred by contemplation. One theory holds that the Upanishads belong to Brahminism, the second stage of Indian religion. The speculations of the Brahmins on the power of sacrifice moved toward an impersonal, salvational mysticism. The union of the human soul (Atman) with the world spirit (Brahman) becomes the goal of salvation. This goal is to be achieved by insight. The famous formula, *tat tvam asi*, "that you are," expresses this identification. Atman-Brahman mysticism unites self and the universe; that is salvation, which is achieved by a kind of miraculous illumination. Sometimes, however, the neutral supreme Brahman also assumes personal features as a ruler of the universe, and thus we find paths opening to a more personalistic divine worship.

All the above-mentioned texts, and many others, are still regarded by pious Hindus as having the force of laws and precepts, whereas they are rejected by reformers such as Buddha and Mahavira. When Hindus think of the Veda, however, they usually mean only the Upanishads, because these contain a clear exposition of the Indian doctrine of karma and rebirth. The *Bhagavadgita* (the Song of the Adorable One) is revered by all Hindus. Based on Atman-Brahman mysticism, it is in many ways typical of Indian religious feeling. Originally a part of the great family epic the *Mahabharata*, it was composed around 500 B.C., and represents human fate in general in the figure of the youthful hero Arjuna. Before the beginning of a great civil war and before the decisive battle, Arjuna on his war chariot holds converse with his charioteer, Krishna, who reveals himself to Arjuna as an avatar of the god Vishnu. Arjuna does not want to fight because he sees many of his kinsmen and friends on the enemy side, but the god convinces him that he may not withdraw from his duty as a warrior. To support this position, Krishna stresses that bodies are transitory, while the spiritual element in man is immortal.

The *Bhagavadgita* links the ethics of bravery and duty with a warrior caste, the Karmamarga (Way of Works) with the Bhaktimarga, the ethics of devotion and practice of love. Bhakti (devotion) to the Sublime or Adored One, that is, to Vishnu-Krishna as a personal god and savior, leads to the way of salvation. Revealing himself to Arjuna as the one and only deity, Krishna states the following doctrine: "Even a wholly bad man, if he devotes himself to me and no other, must be regarded as good. . . . Whoever surrenders to me, is not destroyed."

The implied theology is that God has so unfolded himself to the world that he is all in all (panentheism), even though he continues to overtower the world as ruler of worlds. Krishna-Vishnu graciously inclines toward men who can lovingly surrender themselves to him. We may therefore properly speak, with Söderblom, of a special bhakti religion. The note of personal piety in the *Bhagavadgita* has won it many friends in the West (first translation 1785); and it has also enormously influenced countless Hindus. As Gandhi, for example, declared: "When disappointments confront me, I go to the *Bhagavadgita*. I read a verse here and a verse there, and in the midst of overwhelming tragedies I at once begin to smile."

THE GODS OF HINDUISM

Hinduism is not a founded religion, but one that has grown by historical accretions, without distinctly specified creeds like those of Christianity, without a clearly defined way of salvation like Buddhism. Rather, it includes the most various forms and planes of religious life, including fetishism, animal cults (sanctity of the cow), polytheism, pantheism, henotheism. All exist side by side within the framework of Hinduism. It gives the impression of being a collection of overlapping forms of religion rather than an integral religious system with unambiguous features. Because of this contradictory coexistence of subtle and sublime with crude and primitive views and customs, it has been called an "encyclopedia of all religions."

The absence of specific dogmas, tenets and notions is wholly characteristic of Hinduism, and results in great religious tolerance. The number of venerated objects is boundless; the paths to salvation are many. Consequently, there are Hindus who eat meat and others who are vegetarians, Hindus who celebrate sexual orgies and others who practice strictest asceticism.

Similarly, the gods of Hinduism are exceedingly numerous. Siva and Vishnu have become the most important of them, while many-headed Brahma, who was largely responsible for the creation of the world, has diminished in importance, so that today Hindus regard him mostly as an impersonal universal principle, a kind of world soul. Siva, the antagonist of the demons, is a terrible god whose cult is compounded of gloomily ascetic and wild, cruel and often orgiastic features. As a fertility god his symbol is the phallus, his symbolic animal the bull. The districts most given to the worship of Siva as god of fertility and destruction, and of his son Ganesha as god of rain and growth, lie to the east of Benares.

Vishnu, venerated more to the west of Benares, has kindly and amiable features. In the area in which this kindly, benevolent deity is worshiped, the idea of bhakti has flourished. Vishnu's numerous avatars or incarnations, however, indicate that he was not a single, unified deity. He merged with the heroes Krishna and Prince Rama. When Buddhism ceased to be dangerous to the Brahmins, even Buddha was included among the avatars of Vishnu.

Among the more important of the female deities are Durga (the Inaccessible), Kali (the Black), and Shakti—all of these belonging to the type of *magna mater*, the Great Mother. These three are cruel goddesses; temple paintings depict them with their mouths dripping blood.

All these deities still have large followings in present-day India. The significant fact is that no real rivalry ever arose among all these gods and their cults within the total framework of Hinduism. The Indologist Helmut von Glasenapp has commented: "For the European, such juxtapositions would not work, because he associates the concept of God with certain ideas about divine characteristics or historical facts. The Hindu, on the other hand, sees in the various figures in his pantheon only more or less equal embodiments of an ultimate reality that bridges all contradictions."

THE DOCTRINE OF KARMA

What, then, is this ultimate reality of Hinduism? It is the order of the whole cosmos, which is dominated by a single eternal law: *karma*. Karma is the Indian expression for belief in a moral order. The doctrine holds that every act performed in this life has moral significance and will influence the fate of the living being in subsequent incarnations. Consequently, all beings live under the conditions they have merited by their deeds. If the good suffer misfortunes, they are atoning for misdeeds in an earlier form of existence, and contrariwise, the wicked who fare well are still enjoying the fruit of accumulated earlier merits. Karma works automatically and mercilessly as compensation, settling scores belonging to earlier forms of being. Cosmic law thus shapes all destinies on earth, but without eliminating human free will. Man can decide upon actions which will give him a favorable or an unfavorable karma.

Karma, then, is the total resultant of each existence on earth. The life process itself is without beginning and without end. This idea of karma as the ruler of earthly destinies goes back to the doctrine of reincarnation incorporated in the Upanishads. Every Hindu endeavors by good deeds to assure himself a better reincarnation in the next life. His caste position depends on that —assuming that his sins are not so grave that he must atone in the next rebirth by reappearing on earth as a plant or animal.

Hinduism recognizes no end to existence, and consequently no salvation of the world. This is also the reason that Hindus consider historical events of only passing moment. The wheel of Sansara—the whirlpool of rebirths—will never cease to turn. All beings have had immortal souls since all eternity, souls which merely change their material husks. The direction of change is set forth in a proverb from the Upanishads: "As one does and as one goes, so one becomes. Whose acts are good becomes something good, whose acts are evil something evil." Another proverb explains that he who has led a proper life on earth is reborn as a Brahmin or warrior, while he whose life is unworthy must atone for his deeds in the shape of a dog or a pig.

CASTE

To the Hindu, the doctrine of karma explains the diversity of living creatures, who from the beginning of things (although that is merely a phrase, since he does not believe there ever was a beginning) have been bound to the wheel of fate. The eternal cosmic law accepted by all schools of Hinduism finds its embodiment in a mighty ladder of life which begins with plants and ends with the gods. From this cosmic law follow Indian ideas of caste, on which the entire religious and social system is founded. H. von Glasenapp has defined caste as follows: "A caste is a group of persons who practice the same traditional occupation and are linked to one another by inherited rights, duties and customs. A person is born into this group, which takes care that its members marry only women of the same caste and eat only with persons of the same caste."

The castes, as occupational groups, are organized in corporations that are headed by a committee—usually consisting of five persons. Only the three highest, so-called "pure" castes have special privileges. These are the priests, warriors and peasants. The priests, Brahmins, have as their principal functions performance of sacrifices and teaching. Their caste color is white, their point of the compass the East. The Brahmins must obey numerous restrictions in food, baths and association with others in order to prevent ritual uncleanliness. The caste of warriors, the Kshatryas, to which the kings also belonged, is required to keep in good physical condition. From this caste many government officials are drawn. Its color is red, its point of the compass the North. The peasants and artisans, Vaishyas, work in cattle-raising, agriculture, commerce and the crafts; their caste color is yellow, their point of the compass the South.

These three upper castes undergo a special rite of consecration as a sign of a "second birth," and are therefore known as "the twiceborn." The great mass of Indians, the Shudras, carry out all manner of work and are supposed to serve the twiceborn. Their color is black and their cardinal point the West. There are enormous differences among them, depending on the degree of cleanliness of their occupations. Those who are ritually unclean are declared Untouchables or Pariahs: "Persons who deal with unclean objects, such as laundrymen, or who kill living beings, such as fishermen or leather workers, stand lower than weavers and potters who practice less objectionable occupations. The lowest group of Indian society comprise all those called Pancamas (members of the fifth caste), also known as Pariahs or Asprishyas. These practice occupations considered dishonorable—in the medieval sense—such as street-sweeping, cleaning latrines, etc. Members of the thieves' castes also are included. Since each of these five castes is divided into a large number of subdivisions, Hinduism recognizes from two to three thousand castes, each of which has a specific function within the social organism. Non-Hindus are ranked below all Hindus because they are entirely without caste. From the viewpoint of orthodox Hindus, men of different castes are to be regarded as beings of different species, which may have much in common (as do lions, elephants, buffaloes, etc.), but are radically differentiated by origin and inheritance, mode of life, rights and duties, from the moment of their birth" (H. von Glasenapp).

In the Hindu view, the caste hierarchy constitutes a part of eternal cosmic law. Caste organization has certainly promoted occupational training; it has also resulted in widely different sets of moral standards within the social organism. The marriage and funeral customs, oaths and fasts, food, drink, clothing and work of each caste are binding upon its members. Infraction of caste law can lead to formal excommunication, which in some cases spells a man's doom. Only new karma in later lives can lead to a change in caste.

The development of technology and industry in modern India has had a modifying influence upon the caste system, especially since strict observance of the food rules is practically possible only in the rural areas. In addition, the laicistic Indian constitution of 1949 forbade certain discriminations against the Pariahs—there are seventy million of them! Nevertheless, endogamy—marriage only within the caste—is still very much in force.

The horizontal social groupings of the caste system have given Hinduism an internal unity which it has been unable to find in doctrine or ritual. Yet Hinduism is nevertheless a ritual religion to the extent that all Hindus must follow strict prescriptions for avoiding ritual uncleanliness—although the prescriptions vary for each caste. Moreover, the whole course of everyday Hindu life is accompanied by cultic and liturgical acts.

The caste system as such is three thousand years old in India. Since everyone belongs to a caste by birth, and no one can enter a caste or change castes, Hinduism cannot spread by conversion. It cannot engage in individual missionary work; at best it can take entire folk groups into itself as a new caste. That has happened now and again in regions as far away as Indonesia.

DEVELOPMENTS IN HINDUISM

During the eighth and ninth centuries A.D. the philosophical reformer Sankara undertook to reinterpret the ancient Vedanta texts. His thesis that Brahma, the divine principle, is an impersonal unity, found great favor among cultivated Hindus. Worshipers of Siva, in fact, regard Sankara as an incarnation of their god. Sankara propounded the idea that the various cults were equal ways to reach "Brahma." He divided knowledge into two categories, the lower takes the world for reality, and the higher knowledge which sees the world as Maya (illusion) that distracts men from the solitude of the spirit. The stage of higher knowledge may be reached by study of the Veda and meditation, until at last the soul ascends to Brahma. Following Buddha's example, Sankara founded monastic orders and monasteries all over India.

Two centuries after Sankara a sage named Ramanuja propounded a somewhat more personal concept of God (Brahma incarnated as Vishnu). Ramanuja attempted to lead men to contemplation of the deity's goodness, to the "way of devotion" (*bhaktimarga*) and personal love of God. As Rudolf Otto once commented, Sankara and Ramanuja represent two alternative prototypes of man's search for salvation.

In addition there are at least six other major orthodox systems of Hinduism, and numerous variants, mixed types, sects and reform movements. As a result of Islamic penetration into India (today the majority of India's ninety-five million Mohammedans live in the state of Pakistan, founded in 1947), mixed religions have arisen, such as that of the Sikhs (literally "disciples"). Their founder, Nanak (1469–1538), built this combined Hindu-Moslem religion around the god Rama. Nanak and his ten successors are venerated by the Sikhs as holy teachers, *gurus*. The Sikhs today are isolated from both Hindus and Moslems; in Pakistan they represent a persecuted religious-racial group without a caste system. In India the tall powerful Sikhs are largely soldiers, policemen, chauffeurs and mechanics. Their worship is simple and almost puritanical; they practice two sacraments reminiscent of Protestant baptism and communion.

In modern India atheists, pantheists, polytheists and henotheists live side by side in mutual respect. In addition there are philosophical schools of thought concerned with the operations of karma. Can man liberate himself from the fetters of Sankara of his own accord, by insight and knowledge, or does his salvation depend upon a helpful deity to whom he commends himself by worship and by a good and merciful life? Hindus refer to these two schools of thought as monkey schools and cat schools, because in one man clings to God like the monkey to its mother's neck, while in the other he is dependent on the deity like the kitten that is carried in its mother's mouth.

Thus redemption of the individual remains open to question; but Hinduism knows nothing of a general salvation for the world as a whole. Because of the infinitely large number of living creatures, the wheel of Sankara will never cease to turn, no matter how many souls escape from the cycle of rebirths by attaining the state of bliss, which is usually considered inalienable once secured. Whether bliss means a transfiguration of the individual, or absorption into the world spirit, is a matter on which opinions differ widely.

Because of their lack of dogma, the Hindus find it easy to tolerate other beliefs, and even altogether alien religions. This tolerance contrasts curiously with the rigidity and intolerance of the caste system. In religious matters, Hindu tolerance sometimes approaches indifference, or in the philosophical schools, syncretism. The spirit of prophecy is completely foreign to it, and it gives far more importance to rites and social customs than to doctrines and creeds. As we might expect, Hinduism possesses no supreme authority that issues orders or precepts. Almost everything in Hindu religious life is left to tradition and local custom.

Among the masses of the common people, Hindu religion consists in the worship of innumerable local gods, to whose village chapels rice, fruit and similar offerings are brought. The major gods have magnificent temples, filled with paintings and statues which are wakened in the morning by the ringing of bells, dressed, fed with offerings, and frequently conducted on wagons in processions through the streets. Thus the images of the gods are venerated as if they were beings with human traits and weaknesses. Cultivated Hindus smile at these practices, but they benevolently tolerate them as preparations for forms of higher religious knowledge. Thus a popular and a philosophical view of religion exist side by side in Hinduism.

Hindus at every stage of education and religious development regard the eating of beef as a grave crime and blasphemy, for the cow is a sacred animal, "A poem of mercy, the mother of millions of Indians," as Mahatma Gandhi once put it. Hindus bow reverently before a file of passing cattle, and automobiles swing wide around a cow reclining in the middle of a city street, for no one would dare to make the sacred animal move. Frequently, devout Hindus are also vegetarians, in order to carry out as far as possible the principle of *ahimsa*, non-violence toward man and beast.

MODERN HINDUISM

Modern Hinduism has received great impetus from the appearance of such charismatic personalities as Ramakrishna (1834–1886), a visionary ecstatic who preached the love of God, took up where the reformer Sankara had left off, and regarded all religions as equally valid paths to salvation. Ramakrishna's ideas were couched in a number of pithy sayings, such as: "Different creeds are only different paths to the Almighty. . . . The avatar of saviour in different manifestations is the emissary of God. He resembles the viceroy of a mighty monarch. When disturbances break out in a remote province, the great prince sends a viceroy there to put them down. Thus God sends his avatar into the world whenever, anywhere in the world, religion is being crushed. It is one and the same avatar who has plunged into the ocean of life and appears now as Krishna, now as Christ. Avatars —such as Rama, Krishna, Buddha, Christ—are related to the absolute Brahma as single waves to the whole ocean." For all the tolerance he preached, Ramakrishna exerted great influence in strengthening Hindu pride and self-assurance. Gandhi, Aurobindo and Radhakrishnan, the great names of present-day India, must be understood in terms of the message of Ramakrishna.

Gandhi (1869–1948), the Mahatma ("Great Soul"), turned the principle of ahimsa—borrowed from Jainism—into a political weapon in the struggle for independence from British colonialism. Yet he placed such emphasis upon non-violence that he sometimes abandoned political goals that had almost been attained when he felt that the ethical-religious principle had been infringed. His efforts in behalf of the Pariahs and of reconciliation between Hindus and Mohammedans led to his assassination by a fanatical Hindu.

Gandhi also represented Hinduism's claim to universality; he was firmly convinced of the clear superiority of Indian culture in the face of Occidental Christianity. Gandhi's political disciple,

Pandit Nehru, the late prime minister of India, belonged to the Brahmin caste, but had long ceased to practice the Hindu religion.

Shri Aurobindo (1872–1951) is considered the renewer of Yoga, that ancient discipline that is supposed to lead man beyond himself to a higher plane of consciousness. Aurobindo, too, was a universalistic proponent of the Indian national movement; but his thinking showed the influences of Christianity and Occidental ideas of evolution and progress.

The religious philosopher Sarvepalli Radhakrishnan (born 1888), who in 1952 became vice president of the new Republic of India, has attempted to modernize the Vedanta, in particular the doctrines of Sankara, and to bring Hinduism closer to the West.

A more successful effort in the same direction was undertaken by Vivekananda. Although the caste system has been a major obstacle to Hindu missionary work among individuals, Vivekananda founded in 1897 the Ramakrishna Mission, with headquarters in Bombay, Madras and Calcutta, to propagate the doctrines of the Vedanta. This mission has gained a foothold principally in California. Its goal is a non-dogmatic union of all world religions; Hinduism is regarded as mankind's eternal religion, from which non-Indians have drifted away either out of ignorance or deliberate apostasy. Vivekananda cites a saying of Ramakrishna: "I have tried all religions—Hinduism, Mohammedanism and Christianity —and I have found that all by different roads seek the same God." He goes on to argue that all Indian and non-Indian religions and sects are merely introductions to the universal, unitary vision of the Vedanta, the monistic conception of an all-embracing Oneness of all gods, living beings and things. By attaining the union of Atman and Brahman, the enlightened soul escapes from the eternal cycle of births.

Similar ideas are held by the Theosophical Society, founded by the Russian mystic H. P. Blavatzky in 1875, which has since spread all over the world from its center in Adgar, near Madras. Occultist and spiritistic elements have been included within this syncretistic system; theosophy is hailed as the sum of all the divine truths expressed in all religions.

Modern India is a land of many contradictions which are not

resolved, and of many oddities which most Indians do not feel to be such. The ban on the slaughter of cows results in many grave social and political ills. Burnings of widows, although forbidden by law, still occur. Sadhus (who properly speaking are holy men, but in practice are often nothing but tramps) kidnap babies to be sacrificed to Durga or black Kali. Pampered monkeys, fed in special temples of their own, regarded as holy, inviolable animals because the mythological monkey god Hanuman once aided Rama, run riot and cause immense destruction throughout the country. The caste system prevents any thorough social reform. But in spite of often incredible social and moral abuses, certain ethical standards are common to all Hindus. Or, as a Sanskrit proverb put it: "There is much dispute among scholars regarding holy places, God and religious duties; but that the mother is something sacred and that pity is a virtue, all systems agree."

BUDDHISM

The HISTORY of Buddhism, which is some 560 years older than Christianity, is a curious refutation of its founder's prediction.

For Buddha, according to his favorite disciple Ananda, prophesied that the truth he had preached would last only five hundred years. Then a new revealer of salvation must appear. Nothing of the kind happened. Rather, five hundred years later his teachings reached the height of their influence, although by then they had evolved in a number of respects. Today Buddhism dominates Burma, Thailand, Cambodia, Laos and Ceylon. In many other parts of Asia, it exerts extremely powerful spiritual force.

Buddha, who called himself a *Tathagata* (guide), left behind no written word. His message has come down to us, like the sayings of Jesus, in oral transmission. And as with primitive Christianity, disputes arose early in the Buddhist community over the proper interpretation of the Master's words. Buddha's sermons (Sutta-pitaka) were not written down until two and a half centuries after his death, in the reign of the great Emperor Asoka (273–232 B.C.). This was done at a council of monks in Pataliputra, held in 245, and the language used was Pali, a Central Indian dialect that probably deviated considerably from the language Buddha spoke. However, these differences are not so great as those between the Greek of the Gospels and the Aramaic that was Jesus' mother tongue. This council fixed the canon of southern Buddhism, the "Threefold Basket" (Tripitaka), which contained, among other things, the rules for monastic life (Vinaya-pitaka), the addresses of Buddha (Sutta-pitaka), and scholastic interpretations of his doctrines (Abidhama-pitaka)—the latter of somewhat later date. This vast literature arose between 500 and 250 B.C.; post-canonical texts were added afterward.

The life of the historical Buddha (circa 566–486 B.C.) as represented in the oldest texts seems to have been almost entirely devoted to instructing his followers in what his great Chinese contemporary, Lao-tse, called "Tao," the right way. That life has become of prime symbolic and exemplary importance to all Buddhists. They seek to learn how the Master found the right way which took from him his joy in life, but which in compensation taught him to understand that all birth leads only to suffering and death, that the succession of births is unending unless the path to escape from the cycle of rebirth is found: the way to enter into Nirvana.

THE LIFE OF THE BUDDHA

The story of Prince Siddhartha Gautama, who became a Buddha, an Enlightened One, is that of a young Indian prince of the race of Sakyas in Nepal for whom the pleasures of life became stale. Buddhism has erected this disillusionment with life into a system. One day the young prince rides forth from his sheltered home into the world and sees an ancient, toothless, bent old man by the roadside, tremblingly stretching a wrinkled hand toward him. From his charioteer Prince Siddhartha learns that he is beholding the general lot of man. Thereafter, in spite of all the efforts of his companions to keep him from such encounters, he meets with men afflicted by repulsive diseases, and one day he sees a dead man. The beautiful dancing girls in his palace try to enliven him by their arts; but he sees them as they really are at night: their limbs slack with weariness, saliva drooling from their mouths; some gnash their teeth and others snore. Now his luxurious bedroom seems to the young prince an infirmary, and he decides to depart from his home, for the great lesson that his princely life teaches him is that no power in the world can obscure the true nature of existence, that all life is ultimately torment and suffering, for joys and pleasures are limited by time; when they fade, old age, illness, suffering and death remain. He who asks after the truth in and beyond life comes to the conclusion, like Prince Siddhartha, that all life is suffering. The Hindu does not know the Occidental view of redemption from suffering. Rather, suffering must be extinguished by the extinction of man himself. Man's hunger for life, his thirst for joys, are precisely what lead him to suffering.

Siddhartha Gautama was twenty-nine years old when he decided to give up the life he had hitherto lived and go about the world as a poor, homeless, wandering ascetic. Mara, the evil tempter, accompanied him and promised him an empire if he would desist from his intention. But Buddha would not be swayed. An ancient text thus describes this "great going-forth": "The ascetic Gautama became a monk, leaving behind much money, coined and uncoined, that was held in cellars and in attics. The ascetic Gautama, a black-haired young man in the bloom of youth, left his home and went into homelessness at an early age. The ascetic Gautama, although his parents protested, although they shed tears and wept long, had his hair and beard cut, donned yellow garments, and went out from his home into homelessness."

In the early texts Buddha himself gives his reasons for taking this step. He tells his disciples of the abundance in which he lived, and then continues: "To me, O monks, who lived in such well-being, who was so extraordinarily sheltered, there came the thought: The ignorant, ordinary man, who is himself subject to aging, feels when he sees an old man, and is himself not yet old, uneasiness, shame, disgust, for he applies what he sees to himself. I, too, am subject to aging, am myself not yet old; how then should I not feel uneasiness, shame and disgust in the presence of age? . . . Then, O monks, as I considered these matters, all joy in my youth vanished utterly from me." Similar sentences are repeated in connection with illness and death; for according to the Buddha's doctrine there are three kinds of vanity: vanity of youth, vanity of health and vanity of life. In other words, man forgets that he will become old and sick, and that he must die.

In the search for Nirvana, which is eternal, blissful peace, the Buddha settled for a time near the village of Uruvela and practiced yoga and asceticism with five other hermit monks. After seven years of meditation he came to the insight that the right way leads between the extremes of worldly activity and stark asceticism. His contemporary Mahavira, who founded Jainism likewise as a monastic community, took the contrary view that asceticism is the principal means of salvation; he hailed as a *jina* (victor) the man who so overcomes his desires that he is prepared to fast to death. Jainism, whose symbol is the swastika beneath a starred crescent moon, has survived to the present in India and numbers some one and a half million adherents.

Prince Siddhartha Gautama ended a fast which had brought him to the brink of starvation; he had recognized such fasting as a new form of temptation by Mara. Instead, he wandered on until he came to a fig tree in northern Central India. The site remains a great place of pilgrimage. Here he let himself fall into the fourth and lowest stage of absorption (dhyana). In this stage of "painless and joyless equanimity" there came to him out of the emptiness the *bodhi,* enlightenment, which made him the Buddha. He experienced a state of bliss in which he perceived the insignificance of all that had previously formed the content of his life. This he described as the entrance to Nirvana. After another twenty-eight (or forty-nine) days in stillness he decided to communicate the truth he had seen to other men.

Mara once again tried to frustrate this decision, which was taken in the grove of gazelles in the vicinity of present-day Sarnath in eastern India. But the Buddha persisted, and the moment he began his preaching is regarded as the hour of Buddhism's birth: "Let the gate of immortal salvation be open to all. He who has ears, let him hear the word and believe. . . . I go to the city of Benares to set the wheel of the doctrine in motion. In the world, which is blind, I will beat the drum of truth: salvation from the realm of death. . . . As I teach, so do, and you will soon perceive for yourself that highest goal of holy striving, for whose sake honorable men go forth into homelessness; you will see it and gain it for a lasting possession."

Though opposing the Veda cult and animal sacrifices of the Brahmins, the Buddha nevertheless found his first disciples among them. Like Jesus, he sent them out on missionary journeys, but enjoined them: "Do not go the same ways in pairs." The Buddha himself continued to preach for forty-five years—living a simple monastic life as a wandering teacher in close contact with his disciples—five hundred pupils are said to have accompanied him at times. He died at the age of eighty.

Mara had tried to tempt him into entering Nirvana at once, but after a long struggle he rejected this offer, so that the world might learn the true doctrine. Nevertheless, his whole life was over-shadowed by longing for the end; for all worldly events were incidental and only the teaching important. When one of his disciples asked about the Master as a person, he replied: "Let be, Vakkali; what good will it do you to see my body, which is subject to decay? He who perceives the doctrine, Vakkali, perceives me; he who perceives me, perceives the doctrine." And to his favorite disciple Ananda he spoke the memorable words: "It may be, Ananda, that the thought will come to some of you that the doctrine has lost its Master, that there is no Master any more. You must not look at the matter thus, Ananda. The doctrine (*dharma*) and the discipline (*vinaya*) which I have taught and preached will be your Master after my death."

THE DOCTRINE OF THE BUDDHA

The doctrine of the Buddha is already implicit in the example of his life. Its kernel is contained in the "Four Noble Truths," which he preached in the so-called "Sermon on the Mount" of Benares for the five hermit monks: On man's being, the cessation of craving (thirst), the cessation of pain, and the secret of the Eightfold Way.

Man's being is, in the common Indian view, determined by the necessity of rebirth according to the law of karma, discussed above. Since life brings more suffering and misery than gladness and happiness, the man of insight must try to reduce karma rather than let it prolong itself. Hence the bonds of desire which compel man to remain in the cycle of rebirth must be loosened; his thirst for living must be quenched.

The first sacred Truth of Buddhism, then, is to regard life as pain. The Buddha expressed it in this way: "It is difficult to shoot one arrow after another through a narrow keyhole from a great distance. It is more difficult to take a hair split a hundredfold and with it strike and pierce a similar hair. But it is even more difficult to attain to the insight that all life is suffering." Whoever succeeds in this is already an *arhat*, a perfect saint.

The second Truth is to still the craving for life, which is fed by perceptions and feelings. The life of the ego ceases to trouble when oil is no longer fed to the flame; only then does the flame go

out from lack of nourishment. But the flame is forever being nour-
ished anew by the three principal faults of man: desire, hatred
and blindness. All love of life comes from craving, which rein-
forces the burden of karma and thus repeats the misery of life
endlessly by the turning of the wheel of Sankara. It is necessary
to weaken *skandhas,* the varieties of clinging to earthly things,
by knowledge. Cessation of craving presupposes elimination of
the four fundamental evils in the world: sensual desire, desire
to be, wrong beliefs and ignorance. It is through these that men
mistake the nature of existence and are persuaded to cling to
existence. But one who has attained to knowledge, like the Buddha, and realizes that out of birth come only old age, decay and
death, will crave release from life. Once he has really freed himself from all impressions and emotions, he will no longer have to
undergo new shapes and new rebirths. "That which causes me to
rise again as a god or as a man, namely the four fundamental
evils, are destroyed, annihilated, uprooted in me. As the lovely
lotus in the water is not tainted, so I shall not be tainted by the
world. Therefore I am a Buddha."

The cessation of pain as a result of the cessation of craving (the
third holy Truth) brings man into Nirvana, to the end of the cycle
of rebirth. Nirvana is a state of total peace of soul and indifference to all pleasure and all pain. The disciple of the Buddha escapes the vicious circle of eternal becoming and passing on, and
reaches the goal of existence: peace of soul as a condition of absolute independence from the world. That state is described by
those who have attained it as inexpressible, supernatural delight,
purest bliss. Definitions of Nirvana can only be negative: non-
desire, non-consciousness, non-life but also non-death. In positive
terms it can only be said that Nirvana is the state in which one is
freed from the transmigration of souls. It is possible to think of
Nirvana conceptually only in relation to the endless cycle of life
and death, the wheel of rebirth. But the concept is not so important as the images aroused by the word. The peace achieved
by the Buddha, the "oceanic stillness of the spirit," is so perfect
that it consists in unconditional indifference; indifference not only
toward all pain and pleasure, all happiness and possessions, but
also toward one's own life. An *arhat* no longer has preconceived

opinions or philosophical views; he never discusses things. He does not feel joy or pain; he owns nothing, has cast aside all passions, and is no longer attached even to good or evil. He is quiet, the same under all circumstances, still as deep water. He has found peace, the immutable state of Nirvana. "O monks," the Buddha says, "just as the great ocean has only one taste, that of salt, so this teaching and order has only one taste, that of salvation."

The *fourth* holy Truth—the Eightfold Way to achieve Nirvana —consists essentially of methods of concentration and meditation to subdue the self and curb the craving for life. The prescribed practices will open the inner eye and lead to dhyana, the higher stages of existence within Buddhist absorption. There is a parallel here to the uses of prayer in Christian mysticism. Yoga exercises, breathing control, fasting and mystical concentration are important aspects of the Eightfold Way—but we Westerners tend to see only the externals of these practices. The practical exercises of Yoga, however, must always be coupled with *sankhya,* theoretical understanding, if man is to achieve the path to Nirvana. As we have already mentioned, *sankhya* is the golden mean between the extremes of violent asceticism and worldly activity. The Buddha defined it thus in the Benares sermon:

"There are two extremes, O monks, which he who has given up the world should shun: the habitual practice of those things whose charm depends upon the passions, and especially sensuality—that is low, rude, unworthy, ignoble and unprofitable; and the habitual practice of self-mortification, which is painful, ignoble and unprofitable. There is a middle path discovered by the Tathagata, avoiding these two extremes, O monks—a path which opens the eyes and bestows understanding, which leads to peace of mind, to the higher wisdom, to full enlightenment, to Nirvana. What is that middle path, O monks? It is this noble Eightfold Path: right views, right aspirations, right speech, right conduct, right livelihood, right effort, right mindfulness and right contemplation. This, O monks, is that middle path discovered by the Tathagata, avoiding these two extremes—that path which opens the eyes and bestows understanding, which leads to peace of mind, to the higher wisdom, to full enlightenment, to Nirvana."

BUDDHIST MONASTICISM

The first step taken by a disciple of the Buddha in order to set foot on the path of salvation is voluntary poverty and entrance into a community of monks. The Buddhist monastic community is called *Sangha;* it was founded by the Buddha himself as an order of mendicants, and its organization has proved to be the one unchanging element in the history of Buddhism. The monks had to take strict vows to live ascetically, to cut their beards and hair, to wear the yellow robe, and to accept the "threefold jewel": "I take my refuge in the Buddha, in the Dhamma (law), in the Sangha."

The ultimate goal, at least for the monks of the original order, was to become an arhat in this or some later incarnation. The *Samyuttanikaya,* an ancient book belonging to the canon of the southern Buddhists, has this to say about the right mode of contemplation: "With legs crossed and trunk erect, the monk sits down in some lonely spot and practices earnest composure of his inward self, so that his earnestness is also reflected in his countenance. . . ." In this way the monk eliminates the five obstacles: He casts off worldly desire, ill will, malice, sluggishness, and doubt. He strives for inward peace and clarity, remote from all worldly action, and ceases to experience vacillations concerning good or evil. The highest ideal of Buddhist ethics, which Buddha propounded in the speech at Benares, is *metta,* comprehensive, unlimited but indifferent benevolence without affection, and *karuna,* community of suffering with all living beings, empathy without emotion. He who has made metta and karuna the guiding principles of his life will not repay evil with evil. In the Dhammapada, a kind of Buddhist psalter, one hymn reads: "Enmity does not subside through enmity, but only through amity does enmity subside. Overcome anger by not growing angry; overcome evil with good; overcome the miserly by giving; overcome the liar by truth."

Buddhist monastic life begins with the "going forth" into homelessness, in imitation of Gautama Buddha. Young men are accepted into the novitiate from their fifteenth year on, and finally received into the Sangha at the age of twenty. The monks live in utmost simplicity; aside from certain ritual acts for the laity, they spend most of their time in meditation. A monk owns nothing but his robe, a begging bowl, and a string of one hundred and eight beads, corresponding to the hundred and eight characteristics of the Buddha, on which he is supposed to meditate. Finally, he owns a razor for shaving his head, and a filter to sift insects out of his drinking water, in order to do harm to no living thing. Most of the monks live in celibacy, since Buddhism was originally distinctly antifeminine. But the Buddha, in spite of his scruples, ultimately gave his consent to the founding of an order of nuns. The Buddhist monastic fraternity has now existed for two and a half millennia; it is one of the oldest religious institutions in the world.

EVALUATION OF THE BUDDHA'S DOCTRINE

Because of its fundamentally negative view of worldliness, Buddhism is antipathetic to European thought. Escape from self-hood by meditation is not possible for Occidental man; but for the Indian it is a mode of intense spiritualization. If we accept the Asiatic premises, the doctrine of the Buddha is really nothing but a grandiose epistemology which places the problem of knowledge at the center of all philosophy and with unswerving consistency leads to abolition of the self, to the Nirvana that the Buddha achieved at his death. Buddhism, unlike Western philosophy, does not regard man as an individual, a personal being. Rather, what seems to be ego and selfhood are in reality only impulses of the will and instinctual forces that are constantly changing and passing. Where the ethics of the biblical religions refer to the human person, the Buddha teaches: Let the punishment of evil not strike him who does evil, but also not any other. In reality, neither the one nor the other exist.

Buddha clarifies his meaning by an example: the flame of a lamp burning all night long is, in the second and third hours of the night, no longer identical with the flame that burned the first hour. Yet it is no different, since it is fed by the same fuel. Thus what we regard as our ego is something that is constantly forming anew in the succession of events that comprise our existence. This chain of events is a closed circle without beginning and without end. Therefore neither the same being nor a different being reaches the last phase of cognition, that is to say, the point at which what is in the dying man becomes transformed into a new being. What we call the life of the self comes to rest only when oil is no longer supplied to the flame. Only then does the flame go out from lack of nourishment. Ultimately, then, the Buddha recognizes no individual soul at all, no real "ego." Everything created is insubstantial and transitory; the "individual" is fixed only by the weight of his actions; and the Buddha wishes to free him precisely from this evil.

The Buddha, then, adopted and developed the Indian doctrine of karma. He does not oppose the world as such, but the craving for life. Consequently, Buddhism cannot be identified with nihilism. The Buddha was concerned with something entirely different: with quelling the passions and the will to live altogether. In the Caryapitaka it is stated: "I am equally opposed to those who inflict pain on me and those who give me pleasure. I know neither affection nor hatred. In joy and sorrow I am unmoved, in honor and dishonor I am equable. That is the perfection of my equanimity."

It must be remembered that by pity the Buddha did not mean helping, active love, devotion to fellowmen, but only benign kindliness, the avoidance of unsympathetic acts. Since action is to be avoided, Buddhist ethics could develop only as something purely intellectual. It is devoid of morality in the Occidental sense. Buddhism is, for example, hostile to work, since work implies a clinging to things and therefore is wrong. Aside from the Sangha, moreover, Buddhism rejects all existing forms of Indian community, such as the caste ties. It is indifferent to the family.

The crucial difference between the religions of biblical revelation and Buddhism is inherent in the goal: one seeks redemption and the other extinction. The only salvational element in Buddhism is the prospect of salvation from rebirth. Whereas the Christian West takes a positive view of being in the world, Buddhism sees the highest value in non-being. The Westerner is a man of action; experiencing the resistance of the world, he sets out to master it. The Buddhist only wants to shake it off, and thus extinguish himself. Christians and Jews can have the same experiences in the world as disciples of Buddha: that sorrow cannot be eliminated, that death is the inescapable end of all life, even that reality as a whole ultimately attempts to endure suffering meaningfully, whereas the Buddhist sees ultimate meaning in throwing off suffering by throwing out pleasure, by avoiding life itself as the source of all evil. Thus it is not merely a tragic conception of the world that distinguishes Buddhism from Western religions, but the position of man in relation to natural processes, and the question of how he is to deal with the tragic aspect of these processes.

The major negative concept of Buddhism is suffering, of Christianity guilt. The positive ideas of both religions cannot be understood except in terms of these negatives. Existence is a value in itself, a high good, though perhaps an illusion. Buddhism teaches that this is inevitable, that without this great illusion life would not continue. Life would be confounded in its efforts toward self-perpetuation if it only for a moment appreciated the full reality of suffering. The veil of Maya is the precondition for existence, and only thought can strip off that veil.

For Jews, Mohammedans and Christians, being in the world is not the ultimate, because they regard this world as created, as referring back to a God who has created it. The place of revelation in the monotheistic religions is taken in Buddhism by man's self-understanding, in his seeing through the insubstantiality of the universe and recognizing the will as the greatest obstacle to the bliss of extinction. Original Buddhism—unlike Mahayana Buddhism—is therefore a religion without a deity, without a personal concept of God, and without any theory of salvation. For the Buddhist instructions on the technique of bringing about dissolution of the self are essentially a form of training. Man is sufficient unto himself. Perhaps he even believes that he has power over the gods; in any case, he does not need them to attain bliss.

Consequently, Buddhism regards man not as a being receptive to the summons of the Spirit, but—much like certain modern philosophies—as a purely natural being. The difference is only that just as these philosophies affirm the natural man, Buddhism negates him. The religions of revelation, on the other hand, understand the nature of man not in his own terms, but in terms of something else. In Christianity this something else is the incarnate Son of God, in Judaism the will of God become Word, in Islam the divine Word of the Koran. All three consider man a creature of God whose duty is to do the will of God in this world. Man's failures are not, as they are for the Buddhists, expressions of human transitoriness, but of human sinfulness. Buddhism recognizes no ethical problem in this sense. For the neighbor whom we are bidden to love and yet do not love, so that we fall into sin and guilt, is not regarded as a person by the Buddhist. Buddhism recognizes no positive commandment to love, only the passive requirement to suffer with others. Whether and to what extent this "sympathy" is to be translated into action marks the distinction between the two principal schools in the history of Buddhism. These schools developed around the beginning of the Christian era out of the Buddha's original doctrine.

DEVELOPMENTS IN BUDDHISM

Buddhism spawned a multiplicity of schools, for disagreements early arose among the monks as to how the words of the Buddha were to be interpreted. In the course of time, the doctrines described in the preceding pages—a profound, abstract, purely spiritual teaching intended for the few (Hinayana Buddhism, the Buddhism of "the Small Vehicle")—became a missionary world religion. Around the beginning of our era Buddhists began moving beyond individualistic striving for Nirvana. Some saw their task as rescuing as many people as possible, out of "pity," from the "burning house of the world of evil," and leading them to right knowledge and "salvation." Mahayana ("Great Vehicle") Buddhism considerably altered the original character of Buddhism, transforming it into a cult religion with rich, pompous rituals. Its liturgy with its wax candles, incense and vestments is sometimes reminiscent of Roman Catholicism. Many statues of the Buddha became centers of the cult, whereas older Buddhist art did not depict the Buddha at all. In Mahayana the historical Buddha was transformed into a mythic hero, even a salvational deity. Besides the original Buddha, there appeared numerous heavenly Buddhas, and the exemplary figure of the Bodhisattva, who out of pity for men renounces his own Buddha nature in order to draw as many others as possible out of the ocean of being on to the planks of the Great Vehicle. Gradually, however, this very ideal existence became the object of worship (Bodhisattva cult). Ultimately, the worship of gods—whom, incidentally, Buddha had never repudiated—became characteristic of this worldly form of Buddhism, instead of the original goal of self-salvation by right knowledge.

The Great Vehicle arose in northern India and gradually spread over the entire Far East. In China, Tibet and Japan it underwent numerous assimilations to native deities and was associated with magical notions and various forms of ritual. In these guises it became the dominant spiritual force in the regions it penetrated. But neither hierarchical Lamaism in Tibet nor Japanese Buddhism nor the Chinese folk religion are pure Buddhism. Yet they would not have come into being without the influence of the Buddha's doctrine.

Original Hinayana Buddhism survived only in the South, in Ceylon, Burma and Siam. But it, too, assimilated magical and polytheistic ideas in the course of time and added many new elements to the old stock of ideas. In the country of its origin, India, it degenerated completely. There Hinduism, repressed for some fifteen hundred years, ultimately won out; it had been the native religion of Hindustan, and has become so again. Signs of a revival of Buddhism have, however, been in evidence in recent years, especially among the outcastes. The latest figures indicate 3,250,227 Buddhists in India.

The relationship between Hinayana and Mahayana Buddhism has been trenchantly defined by Gustav Mensching in his book *Buddhistische Geisteswelt:* "Hinayana Buddhism has the appearance of a highly spiritual individual religion, concerned wholly with abstract inner processes, without a cult and without a hierarchy, indeed without any sacral organization. Its creed required the disciple of the Buddha to tread the holy Eightfold Path himself, in order to attain salvation. But Hinayana was in essence a universal religion, and in conformity to the inner law of such religions it gradually turned toward wider and wider circles. Its tendency was to seek to draw all men into the fold. But this goal could be achieved only if it transformed itself into a mass religion. That transformation was accomplished by Mahayana. This does not mean that we are to regard Mahayana as a mere externalization and mechanization of original Buddhism. Quite the contrary. It satisfied genuine religious concerns which were not satisfied in the purely monastic religion of original Buddhism, such as the desire for personal gods and a ritual by which these might be worshiped, for salvation by grace, without the ascetic monasticism that takes men out of secular life. The theologians of Mahayana managed to reconcile these legitimate religious tendencies with the views of Hinayana; but in practice, as adopted by the masses, these tendencies became associated with the typical characteristic of mass religions: the replacement of personal piety by external acts anyone can perform, acts often tainted by magic."

THE PRESENT STATE OF HINAYANA BUDDHISM

The present center of original Buddhism, in addition to Ceylon (5.2 million Buddhists), is to be found in Indo-China. Burma, which became an independent state in 1947, has in fact established Buddhism in its constitution as a kind of state religion, since the majority (some fourteen million) of the population profess it. Buddhism there has served as an ideological weapon for resistance to the Communist peril. In 1957 the major relics of the Buddha were transferred to Rangoon. The situation is similar in Thailand, where again Buddhism is the state religion; the constitution stipulates that the king must be a Buddhist. Bangkok boasts over four hundred Buddhist temples.

Undoubtedly, the laity in Hinayana Buddhism have incorporated a large number of magical notions into the religion. In Vietnam in our time a new hybrid religion has actually arisen, Caodaism, which sprang up in 1925, now has some two million adherents, and uses spiritistic mediums in its ceremonies.

A great many translations and popular accounts have brought the teachings of Gautama Buddha to the West. Today there are small Buddhist communities in many cities of Europe and America.

In 1954 Burma's devout prime minister, U Nu, convoked the Fifth Buddhist World Congress in Rangoon—the Fourth having taken place five hundred years before. Several hundred scholars remained in Rangoon for two years, to purify and retranslate the ancient Pali texts, the bible of Hinayana Buddhism. A theological definition of the person of Buddha was established; it was laid down that he was to be venerated neither as man nor as God, but as the embodiment of the eternal principle of Enlightenment. In May 1956 the work of the congress was concluded with a great celebration in honor of the Buddha's twenty-five hundredth birthday. This celebration was seen by many Buddhists as betokening a new sense of Buddhistic identity with which to counteract the foreign elements that had penetrated even into Southeast Asia. The decision to undertake missionary activities all over the world was confirmed by the congress. Another manifestation of reviving Buddhism was the World Brotherhood of Buddhism, a new organization to combat Communist efforts at undermining the religion. This World Brotherhood held its sixth conference in Cambodia in 1960.

RELIGION IN TIBET

Mahayana Buddhism underwent a peculiar development in the inaccessible highlands of Tibet, the "Roof of the World." At the time of its introduction in the seventh century (A.D. 632, the story goes), it encountered the native *bon* religion, a form of Central Asian animism and shamanism based on magic spells, which still persists in northern and southern Tibet. Here in the high Himalayas men saw the whole universe threatened by fearsome demons and relied for safety upon magicians and exorcisers. With the advent of Buddhism, these wizards gradually became Buddhist priests known as lamas—the word means "superiors." The Mantra school of Mahayana Buddhism—known as Tantrism in Tibet—had already adopted magical rituals, sacred formulas (mantras) and consecrations employing magic spells. These outward observances acquired more and more prominence. The practices that developed are also known as the "Diamond Vehicle" (Vadshrayana). Many Indian texts were translated into Tibetan. Gradually enormous collections of sacred writings were amassed—more than five hundred volumes, some translations from the Sanskrit, some exegetic commentary by Tibetan monks. By about 1300 the Tibetan canon was complete.

The lama hierarchy of Tibet has no counterpart in other forms of Buddhism. A purely ecclesiastical and monastic state arose, since the clergy also exercises secular power and has installed monks in all important offices of government. One-seventh of the population (about five hundred thousand monks) belong to the clergy. Moreover, the five thousand monasteries dominate the economic life of the country. Tibet has been justly called "the paradise of monks."

Originally, celibacy was not imposed on the monks, so that whole dynasties of abbots could develop. But at the beginning of the fifteenth century, after a period of widespread degeneracy, there appeared the great Tibetan reformer Tsong kha-pa (1356–1419), "the man from Onion Valley" in eastern Tibet (Kumbum monastery). This learned and earnest monk introduced monastic celibacy, gave the monks their yellow robe and bowl, and outlawed the use of alcohol and the practice of magic. He also elaborated the hierarchy and placed profession of obedience to the lama even before profession of the Threefold Jewel (Buddha, Dhamma, Sangha). Thus there arose the "Yellow Church," which gave a new meaning to the doctrine of the Bodhisattva: when a Buddha or Bodhisattva passed away, his successor must be sought among children born in the hour of his death. Once the child was found, it was considered the previous saint in a new incarnation: the Dalai Lama, meaning the "mighty lama" who since the days of Tsong kha-pa has resided in the Tibetan capital of Lhasa ("seat of the gods").

The new lama is sought among male children according to the curious laws of "Chubilganic succession" (transformation by incarnation). Instead of succession by blood, as among secular ruling families, or by election as in the Catholic papacy, Tibetan Buddhism since the fifteen century has practiced spiritual succession by incarnation. The great difficulty is, of course, how to recognize the proper successor. For centuries, the search for a new incarnation has proceeded according to the same rules. After an interval of forty-nine days succeeding the death of a Great Lama—the interval may, however, be one of several years—his soul may incarnate anew, generally under miraculous circumstances.

"In order to know what child's body the Bodhisattva has adopted after the death of a Dalai Lama, inquiries are made for children who were born under strikingly miraculous signs, or who after birth assumed strange positions, for example the crossed-leg posture of the Buddha in meditation, or who showed other remarkable characteristics. Families of no particular prestige are preferred, in order to prevent excessive influence of relations upon the future Dalai Lama. A special test decides among the children in question" (Söderblom).

After the death of the thirteenth lama (1933), the following account was given of the discovery of his successor—the search having taken until 1937—in a farmhouse twenty-five miles east of Kumbum monastery. As it happened, this was already in Chinese territory.

"Pabo Dongrub, a boy born on June 6, 1935, was visited. The child came attentively forward toward the monks as they entered, and with a cry of 'Sera Lama' ran toward the leader of the expedition, who was disguised as a servant. Without any shyness, he seized the rosary the lama was carrying, which had belonged to the thirteenth Dalai Lama. Next day the monks came in their proper clothing and subjected the boy to the prescribed examination. First he had to choose once more from among four different rosaries the worn and insignificant-looking one that had belonged to the thirteenth Dalai Lama. The boy also recognized without hesitation a drum of the deceased Lama, with which he had been wont to call his servants, selecting it from among several similar to it. Likewise, he took the old Dalai Lama's worn old walking-stick, not even glancing at a new one decorated with silver and ivory. When the boy's body was examined, it was found to have the requisite signs of a Bodhisattva: large, protruding ears and two birthmarks on the upper part of the body which are said to represent the beginnings of a second pair of arms of the four-armed God Padmapani.

"Transfer of the boy to Tibet proved difficult, and was permitted only after payment of a high ransom to Chiang Kai-shek's Kuomingtang government. Negotiations over the ever-mounting ransom price dragged on. It was 1939 before the boy was allowed to leave China; and in February 1940 his accession was festively celebrated in Lhasa. At that time he was given new names such as: Holy One, Mighty of Speech, Absolute Wisdom, Preserver of the Doctrine, Great Ocean, the Present, Great Jewel of Victory, and so on."

It is obvious that the finding of the child by a procedure which contains remnants of shamanistic, pre-Buddhist beliefs, and his education and training, puts great power in the hands of the clergy who are in charge of him. The Dalai Lama is a "living god," a pope-king. As Bodhisattva and savior, as intermediary between this world and the next, he wields both priestly and political functions. At his side stands the Panchen Lama, whose residence is the monastery of Tashilhumpo. He is found in the

PLATE IX *Germanic Gods.* The runic stone of Hornhausen, Germany, presumably depicts Wotan or Odin armed with round shield, sword, and lance across a field of battle. At the bottom of the stone is a carving of the Midgard snake. Center: The sun cart from Trundholm, Sweden, about 1000 B.C., depicts the deity as disc on the cart. Below left: The urn with the human features was presumably carried across fields in springtime to insure fertility and blessings. Below right: A gravestone from Lund, Sweden, carved with magic runes.

PLATE X *Greek Gods.* Above left: Zeus, the Heavenly Father, King of the Gods. From his seat on Mount Olympus he controls the forces of nature. He is the wisest god, guardian of freedom, supervisor of justice. Above right: Apollo, god of wisdom and music, protector of agriculture and cattle. He confers the gift of prophecy and can cure illnesses. Center: Kairos is the god of the favorable opportunity. Below: Aphrodite, the foam-born goddess. Originally an oriental fertility goddess, she was considered by the Greeks the divinity of love and beauty.

PLATE XI *Greek Temples.*
The sacred area, separated
from the outside world, served
the Greeks for acts of worship,
dances, processions, and sacrifices. Among the oldest religious sites were groves, caves,
grottos, and mountains. The
temple as the house of the
god, and later as a place at
which his worshipers could assemble, was patterned on profane dwellings.

Altar to Zeus from Perga-
mum (the present Bergama) in
Asia Minor. Probably erected
in gratitude for the successful
defense against the Galatians.
The altar was built between
180-160 B.C., high above the
city. A broad staircase led up
to the place of sacrifice, which
was surrounded by a peristyle.

Circular temple in Delphi,
circa 400 B.C., dedicated to
Athena Pronaia. The building
is a *tholos* in the Doric style;
pedestals for statues may still
be seen.

Temple of Poseidon in Paes-
tum, in the Doric style, built
about 450 B.C.—a great example of the high period of Greek
art.

Columns of the Parthenon
on the Acropolis in Athens.
Temples were erected on this
citadel as early as 600 B.C.
The sensitive tapering of the
fluted Doric column's curve
gives them the quality of something alive.

PLATE XII *World of the Romans.* Above: Round marble temple from the first century B.C., dedicated to Vesta, goddess of the hearth. Nineteen Corinthian columns enclose the unadorned cella. Center: Zeus of Doliche, originally a Syrian god, with a goddess. His cult became merged with that of Jupiter in the Roman religions. Below left: Altar of the lares, the protective spirits of family and fields. They were honored at the domestic hearth; their images were kept in shrines. Below right: Temple of Saturn in which the treasure of the state was kept. Today the foundations and eight columns stand.

PLATE XIII *Gods of Hinduism*. Above left: Krishna, the blue god. His dance expresses the everlasting circular motion of life. Above right: Kali, the terrible goddess who combats demons. Center: Krishna and Balarma as cowherds. Persecuted by a king, Krishna grew up among herdsmen. Legends recount his numerous heroic deeds and adventures in love. Below left: Vishnu's incarnation as a fish. Vishnu is said to have incarnated on earth nine times, until at last he revealed himself in human form. Below right: Vishnu resting on the world-serpent Ananta. Its seven heads shield his head. Above him Brahma sits enthroned on a lotus.

PLATE XIV *Statues of the Buddha.* All statues of the Buddha display strict frontality and symmetry. The expression of the face is full of supernatural sublimity, of the radiance of eternal wisdom. Above left: Monumental figure of the Enlightened One in China. Above right: Bhaiskajagura Buddha in Japan. This Buddha heals all diseases and illnesses. Below left: Buddha on lion throne. This sculpture from the Gandhara region influenced all later representations of the Buddha. Below right: A Buddha from the Chinese province of Campong-Thom.

PLATE XV   *Tibetan Religious Life.* Above left: During a funeral the magician lama prays to the gods for a fortunate rebirth. Above right: A monk making *Dormas* of butter. Below: As the Dalai Lama stands at the head of Lamaism, his citadel-palace, the Potala, rises up on the ridge above Lhasa, the capital of Tibet.

PLATE XVI *Chinese Pagodas.* Pagodas consist of several tiers with overhanging roofs. At the corners hang bells whose ringing is meant to carry the holy doctrine over the country. Above left: Pagoda at Nara. The five tiers symbolize the five elements: earth, water, fire, air, and wind. Above right: In the past, the emperor would offer the spring sacrifice in the hall of prayer of the Temple of Heaven in Peking. Below left: A seven-tiered pagoda in Peking. Below right: One of China's largest pagodas, at Hanchow.

same way as the Dalai Lama and is regarded as the incarnation of Buddha Amitabha. The Panchen Lama is the second chief dignitary of Tibet. As his title (from the Sanskrit *pandita,* "learned man") suggests, he is supposed to live in the realm of pure thought and spirit. Gradually, however, conditions changed so that the Dalai Lama became the supreme secular ruler of Tibet, while the Panchen Lama took over more of the religious functions. Recently, this situation has totally changed. After Tibet fell under Red Chinese rule, the Panchen Lama professed himself an adherent of Communism. In consequence, he alone has political influence, while the fourteenth Dalai Lama was forced into exile, and today lives in India.

It would be tedious to list the gods of Lamaism. Gods, goddesses and rituals among the various religious groups have merged with frightful and obscene demons from the ancient Bon religion to form a curiously eclectic pantheon. The cults are excessively pompous, and prayer curiously mechanized: the priests carry prayer scepters and rosaries; strips of paper inscribed with magical formulas and prayers are flown to be fluttered by the wind, or placed in wheels that can be turned by passersby. When the prayer mill rattles, the devotee speaks the sacred formula of Lamaism: *Om mani padme hum. Om* and *hum* are magic words. *Mani padme* has an interpretation in esoteric philosophy: the precious stone (*mani,* that is, the Buddha or his doctrine) is in the lotus (*padme,* that is, the world). In addition, there are purely magical and sexual interpretations. A beneficent power is ascribed to the words, for which reason they are murmured continuously, painted on walls, and placed on paper strips in the gears of mill wheels. Concerning this formula a Bodhisattva once said, according to an ancient text: "I can count every single grain of sand in the oceans. But I would never be able to count the sum of merits acquired by repeating those great six magic syllables: *Om mani padme hum.*"

Lamaism spread to the Himalayan countries bordering on Tibet. The Mongols, the Buryats and the Kalmucks were converted, the latter carrying the religion into European Russia when they began to settle in the area between the Don and Volga after the seventeenth century. Charged in 1942 with opposition to Bolshevist rule and "collaborationism," they were partly resettled, partly exterminated. Lamaism, moreover, contributed greatly to the ethical enlightenment of the savage mountain tribes, although the ordinary man seldom expected more from his lama than magical aid against dangerous forces.

In the eighteenth century China conquered Tibet and made it part of the Chinese Empire. From the very beginning it had to deal with Lamaism as a political power. The Dalai Lama never abandoned his aspirations toward independence. During much of this century England and Russia, the two imperialist colonial powers most concerned, attempted to exploit conditions in the priestly state at the expense of China. After the Chinese revolution of 1912 Tibet, under British influence, broke away from China entirely, but in 1950 it was occupied by a Red Chinese "army of liberation" and in 1951 incorporated into Mao Tsetung's Chinese People's Republic.

As a religious system, Lamaism will remain important only as long as it keeps its hold on the peoples of Tibet and Mongolia. The almost total isolation of the Tibetan theocratic state during the centuries—an isolation breached only in recent years—permitted the evolution of a unique religious and political organization. It is impossible to predict the effect upon this organization of the Chinese occupation and the increasing contact with the outside world through new roads, automobile, and air communications.

RELIGION IN CHINA

Wʜᴀᴛ we today call the Chinese folk religion is a mixture of sectarian Buddhism with Taoist and Confucian elements. That religion includes within its fold nearly five hundred million human beings. From its beginnings, which are lost in the dimness of antiquity, China's folk religion has essentially consisted in veneration of powerful spirits and magic powers of the earth, water and air, which must be placated by rites of prayer and thanksgiving. Some of these animistic notions and traditional superstitions are relics of the earliest stages of Chinese civilization. Elements of an ideal ethical order in the cosmos, which derive from the teachings of the philosopher Kung-tse or Confucius, have mingled with mystical notions of the other great Chinese sage Lao-tse. Many of these ideas were so profound that they almost inevitably had to be debased and diluted by magic. From about the first century A.D. on, however, Mahayana Buddhism with its doctrine of the Bodhisattvas trickled steadily into China, and in both China and Japan entered into curious and intricate alliances with native systems of doctrine. Under Buddhist influence, new schools of religious thought were formed.

CHINESE BUDDHISM

According to ancient traditions, Mahayana Buddhism first entered China in A.D. 61, and by the sixth century had actually become the state religion. The Chinese Buddhists created their own canon of sacred scriptures, seven hundred times more voluminous than the Bible. The greater part of these scriptures consist of translations from Sanskrit Mahayana writings. This vast mass of literature is probably partly responsible for the formation of ten different Buddhist schools or sects in China. These fine-spun philosophical speculations could, of course, never appeal to the majority of the people. Among the common people, only the more practical "School of Meditation" (Chan-tsung; Japanese Zen) and the "School of the Pure Land" (Tsing-tu; Japanese Jodo) have made an impress.

The Chan school, which appeals to an intellectual elite, is concerned with the inward experience of enlightenment; it derives from the Hindu mystic Bodhidharma of the sixth century, who is said to have spent nine years in front of a wall, absorbed in meditation. "Look into your own heart; there you will find the Buddha," was his watchword. The Chan school takes its departure from the legend that the Buddha—called Fo in Chinese—at one time, instead of giving an explanation of his doctrine, held a golden flower toward his audience and smiled at it. No one but a novice monk understood, and he smiled back. The point is that the mystery lies not in words, but in deep contemplation of the flower itself.

The Tsing school is the most widespread; before the revolution sixty per cent of all Chinese Buddhists belonged to it. The "pure land" of its title, also called the "great western paradise," is the heaven in which Buddha Amitabha, the Buddha of Immeasurable Radiance, sits enthroned. Amitabha (Japanese Amida) is the heavenly counterpart of the historical Buddha (Dhyanibuddha), in other words a divine Buddha of pure grace who rules as master of paradise or eternal light and rescues the believers. He is the merciful father to whom innumerable monks and nuns of the Far East have appealed in prayer as "our refuge" for centuries. For the average man who does not desire to become an arhat, it is sufficient to worship the Buddha Amitabha, the heavenly helper of believers of whom neither good works nor asceticism is demanded.

The Buddha Amitabha—not the historical Gautama, that is—is shown in countless temple images as inexpressibly sublime and benign. Usually he is depicted enthroned on a lotus, or else standing erect holding a lotus flower in one hand. At his side stands the Bodhisattva Kwan-yin—frequently regarded as a son of Amitabha. In the course of time Kwan-yin (in Japan Kwannon) became a female goddess of mercy. The Buddhism of the "School of the Pure Land" is on the way to becoming a religion of grace; personal salvation is sought in the heavenly Buddha's paradise, into which his devotees will be received after death. The Nirvana doctrine of the primitive Buddhist communities plays scarcely any part in Amitabha Buddhism.

At present not too much can be known of the situation among Chinese Buddhists under the Communist regime. But even before the Communists took over, the influence of the two principal Buddhist schools on Chinese folk religion was none too great. These schools appealed largely to the educated classes. In general, the Chinese has little taste for metaphysical speculation. His native philosophers have always inclined toward pragmatism.

CHINESE FOLK RELIGION

There never has been a unified Chinese religion. The great masses of Chinese are "religiously" bound together only by the ancestor cult, by certain traditional ceremonies and by a common attitude toward life, consisting in a consciousness of inward identity between man and his surroundings, and a deep respect for nature in all her aspects. A European scholar has called this specifically Chinese attitude toward life "universism." Every Chinese strives to harmonize his life with the rhythm of the universe. More important than all the gods that may be invoked—these vary according to region and social level—and more important than man as an individual is the harmony of the universe. Man can experience that harmony by contemplating the forces that pervade the cosmos, the mystery of Tao. Yin and Yang, the active masculine and the passive feminine principles, are the primal forces, intertwined within a circle. Between them there is no hostile tension and no dualistic opposition; rather, they seek always and everywhere to supplement each other in harmonious cooperation. Female Yin and Male Yang, which represent earth and heaven, are both necessary for the world order. As long as they are in proper accord, they are good; if man treads evil paths, heaven is outraged and earth no longer prospers. The source of their harmony, and thus the origin of all order in the universe, is Tao (pronounced Dow). The idea of Tao appears in the earliest Chinese writings; but it was first placed at the center of Chinese thinking by the philosopher Lao-tse.

The relationships between man and nature, and a longing for man to achieve harmony with nature, were always of paramount importance in China. Veneration of the soil, the mountains and the rivers is connected with this sense of mutual relation. The earthen embankment at the entrance to a Chinese village is supposed to symbolize the fruitfulness of the soil. "In the spring this embankment was the scene of dances and songs, by means of which the land was commended to the blessing of the gods. In the autumn, the harvest thanksgiving festival was held there. To this day Chinese peasants—wherever they are allowed to—sue the favor of the jade-green god of the earth and water with sacrifices and ceremonies."

Veneration of the life-giving forces of the earth is paralleled by reverence for heaven. The actual rituals of the cult of heaven are the province of the emperor, the "Son of Heaven." As mediator between heaven and the people, the Chinese ruler exercised both sacral and political functions. On the night of the winter solstice he made the offering at the altar in the Temple of Heaven; this was the chief religious ceremony of the year. The state cult went on until the dethronement of the Manchu dynasty in 1911.

In addition to the national cults, ancestor worship within the family has long been extremely important in Chinese folk religion. Every family of consequence venerates the souls of ancestors as special patrons; in the southwestern corner of every house there is a home chapel for ancestor worship. These home altars have been a feature of Chinese life since the Shang dynasty (1776–1122 B.C.). The invisible ancestors, whose names are inscribed on the ancestor tablet in every house, are always present to the minds of the Chinese. Offerings of food and other things are made to keep their favor. Ancestor cult, offerings, veneration of local gods and great annual folk festivals have been characteristic of Chinese folk religion for thousands of years. The New Year celebration is one of the most important of these festivals; it is presided over by the smiling god of wealth, Tsai Shen (Japanese Dai-koku), who carries a heavy sack of rice. There are also the Dragon Boat festival, for invoking rain, and various ancestor festivals in memory of the dead. Beneath all the Buddhist overlays and the abstractions of the great philosophical systems, these elements of the folk religion have proved to be the really permanent constituents of the religious life of China. They are part of the innermost nature of the Chinese people, and it is difficult to imagine that they can ever be displaced.

LAO-TSE AND THE TAO-TE-KING

Chinese religious speculation reached its apogee in the work of Lao-tse (literally, "the Old Philosopher"). According to early sources, whose historical value is questionable, Lao-tse was born in South China in the year 604 B.C. He became archivist and chronicler to a prince of the Chow dynasty; but soon became disgusted with court life and political affairs. Retiring to a hut on the slope of a mountain in the district of Han Kvan, he lived in solitude for many decades, wrote a small book, and at last, when he was more than eighty years old, left the hut and tramped off to the west, never to be seen again.

That is all we know with any degree of certainty about Lao-tse; all the rest is legend. The small book he left behind belongs among the most obscure books in the world, which has resisted the efforts of countless translators and interpreters. In size, the Tao-te-king is no larger than the Gospel according to St. Mark. In eighty-one sections, most of them very brief, it deals in ecstatic metaphysical language with Tao and Te. The obscurities begin at once with question of what Tao and Te are. Both are highly ambiguous words that have no precise equivalents in any European language. Tao means something like "ground of being," "way" or "orbit"—the orbit in which the universe moves. Te means approximately "good conduct" or "virtue." Tao-te-king is thus the path of virtue, or the universal law and its effects; it is also Lao-tse's prescription of how man ought to live.

The key to his doctrine is an understanding of the word Tao. What is its meaning? Lao-tse answers in his book: "The standard of man is the earth, the standard of the earth is heaven, the standard of heaven is Tao, the standard of Tao—its own life." It cannot be said that this immanent force does anything—that would be personifying it too much. Nevertheless everything is done by Tao. Tao is eternally without action, and yet there is nothing that it does not do. Rather, the non-doing of all beings helps it to do what it does. By *wu-wei* (doing nothing) and *puh-yen* (saying nothing), the condition of *hu-wu* (equilibrium) is attained. Wu-wei, then, is having effect without acting. Water is a symbol of the Tao; it does not contend, it takes the lowest place, and yet it is the most important thing. Tao is amoral; Lao-tse regards positive moral teachings as a symptom of degeneracy. Everything happens of its own accord; no effort is needed, for action only impairs concentrated sanctity. If the great Tao decays, then humanitarianism and justice, prudence and cleverness arise; and from these stem hypocrisy and ever multiplying conflicts among men.

The ethics of Lao-tse is wholly negative. It is rooted in a quietistic mysticism which assigns no special place to man in the whole realm of existence. The aim is rather to free man from involvements and let him fall back into the ultimate ground, Tao. But for true knowledge of Tao, neither theoretical learning is needed nor practical worldly wisdom such as Confucius taught. Lao-tse says: "Without looking out of the window, one sees the course of heaven. Without going out of the house, one knows the world. The farther one goes away, the less one perceives. Therefore the wise man knows without stirring, gives names to things without seeing them, and completes without acting." Lao-tse approaches primitive Buddhism in these teachings. Not to act, not to interfere in the course of events, is man's duty, he maintains. Some curious conclusions flow from this principle, and are expressed in the Tao-te-king:

Government has no positive tasks. War is condemned. Material progress is despised. Offices and institutions are called useless. Far better for the land to have Tao; everything should be quiet and happen of itself. Politics consists in pursuing no definite ideals, no positive aims; the desirable state is one of stagnation in which hearts are drained of blood and seek only knowledge of Tao. Thus the Tao-te-king states:

> Sincerity begets peaceful governing;
> Skillfulness begets mere struggle.
> Wanting nothing begets orderly community. . . .
> Prohibition begets coercion,

Command begets trouble,
Still begets baseness,
Law begets crime.
Whereas the Perfect One speaks thus:
I observe non-volition,
And the people develop according to their nature.
I observe non-action,
And the people guide themselves as fate wills.
I observe non-sympathy,
And the people thrive, because left to themselves.
I observe non-being,
And the people are as they are, of their own accord.

The morality of the Taoist approaches the idea of the Stoic sage who extolled the golden mean. Equanimity and evenness will overcome all extremes. Thus the twenty-fourth saying runs:

Standing on the toes is not standing,
Spreading the legs is not walking.
He who gets into the light stands in shadow.
He who thinks himself at the goal, goes backward.

From this attitude, not from Christian analogues, springs Lao-tse's rule of life: "I do good to those who do me good, and to those who do not do me good I also do good—and thus it is well with everyone." That sounds like Christian charity, but it is peculiarly unreal because it springs from a mysticism that seeks total devaluation of all the things of the world. In this contemplative mysticism the real ground of things is converted, by absolute emptying of all passions and worldly interests out of the ego, into a totally effectual ineffectiveness: Wu-wei. If all striving, bustle and knowledgeableness are abandoned, selflessness, humility, tolerance and peacefulness take their place.

The highest salvation, in Lao-tse, is a spiritual state: the turning back to Tao, quiet growth and ripening by inner union with the ultimate ground of being. What it comes down to is a *unio mystica* but not an active state of grace, as in the West. Non-action is a proof of the state of grace, in the Chinese view; it is evidence that the world can no longer affect the devout soul. Goodness and humility in the world are, for Lao-tse, not personal virtues, and do not help attainment of the *unio mystica* with the divine principle, Tao. When man practices doing nothing, he helps all beings do what they must do. Lao-tse, consistently enough, is said to have wanted to remain nameless; he certainly never intended to found a new religious community.

Kung-tse, or as we call him, Confucius, was like Lao-tse in not regarding himself as the emissary of a divine power. But unlike his near contemporary, he was a much more actively minded political person, whose criticisms of his society were always motivated by a practical desire to improve it.

Confusius' birth date is placed some fifty years after Lao-tse's (551 B.C.). He married, traveled about among a number of small princely courts, and was active as a political adviser until his death (479 B.C.). The story of his life has been so distorted by legend that it can be disregarded. It suffices for us to know that like Jesus he spread his teachings by the spoken word and living example. They were only written down generations after his death. In his lifetime he did not succeed in gaining acceptance for his views. His circle of disciples was regarded as a school of Scribes, of which there were many in China at the time. The school produced the *Annals of Spring and Autumn,* a book of moral and political wisdom for princes, and the *Book of Historical Documents,* a compendium of ancient Chinese institutions and customs. More important than these writings is the *Lun Yü,* "Discourses and Dialogues," written down by the third generation of disciples, which preserves recollections of the master and some of his sayings. It contains twenty books, but we have it only in a late revision of the fifth century A.D. In spite of its glorification of his personality, it furnishes the clearest information on Confucius' moral philosophy and ideas of political reform. He did not ever say much about religion, and what little he did say has an air of reverence but not of warmth, as Söderblom has commented.

Confucius conceived the Tao rather in its moral and social aspect, in terms of proper government of a state. The political basis of his thinking is plain; his mind dwelt chiefly on the ideas of nation and rule. Within society, the Tao operates in two forms: in music and in the *li*, the ritual rules for community life. There are mysterious powers that influence and govern social life. Morality governs behavior, beautiful music governs feeling. Since the generation of these powers can produce political chaos, they must be supervised and regulated by the emperor, who is the guardian and preserver of lawfulness. The emperor stands at the head of the state, and since Tao is specially concentrated in him, he is also the head of the state religion, its supreme priest. Above him, as the protector of his throne, there is only heaven, whose son he is.

Confucius considered rites (*li*) vital for the nation. A people kept in order by threats of punishment would lose its conscience and degenerate, he said, while a people directed by moral principles would have a conscience and strive for goodness. In the *Lun Yü* Confucius is quoted as follows: "The superior man makes honesty the foundation of his existence. He uses it with address and consideration. He speaks of it with modesty, and carries it out with sincerity and faithfulness. Truly, this is the superior man." The superior man, in Chinese the *chen-dsien*, has arrived at the control of his passions by ethical disciplining of himself. That is to say, through *li* and through music he has approached the Tao. Like the Tao, man ought to be passionless, indifferent and silent. Upsetting of spiritual equanimity by irrational passions should be avoided at all costs.

The Confucian does not seek salvation; at most he desires to be saved from cultural barbarism. What he expects as the reward of virtue is long life, health and wealth in this life, and beyond death the preservation of a good name. Ethics has no transcendental meaning, any more than life is directed toward a goal beyond itself. The Christian concept of original sin as well as the philosophical idea of radical evil are incomprehensible in China. Hence the failure of all efforts by Christian missionaries in China to arouse a sense of sin. The very prerequisites are lacking. The cultured Chinese flatly refuses to consider himself permanently tainted by sin. To be sure, he has a phrase for it, but a Chinese, "I have sinned," corresponds most closely to our formula of politeness: "Please excuse me." For the wrongdoing in question consists in offenses against traditional authorities: parents, ancestors, superiors in the official hierarchy, or else infractions of traditional ceremonies or social conventions.

The foundation of Chinese society is the family; the sustaining element in life the religious veneration that is practiced according to a prescribed ceremonial. Confucius deliberately restored the Chinese ancestor cult. "To honor the dead as if they are still living" is, according to Confucius, an expression of supreme childlike submissiveness. To have no son who can continue the ancestor cult is regarded as a grave offense against the family. "There is no greater sign of respect for the father than to consider him as equal to heaven." Confucius commented in one of his discourses: "He sacrificed to his ancestors as if they were present; he sacrificed to the gods as if the gods were present. The master said: To me, sacrificing without the sense of presence is as good as not sacrificing" (Lun Yü). This is the most positive statement on religion that we have from Confucius. Other remarks of his reveal a skeptical reticence, as for example: "Respect religion, but keep your distance from it." Or: "It is long since I have prayed."

The problems of the state and of right government were Confucius' chief interests. If government is good, the subjects obey of their own accord. Therefore he concerned himself far more with the duties of the governors than of the subjects. Only those who realize the Tao in themselves are superior men, and as such fit to lead the state. Much of Confucius' advice on the conduct of life and political philosophy was summed up in little dialogues such as the following:

Dsi Gung, a disciple of the master, asked what was most important in the art of governing. The master said: See to enough food, enough soldiers, and the confidence of the people. Dsi Gung asked: If it were necessary to give up one of these three things, which could best be spared? The master replied: The soldiers. Dsi Gung asked: If it were necessary to give up one of the remaining two, which could best be spared? The master replied: Food, for men have always had to die. But if the people have no confidence in their ruler, he cannot govern.

Prince Ding of Lu asked: Can the explanation for the prosperity of a country be summed up in a single saying? The master replied: There is no saying that could contain so much. But there is a proverb: "To be a ruler is difficult, to be a servant of the state not easy." If one knows only that to be a ruler is difficult, would not that saying alone be nearly enough to make a country prosper? Prince Ding asked: Can the explanation for the downfall of a country be summed up in a single saying? The master replied: There is no one saying that could contain so much. But there is a proverb: What happiness to be a ruler when no one contradicts, no matter what I command. If the commands are right, it is well that no one should contradict them. But if they are not right and no one contradicts them, is not that saying alone sufficient to bring about the downfall of a country?

The political philosophy of Confucius, based on such bits of practical wisdom, served as groundwork for the Chinese Empire for at least two millennia. Confucius himself purported to be a man of tradition, not an original creator. He himself said in the *Lun Yü:* "I add nothing new to my tradition; in my faith I let myself be guided by the love of antiquity." In true Chinese fashion, he regarded culture as the "study of antiquity." Confucian knowledge, therefore, was transmissible study of the Chinese past, out of which the eternal standard of the Tao might be deduced and followed.

Confucianism attempted to reduce all tensions and contradictions in the world to an absolute minimum. Its ideal of existence was the Tao as an equilibrium of all tensions. This Tao was thus neutral and pacifistic. Man ought to be guided by reason toward a rational order. "Better to live as a dog and in peace than as a man and in anarchy," as a Confucian scholar expressed the principle. Ultimately, Confucianism is no religion at all, but a rationalistic ethics based on confidence in the ultimate goodness of human nature. The moral sensibility of all men and their readiness to bow to ethical values once perceived—or to put this differently, the teachability and learnability of goodness—is assumed as a fact in Confucianism. In direct contradiction to Buddhism, it called for practical adaptation to the world and its conventions. Indeed, it seems to be largely a code of political maxims and rules of decent conduct for cultivated Chinese. The morality developed by the successors of Confucius became the dominant political and philosophical system of China, and was regarded as at once a political philosophy and a religion.

Its very worldliness helps explain why Confucianism has retained its fascination for the West ever since seventeenth-century French missionaries brought word of it to civilized Europe. In the age of pigtails and Chinoiserie, Leibnitz, Wolff, Voltaire and other thinkers of the West virtually transformed the Chinese humanist and sage into their patron saint.

Modern Sinologists have pointed out that our version of Confucius is a highly stylized personality, an embodiment of the ideal Chinese. And in fact those Confucian ethical and political doctrines which have become the Chinese way of life can be completely detached from the historical personality of Confucius. Though the figure of Confucius himself was given superhuman traits and he was held in high homage, he was never worshiped.

Confucian philosophy is plain common sense; Confucian ethics is a conventional morality that has permeated all aspects of Chinese life and set up an ideal of perfection well within the capacity of the average man. Precisely because the Chinese have little gift for religion and metaphysics, Confucianism suited their needs. And for that very reason Confucianism achieved something that the peoples of Europe have never accomplished: the creation of a superior way of life valid for millennia.

DEVELOPMENTS IN TAOISM AND CONFUCIANISM

The doctrine of Lao-tse has undergone a development typical in the history of religions. It has congealed into a religion, Taoism, for in the long run it acquired a practical ethics and a fixed priestly organization. The result is that the antiworldly rationalistic doctrine of the aristocratic mystic Lao-tse has merged with the age-old Chinese profession of magi (*tao-shi*). In addition, the hermits—probably in emulation of the Buddhists—joined forces to form monastic communities. Monastic Taoism remained, however, without influence on public life, for its strongly mystic strain made it shun the world. It was never properly understood by the masses.

Soon the Taoist magi were claiming power over all of nature. They sold amulets, and instead of meditation and preaching in the Taoist temples, they practiced exorcism of demons, soothsaying and alchemy. They attempted to make gold out of quicksilver, just like the alchemists of Europe. By borrowings from the ancestor cult, the whole cosmos was peopled with nature gods and local deities. There were even special gods for different occupations. Thus students venerated Wan-chang, the disembodied spirit of an official of the Chow dynasty, as the god of literature—who thereafter frequently appeared in person to famous scholars. Merchants venerated the war god Kvan-ti, a successful soldier of fortune of the Han dynasty. And so on.

Taoism evolved a complex hierarchical organization of priests, monks and even a pope. The Taoist priests assumed the influential functions previously held by soothsayers and magicians. The chief business of the priests, most of whom came from lower-class clans and who were permitted to marry, consisted in purging streets, houses and persons of evil demons. They also manufactured amulets, tended the provincial gods, and practiced geomancy, which is based upon belief in mutual relationships within the cosmos. Taoist geomancy (*feng-shui*) is used in determining the best location for new roads, where they will be least disturbed by dangerous magnetism, or for graves, where the dead can rest untroubled by spirits and demons. The present-day practitioners of this art are encountering major difficulties, since even a telegraph pole, let alone a railroad line, can seriously upset the *feng-shui* of a region.

The Taoistic monks live in celibacy and follow the example of Lao-tse by withdrawing from the world and cultivating passionlessness. Since the first century A.D. there have also been Taoist popes who bear the title *tien-shi*, heavenly master, and live on Lung-hu Mountain in the province of Shiang-hsi. The title was officially bestowed on them by the pro-Taoist Tang dynasty in 748. Somewhat like the Tibetan Dalai Lama, the heavenly master is determined by lot and the spirit of the first pope appears reincarnated in his successors. But unlike the Dalai Lama, he has neither power nor influence in secular matters.

The Taoist church arose during a period of political upheaval of which few details are known. In 666 Lao-tse was formally deified. Under the Tang dynasty, from the seventh to the ninth centuries, Taoism reached the peak of its influence among the people and at court. Subsequently, it more and more degenerated into a superstition of the lower classes, becoming a mere system of exorcism. The Tao was viewed as a mysterious magical force men could acquire for themselves. By using this force, they could, for example, prolong their lives. The first Taoist pope, Chang Tao-ling, was reputed to have invented an elixir that conferred immortality. To this day his descendants reside on the Dragon-Tiger Mountain, where Chang Tao-ling, strengthened by his elixir, rose into the air and vanished.

In general, it may be said that the actual form that Taoism has assumed is nothing but the continuation of the age-old Chinese folk religion. The earth is overrun by innumerable hordes of *rhen* (souls, spirits) and *ruei* (ghosts) who endanger the life and health of men at every moment. In the trivial matters of daily life and the great affairs of state, everyone from the lowest official to the emperor must reckon with their ill-will and attempt to placate them by courteous petitions.

Thus the doctrine of Lao-tse has had the fate of all profound systems when they are taken over by the masses. As an organized religion, Taoism has gone under in China. There are only a few Taoist monasteries left. Its gods and spirits have entered the folk religion, while its philosophical content has been absorbed by Buddhism, which has proved to be, it would seem, the most viable religion of the Far East.

The development of Confucianism has taken a somewhat different course. From 57 B.C. to 1911, with some interruptions, it was the state religion of China. By imperial edict of A.D. 267, an ox had to be sacrificed to Confucius four times a year. In A.D. 555 it was ordered that a Confucian temple be established in every prefectural city, so that the whole country was covered with sanctuaries in honor of the sage. But this cult of the deified philosopher, celebrated with animal sacrifices in ornate temples, to the accompaniment of music, had very little to do with the simple, pure teachings of Kung-tse. Against his wishes he became the founder of a religion which followed its own laws and had its own history, with numerous triumphs and setbacks, until at last the writings of Confucius and his successors became the accepted code of orthodoxy in politics, morality and faith.

This Confucian state religion was a mixture of ancestor cult, nature worship, astrology and the founder's practical morality. It served the purposes of a centralistic state in which the emperor, as the Son of Heaven and head of the religion sacrificed to his symbolic ancestor Confucius in the greatest temple of the empire, the Temple of Heaven, south of Peking. This temple remained for thousands of years the greatest religious sanctuary in history. The rules governing the rites were gradually developed into a scholastic system, and a strict Confucian creed was elaborated. Posts in the civil service were granted only after the candidates had passed examinations in the doctrine of Confucius, and every further step in an official's career depended on more such examinations. Thus we may say that there took place a complete merging of Confucian scholarship with the state bureaucracy.

Revolutionary breezes were already shaking the empire when in 1905, under the last Manchu empress, the examinations in the old Confucian style were abolished and a modern system of schooling instituted in China. The proclamation of the republic in 1911 transformed China into a modern nation-state. Deposition of the "Son of Heaven" was a blow to the very heart of Confucianism, which henceforth ceased to exist as a theocratic political system. The Temple of Heaven near Peking was made into a vast park for the common people.

The revolution produced a total upheaval in the Chinese way of life. It is highly significant, however, that the men of the revolution also avowed their attachment to Confucius, although they reinterpreted his doctrines into a system of enlightenment intended to serve a semisocialistic republic. Dr. Sun Yat-sen, the father of the Chinese Revolution, called upon his people to consider the ethical values implicit in the teachings of the sage when they set about constructing their new society. Holding fast to Confucian tradition, he rejected the class struggle as a concept alien to Chinese thought. And when nationalistic Generalissimo Chiang Kai-shek took the helm, he, too, attempted to cast the doctrines of Confucius into contemporary terms. His program called for reason, courtesy, honesty and conscientiousness as the prerequisites for salutary lives. "The fact that our country swarms with traitors, communists and dissolute rabble only proves that we have forgotten to cultivate these virtues. If we wish to recover our national health, we must take up these virtues anew and make them the cornerstones of a new life."

Perhaps such revivals are signs that a doctrine which formed and educated a nation for two and a half millennia cannot so easily be excised from the minds of the people. Optimists hold that the basic attitudes of thought and emotion in individual Chinese will remain Confucian long after the old teachings have been officially rejected. It is said that this is happening today in Mao Tse-tung's Chinese People's Republic; that ancient religious ideas have merged with the official government ideology of Marxism-Leninism. Since the gulf between the religious attitudes of the cultured class and those of the masses in China was always very great, the doctrine of Confucius is today under strong attack as "feudalistic" and detrimental to the building of socialism. Almost all the Confucian temples in Red China have been allotted to profane purposes. The Chiang Kai-shek government, on the other hand, in 1954 declared the birthday of Confucius an official holiday to be celebrated annually on Taiwan. But in spite of the Bolshevization of the Chinese mainland, the fundamental thinking of the individual Chinese still seems more Confucian than Marxist.

RELIGION IN JAPAN

JAPANESE BUDDHISM

THE OFFICIAL introduction of Buddhism into Japan is specifically dated as either A.D. 538 or 552, when the Japanese court received the first detailed account of the hitherto alien religion. During the following centuries Japan was heavily influenced by China and Korea, where the study of Buddhism was already flourishing. In Japan, Buddhism tended to adapt to the character of the people and to enter into an alliance with native Shintoism. But there was no question of its totally merging with the old religion of the country, for unworldly Buddhism was none too compatible with Shintoism's devotion to earthly matters. Some adaptation took place, however; soothsaying and the sale of amulets entered Japanese Buddhism. Furthermore, a good deal of sectarianism developed, as in native Shinto.

The various branches of Buddhism, the Small Vehicle (Shojo), the Great Vehicle (Daijo) and the Diamond Vehicle, are represented in Japan. The most striking development, however, is the Japanese evolution of the Amitabha Buddha into Amida Butsu. The "True Sect of the Pure Land," founded by Shinran Shonin at the beginning of the thirteenth century, corresponds to the Chinese school discussed above. It developed out of Honen Shonin's Jodo school (1175), which to this day has some eight thousand temples in Japan and claims some thirteen million followers, especially in the cities. But Shinran's sect won far wider popularity by dispensing with asceticism, celibacy and monastic life, and advocating religious equality for women. Shinran has often been compared with Luther, for Shinran, too, advocated a religion of pure grace and proclaimed that Amida Butsu would save the wicked as well as the good, and that he conferred faith in him as a pure gift.

The "Sect of the Flower of the Law," founded by the reformer

Nichiren in 1253, is based on a widely disseminated chapbook of Mahayana Buddhism concerning the Lotus of the Good Law. In this book the Buddha is transformed into a supernatural savior deity. A sect particularly favored by the samurai, the Japanese warrior class, it is marked by uncharacteristic intolerance toward other Buddhist sects, strong Japanese nationalism, and an apocalyptic, prophetic tone that is far removed from the impersonal benevolence of Gautama Buddha.

The magical Bodhisattva cult of Tibetan Tantrism has assumed a sober Japanese form in the Shingon school (7.5 million adherents). Like the Tendai school (2.1 million adherents), which advances an esoteric philosophy, it was established in Kyoto in the ninth century, and spread rapidly among the nobility in the early Middle Ages. Both cults have imbibed strong admixtures of mysticism, but stay within the doctrinal framework of the Diamond Vehicle. The sectarian forms of the Small Vehicle are no longer extant in present-day Japan.

A keen interest in Zen Buddhism has recently been manifested in Europe and America. Zen ("meditation"), which corresponds approximately to the Chinese Chan School, is a school of strict self-discipline and meditation which has greatly influenced Japanese art (for example, watercoloring). But it has also taken a strong hold on Japanese military men. The samurai found in Zen, with its manly discipline and contempt for death, the ideals they needed. The life-style developed by Zen has shaped the simplest daily acts, such as the ceremony of tea-drinking, garden culture, archery, sitting postures, breathing rhythms, and so on. The aim of Zen is to disclose to the meditative person the religious significance of everyday acts, so that he will become capable of harmony with the ground of being. A curious aspect of the instruction of Zen pupils is the use of shock therapy, which extends even to slaps and beatings with sticks, to promote the religious breakthrough to spontaneous intuition. Zen is a way of life to be attained by spiritual illumination (*satori*), and must be classed as a form of mysticism; only in its secularized form does it become a purely psychological technique. The Zen monasteries have been training centers for many great men in Japanese public life, both statesmen and artists. The adherents of Japanese Zen Buddhism

are estimated at from four to nine million, and the number of
Zen monasteries at twenty-seven thousand.

Since all these and still other sects have developed in the
course of time, and the existing sects have split into many subsects since the American occupation in 1945, it is impossible to
speak of Japanese Buddhism as a unitary phenomenon. At present there are said to be 13 principal sects and 262 subsects. Nevertheless, it can be said that Buddhism has become a religion for
the Japanese, one to which they appeal in all the sorrows of life,
for Shintoism has no answers to blows of fate, illnesses and death.
Among the multitude of Buddhas, many Japanese turn to the
goddess Kwannon; with her many arms and hands, she symbolizes all-embracing kindness and mercy.

The Sunday day of rest, introduced legally into Japan in 1868,
was slow to win acceptance. As a result, the old Buddhist temple
festivals are also celebrated as days of rest by the Japanese:
February 15, the festival of the Buddha's entry into Nirvana;
April 8, the Buddha's birthday; June 7, the festival of Kwannon.
The Bon festival takes place from July 13–15, when the dead are
said to visit the homes of their families. Small paper boats with
burning candles aboard are placed on running water to conduct
the ghosts back to their dwellings in the other world. October 12–
13 is the feast of Nichiren, November 28 the memorial day for
Shinran. In addition there are special holidays and memorials at
particular temple sites. Although the old Japanese ancestor cult
did not fit into the Buddhist doctrinal system, it has been preserved. Buddhistic and Shintoistic ancestor worship have been
assimilated to one another, for in practice most Japanese are
jointly Buddhists and Shintoists.

SHINTOISM

Shintoism (Way of the Sublime, Path of the Gods) is the real,
national religion of Japan, of pure Japanese origin, without any
foreign admixture. It differs from most other religions in having
no founder, no dogmatic scriptures, and in being a pure religion
of this world, concentrating upon the family and the national
community. The closest historical parallel to it is to be found in
the folk religions of the ancient Greeks, Romans and Teutons.

The Japanese soul and the principles behind Japanese government are most authentically revealed in the Shintoist creed, especially the disposition of the individual to take his place within his clan and within the community of his nation.

Shinto may be divided into three periods. The first extends to the introduction of Buddhism, the second from 538 or 552 to 1868, when Shintoism and Buddhism mingled, and the third from 1868, when reformed Shintoism became the state religion. Primitive Shinto had neither a name nor literature. The oldest period is devoid of sacred writings because the Japanese had no script before the introduction of Chinese characters (fifth to seventh centuries). All traditions were handed down orally; these included the rituals recited at sacrifices, and the mythic tales of the grandson of the sun goddess who descended upon the island of Kyushu to govern the country. The Japanese imperial house was said to have descended from this grandson. Since the fourth century A.D. the Tenno ("Son of Heaven") or Mikado ("High Portal") consistently held the same position in Japanese religious life until MacArthur in 1945 attempted to strip him of his sacral dignity.

Japanese mythology abounds in personifications of the forces of nature, represented as innumerable local deities. In the Shinto of the second period every deceased person could become a *kami* ("supernatural being"), that is, the embodiment of a family's vital force, and as such eternally present. This idea is the root of the ancestor cult so characteristic of Japan and China. The kami is worshiped on certain memorial days, prayers and sacrifices being offered to it. The members of the family stand before the ancestor tablet and say: "I speak to you, exalted soul of our father who has become a god." Or else the prayer may begin: "Today, on the three hundred and thirtieth anniversary of the day you departed from us . . ." The tablets are called *tama-shiro* ("soul representatives") and consist of a simple board about eight inches high, of white, unlacquered wood. On them are inscribed the real name of the deceased person with the additional phrase: *no mitama* ("soul of . . .") or *no mikoto* ("life of . . .").

If you ask a Japanese with old-fashioned views where he lives, he will name the site of his family graves as his "eternal home," even if his present residence is very far from it. The Japanese ancestor cult leaves no room for individual freedom. The dead become tyrants over the living. Every day they are appealed to; every day they must be thanked: "For help given by day and night receive, you exalted ones, our respectful gratitude." Daily, they are permitted to participate as living, present beings in all family events; they are informed of the birth of children and of all other important happenings, and in periods of distress they are asked for aid. But in contradistinction to China, the state cult (the Japanese word for government is *matsuri-goto*, meaning "religious affairs") takes precedence over the private ancestor cult. The duty of submission to the emperor, the highest sacral power, ranks higher than duty toward ancestors, for which reason Shintoism has also been called Tennoism.

The first mention of divine honors being paid to deceased emperors occurs in the literature of the ninth century, where reference is made to prayers for rain or protection against evils being addressed to them. The number of emperors officially worshiped as gods after death is, however, quite small; of 122 there are only 12 such emperors and 3 empresses, including Tenno Meiji, who died in 1912, and his wife. In addition there are a number of celebrated war heroes and scholars who won popularity, such as Sugahare Michizane, who received ritual honors as god of calligraphy and scholarship.

In the folk religion, sacred animals such as the fox also play some part, as may be seen from images in Shinto shrines; but there is no trace of genuine totemism even in the oldest forms of Shinto. The primitive Japanese venerated everything in the world around him that was grand, mighty, extraordinary and mysterious, or that had some connection with his earthly needs and promoted his well-being. The deification of natural forces, apparent in the oldest mythology, is still a living faith. The sun goddess Amaterasu takes first place. Originally conceived as the material sun, she became a spirit, the ancestral mother of the human emperor, and holds the central position in the Japanese nature cult—the sun's disk may also be seen on the national flag. Amaterasu's principal temple is in Ise. From time immemorial every new emperor presents himself to her there at the time of his accession. To this day Japanese farmers and city dwellers will step out of their houses at dawn, after they have washed their hands and rinsed their mouths, to bow toward the East, clap their hands several times, and wish themselves good fortune for the new day.

Ancient Shinto also had an active moon cult, but in recent times this has greatly dwindled. The moon god Tsuki-Yomi is masculine, unlike the corresponding god in China. Japan also has a storm and sea god, Susanowo ("the Rager"), as well as numerous river gods and sea nymphs who use crocodiles and sharks as their messengers. They are usually represented in the shape of dragons. In addition there is a harmful god of fire who causes devastating conflagrations. For protection against these, amulets and talismans are commonly used. Another type of ritually purifying fire is venerated. Numerous holy wells, springs and mountain peaks are also venerated in Japan. Since the country is prone to earthquakes, there is an earthquake god in Shintoism, represented as a gigantic fish who lies under the surface of the earth and creates quakes by moving his scales. A cataloging of Japanese myths and gods made in 1901 resulted in a list of 3,132 deities. This large number included, however, many of the domestic gods connected with the ancestor cult.

Shinto priests usually have a civil occupation; their priestly office is only an avocation, as it were. The office of priest is hereditary and organized by rank; but the priests do not, as in Buddhism, form a class sharply separated from the laity. The priests are the guardians of the Shinto shrines, which unlike the Buddhist temples are beautiful for their very simplicity. Most Shinto shrines are situated in carefully tended, fenced groves. Shrines, too, are hierarchically ranked.

In addition to male priests, there are priestesses and sacred dancing girls (*maikos*) in all larger temples. Usually little more than children, the maikos dance in red skirts and white bodices, their faces powdered to a corpselike white. To monotonous music they wheel in slow round-dances. They also help at festivals in bringing the offerings, which usually consist of saki, meat, fruit and vegetables. Japanese religious folk festivals are always characterized by gaiety. Frequently they turn somewhat wild, and under the influence of saki take on an orgiastic quality.

Public houses stand right beside the temples, and the celebrants go in and out of them without shame. Even the temples in Ise are noted for the joys of this world; as the proverb says: "One does not take one's wife to Ise." This rejoicing may strike the foreigner as somewhat tame; but he must remember that as a people the Japanese are conditioned to practice extreme self-restraint in all outward manifestations of passion.

THE PRESENT SITUATION

Revival of a pure Shinto, independent of Buddhism, began in the eighteenth century, and since then a number of sects have formed, some of them borrowing from Chinese Confucian models. There are now some thirteen such sects, firmly anchored in the lower classes. They seem on the whole to be lacking in emotional force and in ideas. This folk Shinto seems to be an answer to the fact that official Shinto, with its rites and ceremonies in palace and shrine, has been long isolated from the people. The sects owe their great success to the touching naiveté of the Japanese masses, and to all sorts of dubious practices, such as prayer-healing. Official state Shinto, with its formalized sobriety, became a system of practical rituals. Insofar as it offered so little satisfaction to emotional needs, it opened the way for the penetration of Buddhism into Japan, but also led to the growth of Shinto sects.

In 1868 Japan officially declared her commitment to Western culture. With the fall of the pro-Buddhist Tokugawa government, Buddhism lost its privileged position; and although Shintoism has no real religious content, it became the state religion to the extent that the divine origin of the Tenno was officially proclaimed. The portrait of the emperor in the schools was regarded as the supreme symbol of religion, and year in, year out, there had always to be a teacher on hand to guard each of these portraits, even sleeping in the school building. The Shinto monopoly was not maintained, however, and as early as 1875 religious liberty was introduced. In the new constitution, no state religion was established. The principle was: "As long as Japan has the imperial family, she needs no religion." Shinto was declared to differ in ritual from all other religions. In practical terms, Shinto was the equivalent of Japanese nationalism and the political loyalty of Japanese subjects.

Only from this point of view can we understand what the American secularization of the emperor after 1945 meant to Japan. That the emperor is no longer to be regarded as a descendant of the sun goddess has produced a revolutionary swing in the direction of ideological nihilism. A good many Japanese of the political and intellectual upper stratum committed suicide by shooting themselves (the new method of suicide being another sign of the change in the times). All in all, Japan has encountered great difficulties in the process of democratization, which in effect has meant the separation of state Shinto from politics. It is moreover very much open to question whether Shintoism without veneration of the emperor is actually in process of being modernized and is adapting to Christian models. Hopes might have been held that, with the edict putting an end to the emperor cult the major obstacle to Christian missionary work would be removed. However, such missions have had little success in postwar Japan.

In spite of officially proclaimed religious freedom, the bond between Shintoism and the people seems to have become no looser than the relationship toward the Tenno. Both still represent the real content of Japanese nationalism. An imperial house that has reigned for some seventeen hundred years has another quality from the innumerable dynasties in the rest of the world. Perhaps Japan is the only country on earth in which sacred kingship has defied all the disintegrating tendencies of Western thought. In the eyes of millions of Japanese to this day Emperor Hirohito is a descendant of the sun goddess Amaterasu, and thus an "incarnate supernatural being." In the immediate postwar era, state Shintoism seemed doomed. But since Japan has regained her sovereignty, its star is once more in the ascendant.

The Religions of
Biblical Revelation

JUDAISM

THE TERM Judaism does not express either a religion only, or a race, or a modern nation. Judaism has its place in an intermediate realm difficult to define, for which there are scarcely any analogies or parallels in religious history. Even the pagan Balaam in the biblical tale was forced to recognize something different in Israel: "Lo, a people dwelling alone, and not reckoning itself among the nations" (Numbers 23: 9).

This unique community came into being by an act of foundation: the tribe of Israel was chosen by God out of the multitude of peoples and led to Sinai, there—according to the Jewish belief—to be deemed worthy of partnership in a divine covenant and to receive the Torah, the commands of the Lord of heaven and earth. Because Israel is the physical seed of Father Abraham, the people remain through the millennia bound to a common destiny. Their historical task is to testify to the nation's God's supreme rule. The most impressive testimony of this is Israel's mere existence, for it is the only still-living people of antiquity. To that extent, every Jew today by his sheer physical existence is a miracle of divine providence, as Johann Georg Hamann, the German theologian who was called the "Magus of the North," observed two centuries ago. Frederick the Great, the freethinking Prussian king, also remarked that the existence of the Jews was the only possible proof of God.

Among world religions, Judaism with its somewhat less than thirteen million adherents, is numerically one of the smallest— and during the years 1933 to 1945 its total numbers were diminished by almost a third. At the same time, however, it is the oldest existing religious community. As such, it arose out of an alliance of Israelitic tribes whose settlement of the land of Canaan, later called Palestine, may be dated from 1550 B.C. The name Israel, Genesis 32: 28, is interpreted to mean "He who strives with God." It is first encountered on the victory stele of an Egyptian pharaoh. Only much later, after the Babylonian exile, were the Israelites called Jews.

Among the living traditions of the Twelve Tribes of Israel are the stories of the forefathers and their exodus from Egypt, the long wandering in the desert to Mount Sinai, and the revelation of God that was there granted them. Moses, the leader of the people, became the ear and mouth of the people, the recipient and transmitter of the divine message.

According to the biblical account, on Sinai a sacred bond was forged between the hitherto seminomadic tribes of Israel and the God of their fathers. The covenant was based on reciprocal services. The people acknowledged "the God of Israel" as ruler of the worlds and creator of heaven and earth, while God recognized the people of Israel as his followers among the nations of the earth. This "choosing" of Israel to be the people of the covenant was accompanied by the establishment of a code of laws consisting of 613 commandments and prohibitions. These are set forth in the Torah (otherwise called the Five Books of Moses, or in Greek, the Pentateuch).

In pre-Mosaic times the God of the fathers had had his throne in the Ark of the Covenant, which went with the Israelites on their nomadic treks. When the tribes settled down, so did the place of God. When the psalmist King David (1000–960) conquered Jerusalem and made it his capital, the Ark was transferred there, until his son Solomon built God a resplendent temple as the chief sanctuary of Israel.

In 922 a division of the kingdom took place. The northern tribes elected as their king Solomon's son Jeroboam I. Both kingdoms, the Kingdom of Judah and the Kingdom of Israel, waged numerous wars during the following centuries, against one another and against the dangerous adjacent countries of Egypt and Assyria. Both kingdoms were ultimately toppled. In 772 the Kingdom of Israel was destroyed by the Assyrians, and its inhabitants vanished from the face of the earth—these are the "Ten Lost Tribes." In 586 Jerusalem was captured by the Babylonians under Nebuchadnezzar, the temple destroyed, the last

King of Judah, Zedekiah, taken prisoner, and the majority of the population sent into exile in Babylonia.

After King Cyrus of Persia permitted the tribe of Judah to return from the Babylonian exile (about 520 B.C.), the priest Ezra once more proclaimed the law of the Torah (about 450 or later). Since then, Judaism has represented a conscious amalgam of religious and national elements. Thus from common descent ("the seed of Abraham") arose a national religion which, however, in the shape given it particularly by the prophets embodied a universal message, directed toward the whole world. This is the unique element in Judaism which raises it above all merely racial and merely denominational approaches to religion.

THE JEWISH CREED

Judaism does not have dogmatic standardization of its beliefs, but it nevertheless possesses specific doctrines. Thus it teaches the oneness and unity of God, who revealed his will—contained in the Torah—to the world at Sinai. This revelation was continued first in the prophets (Isaiah, Jeremiah, Ezekiel, Amos, Hosea, and so on), and later in the Talmudic rabbinical writings. Furthermore, the Jews regard the world as God's creation. The Jewish calendar dates from the creation of the world 5726 years ago. Worship of God as the ruler of the universe is a spiritual act. "Hear, O Israel: The Lord our God is one Lord" (Deuteronomy 6: 4), the Jewish credo runs. Thus the intercessor figure, or Son of God, is rejected. Man has been given the freedom to do good (God's will), or to separate himself from God and thus to sin. Original sin, viewed as an inescapable compulsion to sin, is likewise rejected, but an innate tendency in man toward evil is recognized. According to Jewish belief, man may, by penitence and change of heart, overcome this susceptibility to the world's corruptions. Judaism believes in punishment beyond the grave of man's good and bad deeds, and in the resurrection of the dead. It expects the coming of the Messiah or of the messianic age, in which the evil impulses will be extirpated from men's hearts and an eternal kingdom of peace will dawn. For this reason Judaism rejects the Christian belief that salvation has already taken place, or at least has begun.

The Jewish religious philosopher Maimonides (1135–1204), whose real name was Rabbi Moses ben Maimon, in his commentary on the Mishna attempted to formulate the content of the Jewish creed. His thirteen doctrinal truths are cited here in the later form in which they were fixed in the Jewish prayer book:

I believe with perfect faith that God, blessed be his name, is the Creator and Guide of everything that has been created, and that he alone has made, does make, and will make all things.

I believe with perfect faith that the Creator, blessed be his name, is one God, and that there is no unity in any manner like unto his, and that he alone is our God, who was, is, and will be.

I believe with perfect faith that the Creator, blessed be his name, is not corporeal, and that he is free from all the accidents of matter and that he has not any form whatsoever.

I believe with perfect faith that the Creator, blessed be his name, is the first and the last.

I believe with perfect faith that to the Creator, blessed be his name, and to him alone, it is proper to pray, and that it is not proper to pray to any being besides him.

I believe with perfect faith that all the words of the prophets are true.

I believe with perfect faith that the prophecy of Moses, our teacher, may his soul rest in peace, was true, and that he was the chief of the prophets, both of those that preceded and of those that followed him.

I believe with perfect faith that the whole Law, now in our possession, is the same that was given to Moses our teacher, may his soul rest in peace.

I believe with perfect faith that this Law will not be changed, and that there will never be any other law from the Creator, blessed be his name.

I believe with perfect faith that the Creator, blessed be his name, knows every action of the children of men, and all their thoughts, as it is said. It is he that fashioneth the hearts of them all, that giveth heed to all their works.

I believe with perfect faith that the Creator, blessed be his name, rewards those who observe his commandments, and punishes those that transgress them.

I believe with perfect faith in the coming of the Messiah, and, though he tarry, I will patiently await his speedy appearance.

I believe with perfect faith that there will be a resurrection of the dead at the time when it shall please the Creator, blessed be his name, and exalted be the remembrance of him for ever and ever.

In historical terms Judaism is a family religion. For an orthodox family, the whole of life is dominated by the religious element. Affixed to the door to the home is a mezuzah, a small capsule containing fifteen verses from scripture, signifying that the house serves God just as does the synagogue as a place of assembly for the faithful, a temple of God. The dietary laws of the Torah, which again are religious in nature, being means for the sanctification of Israel, are faithfully observed. It is forbidden to eat the flesh of impure animals, the most prominent of which is the swine. This taboo was probably not so much hygienic as demonological, for the pig was a sacred animal in the cult of the god Moloch. The snake, too, was regarded as demonic. The law furthermore prohibits the eating of carrion, and of mammals and birds that are not slaughtered in the prescribed fashion; also certain parts of the fat and the blood, which by ancient Oriental ideas was the seat of the soul. The proper method of slaughtering by the "kosher butcher" aims at complete bleeding of the meat that is intended for human consumption. Equally under ban are animals which prove to have diseased internal organs. There is a special proscription against eating the sinew of the hip in mammals, because in Jacob's nocturnal struggle the angel dislocated his hip. "Therefore to this day the Israelites do not eat the sinew of the hip which is upon the hollow of the thigh, because he touched the hollow of Jacob's thigh on the sinew of the hip" (Genesis 32: 32).

One of the most severe bans concerned the eating of mixed dishes of meat and milk products. The law is based on Exodus 23: 19 and Deuteronomy 14: 21 ("You shall not boil a kid in its mother's milk"). A household conducted along ritual principles therefore requires two sets of pots, dishes and silverware, one reserved for meat, the other for milk dishes.

The cleanliness laws of the Torah are also an essential part of Jewish ritual.

Prayer at home and in the synagogue are both of major importance in Jewish religious life. The basic form of such prayer is the *beracha* (prayer of praise and thanksgiving, hymn), which should be made with heartfelt intensity. Jewish mysticism in particular laid stress on prayer as a bridge to God. Every day has three prayer periods: evening, morning and afternoon, with special additions to the morning prayer on feast days and new moon days. Men pray with covered head; in the morning they wear a prayer shawl, a four-cornered cloth of wool or silk, with tassels. For weekday morning prayers prayer straps are fastened on the left arm, opposite the heart, and on the forehead. A capsule with a little roll of parchment, on which important verses from the Torah are inscribed, is attached to these straps.

Worship, which consists of prayer and instruction, is the same throughout the year; the basic prayer texts have remained the same for some fifteen hundred years, and are common to all Jews throughout the world. On feast days, of course, additional texts are used. Certain symbolic acts of temple worship in Jerusalem, such as the blowing of the shofar, have been preserved in present-day services.

Instruction consists in reading of the scriptures, a practice taken over by both Christianity and Mohammedanism. In the Jewish service the Torah is read in fifty-four weekly sections throughout the liturgical year (from autumn to autumn). A section is read every Sabbath. There are also readings from the prophetic books, framed within the singing of hymns.

The high point of Jewish religious and family life is the Sabbath. Rabbis have often hailed the Sabbath as a foretaste of the world to come. On this day orthodox Jews refrain from all work, do not travel, use the telephone, write or touch money. These traditional Sabbath stringencies have given to the whole world the seventh day as a day of rest—one of man's most important institutions. Like the Christian Sunday, however, the Jewish Sabbath rest is no longer kept so strictly among many groups. The synagogue Sabbath worship begins at sunset on Friday evening, and is continued at the home evening meal, at which time the housewife lights the traditional Sabbath candles and the father of the family blesses the wine and breaks the Sabbath bread.

The principal holidays of the Jewish year are the New Year, in September or October, and Yom Kippur, the Day of Atonement. Between these two holy days is a ten-day period of penitence, recollection and return to God. In biblical times it was customary, on the day before the Day of Atonement, to drive a goat into the desert "who shall bear all the iniquities of the children of Israel, and all their transgressions, all their sins" (Leviticus 16: 21–22). From that custom comes the concept of the scapegoat. A strict fast of twenty-four hours is prescribed for Yom Kippur, accompanied by self-examination and an accounting with oneself of all the acts and omissions of the preceding year. Throughout the day, prayers are conducted in the synagogue for God's grace and mercy.

Devout Jews also fast on 9 Av (in August), in memory of the destruction of the second temple in Jerusalem in A.D. 70, by the soldiers of the Roman emperor Titus, whose triumph was memorialized in the Arch of Titus, still standing in Rome.

Among the important holidays of the liturgical year is the Feast of Passover in March or April, commemorating the time that the Angel of Death passed over the houses of the Israelites in Egypt (Exodus 12). It reminds the people of the liberation of the children of Israel from Egyptian bondage, and is celebrated for seven days by the eating of unleavened bread. The prayers and dietary prescripts of the passover meal (*seder*) are set forth in detail in the Haggadah. The thin, unleavened breads are the "bread of affliction" (Deuteronomy 16: 3): *moraur* is the bitter herb; and *charosset*, a mixture of apples and nuts, symbolizes the mortar that the Jews used when they performed forced labor for the pharaoh. At the seder meal on the eve of Passover the father of the family, holding a piece of matzoth in his raised hand speaks the traditional words: "This is the bread of affliction that our fathers ate in Egypt; whoever is hungry, let him come and eat with us." The participants in the meal sit leaning to the left—in antiquity, the posture of free men.

Finally, the pilgrimage feasts must be mentioned: Shavuot, the Feast of Weeks or First Fruits, in May or June, which is intended as a reminder of the reception of the Ten Commandments; Sukkoth, the Feast of Tabernacles, an eight-day harvest thanksgiving in the fall; the Feast of Lights, Chanukah, which is comparable to the Christian Christmas and celebrates the victory of Judas Maccabaeus over the Syrians and the relighting of the temple light. Each evening of the eight-day festival one more candle is lit in the eight-armed candelabrum, and children receive presents. Chanukah, like Purim in the spring—which is a kind of Jewish carnival—is a festival of joy recalling the rescue of the Jews from oppression.

Aside from the feast days, Jewish ceremonial also follows the course of human life. On the eighth day after birth boys are circumcised (Genesis 17: 10) as a sign of the covenant between God and Israel and in memory of God's covenant with Abraham. At the age of thirteen boys become a *bar mitzvah,* a son of the law, and assume the religious duties of an adult. The other high points in life, such as marriage and death, are subordinated to man's duties toward God and have their special ceremonial expressions.

Judaism recognizes no supernaturally founded institution for salvation. The synagogue is only a house of worship. The individual sustains the religious life of the community; in that sense every Jew is a priest. The rabbi is at once pastor, teacher of the traditions and judge in questions of religious law. Where by state legislation or voluntary agreement, Jewish communities have joined in an association, this organization only deals with administrative questions. The congregation provides for worship in the synagogue and for religious instruction of children; it also makes it possible for its members to keep the dietary laws by appointing kosher butchers. Traditionally, the congregation is also supposed to maintain a bathhouse, which menstruating women are required to use according to the precepts laid down in the Bible. Another characteristic feature of the orthodox Jewish congregation is the Holy Brotherhood, which assumes the duties of washing, anointing and burying the dead without distinction of position and economic condition of the members of the community. Service in this brotherhood is performed on an honorary basis.

JEWISH ETHICS

Jewish monotheism regards righteousness as the supreme ethical quality. Man has ethical duties toward God as well as toward his fellowmen, no matter what their nationality. These duties are set forth in the laws of Moses, in the enunciations of the prophets, and in later traditional interpretations.

In Judaism, ethics is not a subdivision of religion, but part and parcel of it. The Hebrew idea of *kadosh* (holy) as the supreme standard of existence and conduct merges ethics and religion: "You shall be holy, for I the Lord your God am holy" (Leviticus 19: 2). The supreme quality of God is righteousness; since man was created in the image of God, it is his highest task to imitate God and acquire the attributes that God taught to Moses on Mount Sinai: "The Lord, the Lord, a God merciful and gracious, slow to anger, and abounding in steadfast love and faithfulness, keeping steadfast love for thousands, forgiving iniquity and transgression and sin" (Exodus 34: 6–7). Similarly, in Deuteronomy 13: 4 the command is given: "You shall walk after the Lord your God." The Talmud gives this interpretation of that command: Is it possible for men to walk after the deity, when it is said after all: "The Lord your God is a devouring fire"? Rather, man must imitate the ways in which God works: the way he visits the sick (Abraham in the grove of Mamre); the way he consoles the mourner (Isaac after Abraham's death); the way he buries the dead (burial of Moses)—so shall man act. God defined what was good for man in the Torah; ethics develops out of the commandment to love your neighbor as yourself (Leviticus 19: 18).

No ethical distinction was drawn between Jews and non-Jews. That is apparent from the laws on foreigners in the Bible: "When a stranger sojourns with you in your land, you shall not do him wrong. The stranger who sojourns with you shall be to you as the native among you, and you shall love him as yourself; for you were strangers in the land of Egypt. I am the Lord your God (Leviticus 19: 33–34). Robbery, blackmail, theft, embezzlement, any appropriation of the property of others, are considered a sin against God as well as an offense against man. All trickery in trading is forbidden; any business dealings that violate good morals are invalid before the law; excessive profits, price-gouging and unfair competition are decried. For "let the property of your neighbor be as dear to you as your own" (from the Talmud tract *Proverbs of the Fathers* 2: 12).

In biblical times a portion of the harvest was set aside for the care of the poor, and the tithe, comparable to modern taxes, was also used for this purpose. Land speculation was discouraged by the institution of the year of jubilee, which in biblical times made land revert to its original ownership every forty-nine years; later, however, this provision was abandoned as unenforceable. Workmen had the protection of laws; minor orphans could not be sued. In postbiblical times charitable institutions were established to meet changed social conditions. Those who refused charity were likened by the Talmud to idolators. Jewish charitable activities have persisted through the centuries; originally only individual and planless, they developed in the nineteenth and twentieth centuries into great international associations of Jewish welfare and social organizations, comparable to similar Christian institutions.

THE TALMUD

Man's ethical duties toward his fellows and toward God are set forth in the Bible. How these precepts were to be translated to the daily life of men who lived a thousand years later in altogether different countries was the content of the Talmud. Even in biblical times numerous instructions, for fulfilling the precepts of the Torah, had been handed down by oral tradition. These were collected and written down in the Mishnah, completed around A.D. 200 by Rabbi Yehuda ha-Nassi. The Mishnah, as a canonical collection of oral traditions, is thus a commentary on the Torah, on the legislative parts of the Bible. But since the Mishnah left many matters unclarified, the process of standardizing the law continued. The rabbinical schools of Palestine and Babylonia carried on unending discussion of all controversial questions. The much more extensive writings embodying these discussions are called the Gemara. The Mishnah and Gemara together constitute the Talmud.

The discussions of the rabbinical academies between 200 B.C. and A.D. 500 are recorded in the twelve thick folio volumes of the Babylonian Talmud. There is a Babylonian and a Palestinian Talmud; the former was more widely distributed and enjoyed greater prestige. The nature of the Talmud may best be grasped if we compare it to the minutes of modern parliamentary debates, for the discussions concerned all the important problems of life faced by Jews. Law, doctrine, exegesis of the Bible, sermons, history and anecdote stand side by side. Its great value for the practical conduct of life lay in its wealth of precise prescripts and prohibitions, covering all conceivable cases and situations, based on the letter of the Bible and on oral tradition.

This process of fixing the rules of life was never ended, and in principle can never be ended. The conclusion of the Talmud around 500, the codification of the Mishnah-Torah by Maimonides in 1180 and the systematic compendium of rituals known as the Shulchan Aruch (1565) are merely important milestones on a road that represented an essential and logical religio-historical evolution.

The vast masses of material in the Talmud are divided into Halakah and Haggadah. By Halakah is meant the part of the Talmud that deals with the 613 precepts of the Torah (by rabbinical count: 248 commandments and 365 prohibitions) in their concrete applications. The Haggadah, on the other hand, contains more narrative material: ethical teachings, proverbial wisdom, legends, parables, sermons, allegorical tales. Only the Halakah has the binding force of religious law. The Haggadah is more concerned with stirring the emotions. Both Halakah and Haggadah were elaborated and exposited in the frequently poetical or allegorical Midrash, which attempted to draw lessons for the present from the past.

The peculiarities and spirit of the Haggadah can perhaps best be seen from a few edifying fragments taken from the *Proverbs of the Fathers,* a Mishnah tract which contains no Halakhic doctrines, but only proverbial wisdom of a religious nature.

Aqabya ben Mahalel said: Contemplate three things, and you will not sin: Know where you come from; know where you are going; and know before whom you will some day deliver an accounting. Where you come from: from a stinking drop; where you are going: to a place of dust, mould and worms; before whom you will deliver an accounting: before the King of Kings, the Holy One, praised be his name (III, 1).

Rabbi Chanina, the chief priest, said: Pray for the welfare of the government, for but for fear of it one man would devour another alive (III, 2).

Rabbi Jacob said, This room is an anteroom for the future world; prepare yourself in the anteroom so that you will be admitted to the hall (IV, 21).

He said further: Better an hour in penance and good works than a whole life in the future world, and better an hour of bliss in the future world than all life in this world (IV, 22).

Samuel the Small said (after Proverbs 17, 18): Do not rejoice when your enemy falls, and let not your heart be glad when he stumbles, lest the Lord see it, and be displeased, and turn away his anger from him—and upon you (IV, 24).

DEVELOPMENT OF JEWISH MYSTICISM

Side by side with the Talmudic line of doctrine there has run since very early times an underground mystical current in Judaism, which grew particularly strong during the Middle Ages. Like all religious mysticism, the Jewish brand reflected an existential experience in which the subject-object dichotomy of intellectual cognition are left behind. This mysticism is particularly hard to understand, however, because there is a closed cosmological system underlying it, and one which has passed through several stages of development. Speculations on the hoped-for, imminent coming of the Messiah are closely linked with almost all manifestations of Jewish mysticism.

Jewish mysticism spread from Spain and Southern France in the thirteenth century. It incorporated, under the name of Cabbala, older traditions, some of which probably stemmed from ancient Gnosticism. Its principal document, the Book of Sohar ("radiance"), written in frequently obscure Aramaic, was ascribed to Rabbi Simon bar Yochai and supposedly dated from the second century. In fact, most of this rather incoherent re-mythologizing of commentary on the Pentateuch was probably the product of Moshe ben Shemtob de Leon of Guadalajara, a Cabbalist who died in 1305. The Book of Sohar was first printed in Cremona and Mantua in 1558.

The major themes of Jewish mysticism are the state of being before the Creation, and the primordial light above the visible sky; the doctrine of the ten spheres, which are permeated by divinity; the conception that heavenly sparks in all earthly things must be liberated from their husks. In addition, there are allegorical interpretations of the deeper meanings of the Torah, based on numerological manipulation of the Hebrew letters; similar interpretations of biblical persons and of all of Jewish history; and an extensive doctrine dealing with angels and demons. Since there are such evil powers from the "other side" in the world, "practical Cabbala" also deals in magic and counterspells. The goal of Cabbalistic efforts is spiritual understanding of the ultimate mysteries and hence the *unio mystica* of man, made in God's image, with the *deus absconditus,* the hidden God.

The spiritual life of European Judaism in the sixteenth and seventeenth centuries was strongly influenced by the Cabbalistic mysticism of Moses Cordovero (1522–1570) and Isaac Luria (1534–1572). Throughout the seventeenth century it was evident that the old Talmudic scholarly impulse no longer served the needs of the schools. A great change was felt to be in the offing— a change that ultimately took the form of the emancipation of the Jews. The entire preceding period suffered from a spiritual crisis, arising from the fact that the Jewish ghetto, which had stood still while the world was modernizing, began to be riven by great internal and external shocks.

In 1626 Sabbatai Zevi was born. An ecstatic personality, early seized by a messianic conviction, he entered into a mystic marriage, solemnized at a feast in Salonika, with the Torah, which he proclaimed the daughter of God. In the year of salvation that had been reckoned out by the Cabbalists, 5408 (1648), Sabbatai Zevi for the first time declared himself the Messiah. Believers were convinced that the time of salvation had dawned; they even celebrated his birthday, the anniversary of the destruction of the temple and Judaism's great day of mourning (9 Av), as a messianic day of rejoicing. According to Sabbatai Zevi's pronouncement, the day of salvation was to come in the year 1666. The year arrived, but expectations were not fulfilled; in the meanwhile the Messiah had fallen into the hands of the sultan of Turkey, whom he had set out to convert. Confronted with the choice of abandoning his claim to be the Messiah or accepting Mohammedanism, Sabbatai Zevi became an apostate, and after ten restive years died as a Moslem.

This disgraceful apostasy of the false Messiah in 1666 proved to be, however, by no means the end of the shameful incident. Amazingly enough, it gave birth to the Sabbatian movement, which for another generation exerted an irresistible fascination upon hundreds of thousands of Jews. As secret Sabbatians, they were prepared to believe the impossible rather than sink into the abyss of despair that awaited them if they acknowledged that salvation was not soon at hand. Sabbatai Zevi and the movement he started continued, in the person of the messianic pretender Jacob Frank and his daughter Eva, down to the time of the French Revolution. This movement had graver and more fateful consequences for the religious and intellectual history of Judaism than the divorce, 1600 years before, of the new Christian movement from the Jewish religious community.

The last wave of Cabbalistic, messianic mysticism was Chassidism. In contrast to the official rabbinical doctrines, Chassidism was a movement to renew the faith among the Jews of Eastern Europe. The concept of *Chassid* is biblical; the word is connected with grace, holiness and also love, and in later times the noun *chassiduth* was rendered as: to love the world in God. The ideal representative of the new movement was not the learned scholar but the zaddik, the mediator between the upper and the lower worlds. The Chassidim regarded themselves as representatives of genuine, devout Judaism. Chassidism, by breaking through the elaborate and ossified system of casuistic interpretation of the Law, transformed a sizable section of Jewry once again into religious enthusiasts. As we now know, there were intermediate links between it and the Sabbatian and Frankist movements.

The founder of Chassidism, Rabbi Israel ben Eliezer of Miedzyborz (1700–1760), who bore the epithet Baal-Shem-Tob (Master of the Good Name), was an itinerant preacher and miracle worker who perceived guises of divinity in all the phenomena of the world—even the very lowest and basest. As a *homo-religiosus* he takes his place beside such Catholics as Blaise Pascal, such Protestants as Sören Kierkegaard, and such devouts of Russian Orthodoxy as Fyodor Dostoevsky.

The Baal-Shem stands at the center of Chassidic legend, which has more to tell about him than does history—a fate he shares with many charismatic personalities. The doctrines and maxims of the Baal-Shem and his disciples of the first and second generation were handed down orally, in the style of Jewish traditional literature, and committed to writing long afterward. But from the legends it is plain that immediacy of religious experience was the essence of original Chassidism. Martin Buber has done a great deal, in his poetic retellings of these stories, to convey the fundamental motifs of Chassidism: nearness to God; the effect of human actions upon the higher spheres; joy; the ecstasy of prayer. Thus Rabbi Pinchas of Korets is quoted as saying: "Joy exists upon a higher stage than sorrow. Even a newborn infant weeps at first; only later does it also laugh. For then it has already attained a higher stage. Joy wells from higher worlds: from the aureole of God. Therefore, too, joy washes all sins away."

In its historical development, Chassidism suffered the fate of all revivalist movements, gradually petrifying in observance of outward forms, dogmatism and tyranny. In the nineteenth century it degenerated into magic and superstition: all that remained was the "wonder rabbi," who seldom knew anything of the mysteries of inner vision, which had been truly present in the mysticism of the Baal-Shem and his disciples.

RECENT RELIGIOUS HISTORY OF JUDAISM

All through the Middle Ages—which for European Jews did not terminate until the end of the eighteenth century—the forms of religious worship remained in general unchanging. In all the previous centuries the ceremonials and rites of the Jews had been so wholly isolated from their surroundings that virtually no social interchange took place. The opening of the ghetto gates meant a revolutionary upheaval for European Jews. Within a generation they had to encompass an intellectual evolution that had taken the Christian West three centuries. Once the walls of the medieval ghetto came down, the reformers tried to wipe out the "inner ghetto," in order to make the Jews capable of taking their place in society with all the rights and duties of other citizens. As a result, during the century of emancipation the traditional forms of worship were increasingly abandoned or transformed. However, the religious liberals did not succeed in establishing a generally binding new way of life which would bring the religious laws of biblical and postbiblical times into conformity with the realities of the nineteenth and twentieth centuries.

The age of emancipation, initiated by the work of Moses Mendelssohn (1729–1786) and the effects of the French Revolution, undermined the traditional forms of Judaism. Since then, there have been orthodox, conservative and liberal schools, arising from diverse approaches to questions of religious practice—rather than to fundamental questions of belief. Only extreme liberals and Zionists have advocated a revision of Judaism to bring it closer to the views and manners of unbelievers or believers in other religions. In 1948 the state of Israel was founded, partly as a reaction to the terrible Nazi persecutions. The official language is a modernized Biblical Hebrew (Ivrith), and the national flag displays the Star of David between two horizontal blue and white stripes. The establishment of the state marked a new era in the history of the people and religion of Israel. The overwhelming majority of the citizens of Israel profess Judaism as their religion; but only some twenty per cent of them can be called orthodox. The state of Israel, in which about fifteen per cent of all Jews now live (about 1.9 million) is by no means identical with Judaism as such. A great many present-day Jews regard their worldwide dispersal as their mission, and therefore reject nationalistic limitations.

Among the various schools within the synagogue, the most controversial subject is that of the ceremonial laws. The orthodox regard these as unconditional and immutable. The liberals abbreviate them a good deal, since they accept only those parts of the ceremonial that seem to express their own religious feeling. The conservatives—in America called Reconstructionists—take a middle position. The question of the use and extent of the vernacular in community prayers—which until the beginning of the nineteenth century were conducted solely in Hebrew—is one of the most hotly debated points. At any rate, it may be said that the previous unity of Judaism has been dissolved. Since the end of the Second World War, half of those who profess Judaism as their religion may be found in the Americas; Europe now contains only 2.9 million Jews (as against 9.5 million in 1939)—not even a third of the number before the war.

Through the centuries Judaism has proclaimed its message to

the world in multifarious shapes. That message is essentially the simple one that the world itself is not the measure of all things, that it has a Master before whom man must bow down. This mission unites the synagogue with the church and the mosque—and, indeed, the latter two proceeded from the former. If man does the will of God—and according to the Jewish belief, man has the freedom and the power at least to broach that task—the Kingdom of God grows. That kingdom, in the Jewish belief, has not yet dawned, but it is on the way. Jew, Christian, Moslem and pagan are eternally being called to Sinai. The Jewish world mission consists in making that call audible again and again.

The call to Sinai, the proclamation to man that the righteousness of God exists eternally within human injustice—that is what is eternally Jewish. The message of Judaism applies particularly to the man of our time, cut off from God's word and thrown upon his own devices. Through the centuries and the millennia, that message has fundamentally remained unchanged. As a Chassidic rabbi said to his disciples: "The great guilt of man is not the sin he commits—for temptation is mighty and man's strength small. The great guilt of man is that at any moment he can repent and does not do so." For in the repentant man, Jewish belief holds, Creation is created anew.

JUDAISM AND CHRISTIANITY

For nineteen hundred years Jews and Christians have walked side by side through this world. They certainly have glanced often enough at one another; but no real dialogue between them has arisen—and could not. During the first centuries the Jews were intent upon defending Jewish doctrine from Christian reinterpretations. Their "refutations" of the opponent shut off real debate. And when Christianity had come to power, the Christians no longer cared to engage in serious discussions with the Jews crammed into the medieval ghettos, for their very powerlessness was taken as plain proof that God was punishing them. In the intellectual atmosphere of medieval scholasticism, Jews and Christians could only be concerned with justifying each his own religion and denying the other's claim to truth. When, in modern times, the premises changed, the first discussion took place within the framework of a new "religion," that of the Enlightenment. Yet under the dominion of Reason, neither Christianity nor Judaism could be given a fair hearing.

When in the course of the nineteenth century, political and religious liberalism grew increasingly strong, the premises for a real encounter were laid. Real encounter can take place only in areas of freedom, in which the various partners to a dialogue can speak the truth as they see it without constant fear of endangering themselves or of meeting at the very first step insuperable prejudices on the other side. Only in such an atmosphere of external freedom is there inner freedom to ask and be asked openly, to express one's own concerns and take seriously the other's, to understand him on his own terms without relativizing one's own position. Such real understanding, aimed at genuine dialogue, at clarification rather than at domination, has become possible only in the twentieth century, and has produced results of epoch-making importance. This precious product of liberalism, which today is in danger of being lost again, along with the gift of dialogue altogether, is perhaps the one real element of "progress" the twentieth century can boast of as against the Middle Ages.

The last religious dialogue between Christian and Jews in Germany, before the night fell, took place as late as January 1933 in the Jewish Academy in Stuttgart between Martin Buber and Karl Ludwig Schmidt. The late religious philosopher Martin Buber is regarded as a restorer of Chassidism. On this occasion he attempted to interpret the Jewish nature and the history of Judaism. Sacrifice for the common good and for an idea is characteristic of the innermost strivings of Jews, he declared. The mark of the believer should not be a pedantic keeping of the Law, or asceticism, but joyfulness, reverence and humility.

Buber's concluding remarks, which must be quoted *in extenso*, contain everything that need be said about the relationship to Christianity, seen from within the Jewish fold. Here the true Jewish faith is expressed:

I live quite close to the city of Worms, to which I am also linked by ancestral tradition, and from time to time I go there. When I do, I always walk straight to the cathedral. It is a visible harmony of members, a whole in which no part veers from perfection. I walk around the cathedral, looking at it with a perfect joy. Then I go across to the Jewish cemetery. That consists of slanting, shattered, formless stones placed every which way. I stand in it, look from this chaos of the cemetery up to the glorious harmony of the cathedral, and it is as if I were looking at the Church from Israel. Down here you do not have an iota of form; you have only the stones and the ashes under the stones. You have the ashes, no matter how much they may have vanished. You have the physical being of the people who have become dust and ashes. You have them. I have them. I do not have them as physical beings within the space of this planet, but as physical beings of my memory back into the abysses of history, back to Mount Sinai. I have stood there; I was connected with those ashes and through them with our forefathers. That is the recollection of an event and a relationship with God which is given to all Jews. The perfection of the Christian house of God cannot divert me from that. Nothing can take from me Israel's time with God. I have stood there and have experienced it all myself; all that death has happened to me; all the ashes, all the shatterings, all the soundless lamentation is mine; but I was not given notice that the covenant is terminated. I lie on the ground, stretched out like these stones. But I was not given notice.

The cathedral stands as it stood. The cemetery lies as it lay. But we were not given notice.

If the Church were more Christian, if Christians met her requirements better, if they did not have to contend so much with themselves, then—Karl Ludwig Schmidt says—a keener debate would be possible between them and us.

If Judaism became Israel again, if the holy countenance emerged from behind the mask, then—I reply—what divides us would not be weakened, but no keener debate between us and the Church would take place. Rather, something entirely different, which today is still inexpressible, would happen.

I ask you, by way of conclusion, to listen to two sayings which seem to contradict one another, but are not really contradictory.

In the Talmud it is taught: The proselyte who comes in this age to be taken into Judaism must be asked: "What have you seen in us, that you wish to be converted? Do you not know that those of Israel in these times are tormented, driven, hurled hither and yon; that sufferings have come upon them?" If he says: "I know, and I am not worthy," then take him in at once.

That may seem like Jewish arrogance. It is not. It is nothing but a venting of what cannot be dismissed. The distress is real distress and the disgrace is real disgrace. But there is a divine meaning in it; we are assured that God, as he promised us (Isaiah 54: 10), will not let us fall from his hand.

And in the Midrash (to Leviticus 18: 5) it is said: "The Holy One, blessed be he, declares no creature unworthy, but he takes up all. The gates are opened at every hour, and whoever seeks to enter, may enter." And so he speaks (Isaiah 26: 2): "Open the gates,/ that the righteous nation (*goy zaddik*) which keeps faith/ may enter in." It is not said that priests may enter, that Levites may enter, that Israelites may enter, but that a *goy zaddik*, a righteous nation, may enter.

The first saying deals with proselytes, the second deals with the human race. The gates of God are open to all. The Christian need not pass through Judaism, nor the Jew through Christianity, in order to come to God.

THE RELIGION OF ISLAM

THE THIRD and so far the latest comer to the ranks of world religions, based on the biblical revelation of the God who created heaven and earth, is Islam. Like Judaism, Islam is also a national religion with universal claims. Mohammed, the prophet of Arabia, considered himself to be perfecting the work of Moses and Jesus, and proclaiming the newest covenant after the Old and the New Covenant. More than 350 million Mohammedans—including 70 million in India, where they form the chief obstacle to national unity—proclaim five times daily in their prayers the fundamental formula of the Moslem creed: "There is no God but Allah and Mohammed is his Prophet." Surah 112 of the Koran takes sharp issue with the Christian doctrine of the Trinity: "Say, He is God alone! God the Eternal! He begets not and is not begotten. Nor is there like unto him any one!" This verse is spoken by the Moslem when he kisses the black stone of the Kaaba.

The Mohammedan name for God, Allah, is composed of the definite article *al* and the ancient Semitic word for deity: Arabic *ilah*, Babylonian *ilu*, Hebrew *el*, *elohim*.

Mohammed was the recipient of revelation; to him Allah communicated a sacred book for the Arabic people. He was sent into the land as a *rasul* (apostle), for Arabia had not yet had a revelation. In Islamic belief, however, the revelation is not a mystery of salvation, as in Christianity, but primarily a set of instructions on how to live a life of blessedness.

Pre-Islamic Arabia had many loosely related tribal cults from which Mohammed took various elements: for example belief in jinns and iblis, spirits and devils arising out of the fierce heat of the desert. In the series of seven heavenly messengers whom Mohammed acknowledges as his forerunners, three are Arabic.

He also took over cults dating from the early history of the Arab tribes, such as the fetishistic cult of the black stone known as the Kaaba in Mecca, which was probably a meteor. The god of the sanctuary was simply called the master of the house, the God of the Kaaba—the word meaning cube. The territory in which the Kaaba is located had been inhabited since the fifth century by the tribe of Koreish, to which Mohammed belonged. Every year it celebrated with great pomp the pilgrimage to the Kaaba, which was also the site of the greatest fair in Central Arabia.

In addition to the religious practices of his native land, the chief influences upon the religion of Mohammed were Judaism and Christianity. From Judaism the prophet took the monotheistic concept of God. Jewish influence in Yeman had been considerable since ancient times; there had been Jewish kingdoms there in the past. Certainly the son of the desert could not comprehend Jewish theology; but much narrative material from the Bible, and much of the elaborating Haggadah, had come to Mohammed by oral tradition. He also misunderstood many details, or else his memory so distorted them that, for example, he confused Moses' sister Miriam with Mary, the mother of Jesus. When the Jews attempted to show him the errors in his Surahs, he rejoined that it had all been revealed to him by Allah, and that Allah could not err.

The Christianity of Arabia, with which Mohammed became acquainted on caravan journeys, was of a special kind. It was not that of the imperial Church of Byzantium, but that of Monophysite Nestorian sects, strongly influenced by the ascetic piety of monastic religion. Mohammed, who probably could not read or write, learned about Christianity not from literary sources, but from personal association with Christians.

He knew of the Taurat and Indjil, the Torah and the Gospels, only from hearsay and concluded that both derived from the original book preserved in heaven by Allah. In point of fact, Moslems have never paid much heed to the Old and New Testaments even though the Koran calls Jews and Christians *ahl al-kitah* (possessors of the scriptures)—in other words, sharers in the divine Book.

LIFE OF THE PROPHET AND ORIGIN OF ISLAM

Mohammed himself was the great architect of the Islamic religion. It bears the clearest imprint of his life and doctrines. For a portrait of Mohammed, we cannot do better than to turn to the Koran, which, unlike later traditions, contains authentic sayings of the Prophet. Mohammed was born about A.D. 570 in Mecca, the son of a Koreishite family. Orphaned early, he grew up under the care of his nearest relatives. As a boy he was a shepherd. At the age of about twenty-five he seems to have become a kind of business adviser to a rich widow named Khadija, who was fifteen years his senior. Eventually he became her third husband. Concerning the early religious development of this merchant of Mecca, we know nothing. He seems, however, to have begun early to meditate on the values of life, and to have had an unusually nervous, high-strung constitution.

At the age of forty Mohammed began having visions. Tradition relates that in his deep piety he withdrew one night to Mount Hira in the vicinity of Mecca, where the angel Gabriel visited him and had him memorize the contents of a scroll the angel had brought with him. This contained the beginning of Surah 96 of the Koran, and is known by the title "Congealed Blood." At dawn the figure of the angel stood against the clear horizon, wherever Mohammed turned. Tradition says that Mohammed was at first very frightened and resisted the call. But he soon found believers who strengthened his own faith; the first were his wife Khadija and his cousin Ali. Under their influence he became persuaded that the holy spirit of prophesy had come over him. But he had to wait another three years before a new vision gave him the certainty that he was indeed a *rasul* of Allah. He had been wandering anxiously about in the mountains, when a vision from the other world shone before him, filling his heart with certainty. He felt that he was on the point of fainting, and hurried home, shaking with fever. "Wrap me up," he called to his family; and then, in a violent nervous fit, he seemed to hear the words: "O wrapped one, stand up, yes, admonish your Lord, yes praise him. Your clothes, yes, cleanse them. Be not kind out of selfishness. And your Lord, yes, wait for him." From then on, according to tradition, the revelations followed one another regularly.

We encounter here an extremely important characteristic of Islam. The revelation is not actually a living experience between God and man, a happening into which God himself enters; but it is a book. The first word of Mohammed's revelation is: "Read!" The page of a book is shown to him, the book the angel has brought down from heaven. Jesus, by contrast, left no written word to his followers. Islam was a book religion from the first moment on. God did not descend from heaven and give himself to man—he gave a book.

Now the first adherents from his own family and slaves joined his small group of believers. The first prominent man from another family was Abu Bekr, the wool dealer, who became Mohammed's faithful friend. The first believers held regular meetings, at which Mohammed imparted the revelations that had been accorded to him. But when he wanted to preach in the streets of Mecca, he encountered mostly mockery and incomprehension. It took many years of struggle before his message was accepted by his fellow countrymen, years during which that message also had to mature, before it was fully ripe for annunciation.

Gradually a small circle grew up in Mecca that listened to Mohammed's warning of a judgment about to fall on the city of Mecca because it would not acknowledge him. Many members of the lower classes joined the new party around Mohammed. But there was also a distinguished man named Omar. The attitude of the majority of the Koreish grew more and more hostile; they thought Mohammed possessed by evil spirits, especially after he began to proclaim that all the Kaaba ceremonies were superstition and idolatry, that idols were nothing and the only reality was Allah, while man's only duty was submission to Allah. The Arabic word for submission is *Islam.*

When pilgrims came for the annual pilgrimage from the city of Yathrib, then ruled by Jews, and proposed to Mohammed that he move there, where they would assure him a friendly reception, Mohammed and his band accepted the invitation. The people of Yathrib pledged themselves to protect him and his followers like their own blood relations. This alliance, so fateful for the history of Arabia, was sealed by a formula of agreement borrowed from the age-old Arabic tribal treaties. The city of Yathrib took a new name, Medinet al nebi, City of the Prophet, or Medina for short. This hejira (flight) took place in A.D. 622 and marks the beginning of Mohammedan chronology.

During his first few years in Medina, Mohammed tried unsuccessfully to convert the Jews living there. The Jews concluded that he was not their Messiah—especially since he did not observe their Sabbath or their dietary laws. Mohammed thereupon declared that some of their laws were falsifications, others a bane imposed on them by God. In the end he realized the futility of his efforts to convert the Jews. One day during prayer in the courtyard of his home he testified publicly that he was abandoning the attempt. Instead of praying in the direction of Jerusalem, as he had previously done, he turned toward Mecca. Henceforth, Mecca became the point of orientation (*qibla*) for all Moslems during prayers, for burial of the dead, and for all Mohammedan mosques. By this act, the pagan Kaaba became the central sanctuary of Islam, and Mohammed had taken the first great step toward the conquest of Mecca.

In Medina Mohammed organized a religious community as a theocratic city-state. Claiming to be Allah's plenipotentiary, the transmitter of Allah's commandments to the people, he imposed dictatorial rule on all the inhabitants of the district. The courtyard of his home became the inner court of the first mosque. Followers who came to him from Mecca supported themselves by preying on the caravans on their way to Mecca, despite the time-honored four-month truce of God during the time of pilgrimages. The Moslems, thanks to their strict discipline and contempt for death, defeated a Meccan army of nine hundred men at Bedr, near Medina. Mohammed had wisely promised a paradise of inexpressible wonders in which all sensual desires would be gratified, as the reward for those who died a hero's death. The Meccans, however, won a second battle, the Battle of Ohod, because of their numerical superiority. The holy war for the possession of Mecca went on for several years, with shifting fortunes, until at last in the year 8 of the new era (A.D. 630) Mohammed was able to march into Mecca at the head of his conquering army. He solemnly took possession of the Kaaba and destroyed the idols in and around Mecca. Henceforth, the rise of Mohammed to a position of supreme power in Arabia proceeded rapidly. By the following year ambassadors were pouring into Mecca to submit to the Prophet. Many of the tribes of Arabia, including a number of Jewish and Christian ones, converted to Islam. Mohammed, however, did not live to see the complete conversion of all of Arabia. The *la-ilaha illa-'llah, muhammad rasula-Ilah* (there is no God but Allah and Mohammed is his Prophet) became a battle cry for the unification of the tribes of Arabia and later for many of the nations of the Orient.

At the end of the year 10 there took place the so-called Farewell Pilgrimage, the first pilgrimage to Mecca instituted by Mohammed himself. There the Prophet made a number of important decisions on ritual, which henceforth remained binding upon all Moslems—for example, he forbade unbelievers to set foot in Mecca. He also introduced the ceremony of the *haj* procession around the Kaaba, now purified of idols, and the kissing of the black stone. Yet a man like Omar could object to this vestige of paganism, and in the course of a later pilgrimage is said to have spoken thus to the black stone: "You are only a stone after all, which can do neither good nor harm. If I had not seen the Prophet kiss you, I would not kiss you."

Mohammed's political gifts and organizational ability were indubitably remarkable. He used every possible means to unite the Arab tribes: kindness and mildness, persuasion by missionaries, but also holy war against unbelievers who had to be brought to acknowledge Allah by force. He made conversion of all still pagan Arabs a religious prescript for Moslems. Pagans had only the choice between accepting Islam or death. But he allowed the believers in monotheistic religions and "peoples of the Book" (Jews, Christians, Sabians) completely free exercise of their religion. They were compelled, however, to wear different clothing from believers and to acknowledge the political supremacy of Islam by paying a toleration tax (jitsya). Thus the alternative was not Islam or annihilation, but Islam or tax. Converts were accorded the rights and duties of full citizens; those who clung to their old faith were relieved of both rights and duties in return for their contribution to the treasury. They became *dimmi* (protected citizens). Such a degree of tolerance was to remain foreign to Christian Europe for many centuries.

To return to the life of the Prophet: after Khadija's death Mohammed began keeping a harem of young women, including even his adoptive son's wife. A saying of the Koran set four wives as the maximum for a free man; but the Prophet's sensuality would not be confined; his harem grew beyond that number, and was legalized by a divine commandment. Altogether Mohammed married thirteen times. Harem intrigues and the discord of wives competing for his favor occupy a large part of his biography. According to tradition Mohammed once said: "I have loved two things in this world, women and pleasant scents, but have found refreshment of my heart only in prayer."

On June 8, 632, A.H. 11, a short time after his return to Medina from the Farewell Pilgrimage, the Prophet died, at the age of sixty-one, in the arms of his favorite wife Aisha, the daughter of Abu Bekr. An eclipse of the sun is said to have taken place at the hour of his death.

He had already laid the foundation for the unprecedented rapid development that was to make Islam the third great religion of the world. The Prophet's grave in Medina became, along with the Kaaba, the great pilgrimage sanctuary of the Mohammedan world, and has remained that to this day.

Mohammed regarded himself as the *khatam al-anbiya,* the seal of the Prophet, or in other words the fulfillment of the work of Moses and Jesus. He always stressed the purely human nature of Jesus. He never conceived of himself as a mediator between God and man, but as the Apostle whose task it was to communicate the holy book, the written revelation, to the Arab people. His sense of mission is reflected in Surah 46: 8: "I am not an innovator among the apostles; nor do I know what will be done with me or with you if I follow aught but what I am inspired with; nor am I aught but a plain warner." According to an old tradition, he said: "Praise me not as Issa (Jesus), the son of Miriam, is praised." Belief in Mohammed was not the same thing as the Christian belief in Jesus. Later developments in the religion, however—especially under the influence of the cult of saints in the folk religion—made Mohammed into an exemplar for believers, and this was even carried so far as a Moslem cult of relics. Later on, Mohammed was regarded as the friend, the *habib* (beloved) of Allah, superior even to Abraham. Moslem mysticism made him the crown of Creation, the "perfect man"; he was even called the pre-existent light of revelation. Such transfigurations of the founder are typical in the history of religions.

Nevertheless, Mohammed may be compared rather with Moses than with Jesus. Like Moses, he was leader of a nation, prophet and transmitter of revelation. But the political elements in his makeup are far more prominent. His historical importance is in fact political. Mohammed succeeded in accelerating the transition from nomadism to settled community life in Arabia, and in bringing the greater part of the population of the peninsula under a hitherto inconceivable iron discipline.

THE MESSAGE OF THE PROPHET

Unlike Judaism and Christianity, Islam is founded not on an event but upon the Being of Allah. Islam stresses contemplation of the divine being, which manifests itself as will and prescript. The freedom of man's will depends on this ability to perceive God. Mohammed's message was initially a sermon on the judgment, a portrayal of the flames of hell awaiting those who refused to believe. In general, eschatological notions of retribution, paradise, hell, resurrection of the dead and last judgment play a large part in Mohammedanism. It has been calculated that a fifth of the Koran consists of descriptions of these "last things." Persian and Judaeo-Christian models are recognizable in many of them. The noblest title of Allah is "Lord of the great Judgment Day."

After Mohammed settled in Medina, ethical and religious prescripts began to predominate in the Surahs. Mohammed also borrowed Christian and Arabic ritual customs and adapted them as he saw fit. Thus he took over the idea of the Sabbath from the Jews, changing the day to Friday. Initially, too, he included in his law the Jewish Day of Atonement, but subsequently substituted Ramadan as a month of fasting. He also strictly forbade, as in the apostolic decree (Acts 15: 20), the eating of blood and the meat of animals not properly slaughtered. In addition, he made a prescript against eating the flesh of swine, but permitted the use of camel meat, which was forbidden in Jewish law. After initial vacillation, he strictly forbade wine—Islam is the only world religion that imposes on its believers abstinence from alcohol in all forms. Likewise, the Prophet forbade the taking of interest and the games of chance that were widespread in Arabia. Circumcision, usually between the ages of four and nine, is not prescribed in the Koran, but has been practiced by all Arabs from very ancient times and symbolizes acceptance into the Islamic communion.

Islam is a legalistic and ritualistic religion which lays great stress on observance of the law (*shari'a*) set forth in the Koran. Obedience, man's submission to the will of God, is the sole act of freedom accepted by Islam, which is otherwise a veritably totalitarian religion. "Faith" in Islam means that a man fulfils his religious obligations with painful exactitude. If he does that, Allah, the Almighty and All-merciful will see to the rest. Thus Mohammed reduced the relationship between God and man to an extremely simple formula.

From this there follows the Mohammedan doctrine of predestination, which in many respects is similar to Calvinistic theology. Allah guides man or leads him astray, as he wishes. Given the boundless omnipotence of God, creatures must submit in impotent dependence and utter humility. The consequence is Mohammedan fatalism. If everything is predestined by Allah, life and death, everything that happens, depends upon God's inexorable decree. Submission to *kismet* (fate) results in a passivity that can be dispelled only by some religious requirement, such as that of a holy war; then the passivity is transformed into fatalistic aggression.

Islam does not recognize the need for penitence in the Judaeo-Christian sense. Nor do Moslems experience a real longing for salvation. Allah is irrational and unpredictable; the only tenable attitude for man is therefore total humility. Socially, this submission unites men and makes them equal. Thus Moslems—the word is the Arabic participle of *islam,* and means "surrenderers to God"—regard themselves as members of a great fraternity. There are no distinctions of race or class in the mosque. In Pakistan, Islam has even succeeded in breaking down the stringent Indian caste barriers. The simple community worship of the mosque, without pictures and without music, engenders the char-

acteristic sense of Mohammedan brotherhood. Mohammedans
are exceedingly democratic—if we except the veiled women confined in their harems and possessing few rights. The harem and
the veil, incidentally, were introduced by the Abbasids in the
eighth century; they were a borrowing from Byzantine court
ceremonial. Islam also has no special priestly class, because it has
no real sacraments for priests to administer.

MOHAMMEDAN MYSTICISM

The bedouin ideal of equality in a simple life has continued to
affect Islam and led to the formation of a special monastic group,
which in turn has produced meditation, asceticism and mysticism. Sufism, one of the varieties of Mohammedan mysticism,
is not the product of alien influences, but a legitimate expression of the "monks" of the order of dervishes. Sufism acquired
great influence over Islam, largely due to the work of al-
Ghazali, one of the greatest theological and legal minds of all
time. To become a *sufi* means literally: to don the woolen gar-
ment; to bid farewell to everything that might divert the mind
from God and divine things; and to devote oneself entirely to
contemplation. The oldest orders of sufis started in Iraq in the
twelfth century, but they spread to all Islamic countries.

Today, about five per cent of all Mohammedans are Sufis.
They are divided among a large number of orders and fra-
ternities. More than seventy of these orders consist of fakirs or
dervishes. They do not, however, take vows of chastity—for
which reason dervishes can live secular lives. By simple, popular
preaching the dervishes contributed a great deal to the spread of
Mohammedanism. Among the dervishes (the word probably
comes from the Persian *darvish*, "beggar") are some who howl,
scream and dance in wild ecstasies, the theory being that in this
state they approach closer to Allah. In some countries the orders
of dervishes are restricted or even banned nowadays; but their
power is still great, especially in North Africa. The Sufis and dervishes undoubtedly made great contributions to the deepening
of Mohammedan religious life—although also to veneration of
saints and relics.

THE FIVE PILLARS OF ISLAM AND THE KORAN TRADITION

The five pillars of Islam were developed very early, probably during the lifetime of Mohammed. They are the indispensable duties of a believer:

Shahada, the creed: There is no God but Allah and Mohammed is his Prophet. This is the sole dogmatic profession in Islam, and of the highest importance because it has preserved Islam from any inclination to deify Mohammed.

Salat, canonical performance of liturgical worship three, later five times a day, preceded by ablutions. Specific prayers are recited, and the movements of the body, the bowings and prostrations, are prescribed in every detail.

Zakat, which initially meant alms, but later came to signify payment of taxes for purposes of war.

Sa'am, fasting (associated with sexual continence) during Ramadan, the month of revelation, in which the Koran, God's uncreated word, was communicated to Mohammed by the angel Gabriel. From dawn to sunset the Mohammedan must not eat, drink or smoke. At the end of Ramadan the breaking of the long fast is celebrated as a festival of rejoicing.

Hajj, the pilgrimage to the Kaaba in Mecca, which every adult Moslem is obligated to undertake at least once in his life. Immediately after arrival the pilgrim runs seven times around the Kaaba and tries despite the great crowd to kiss or at least to touch the black stone. There is no greater joy on earth for a Moslem pilgrim. Other sacred places of pilgrimage are Medina and Jerusalem.

One of the other pillars of Islam is veneration of the Koran, the inexhaustible source of edification for the believer. It is not a code of laws, like the Mishna of the Jews, since it is far from exhaustive, although the legislation of ancient Islam was based upon it. The believer regards the Koran as infallible. The Arabs imitated and surpassed the Jews' veneration of the Torah. The revelations are called Koran ("recital") or Surah ("line, chapter"). The Koran was established in its present form under Caliph Othman (644–656). In language and style exceedingly uneven, the Koran consists of 6,206 sentences of varying length—the shortest being a single word, the longest sixty-eight words. The work is divided into 114 Surahs, the shortest of which contain three, the longest 286 verses.

The older, Meccan Surahs at the end of the Koran differ from the younger, Medinan Surahs in their briefer, more poetic form, their many oaths and asseverations, and their focus on the Prophet's favorite theme: the judgment, the unity, the grandeur and mercy of Allah. The revelations in Medina were longer and dealt with all sorts of affairs which needed to be decided by the Prophet. Interpolated among the revelations are tales from the Haggadah and apocryphal material from the Christian Gospels, which Mohammed himself imaginatively embroidered.

The fundamental laws, customs and organization laid down by the Koran were supplemented by the sunna, the traditional customary law. For all questions not covered in the Koran, Moslems turn to the acts of the Prophet himself as recorded by oral tradition. Questions of the conduct of life according to the sunna are settled by another non-canonical collection of Mohammed's sayings, the *hadith*, the oral doctrine of Islam. If the Koran corresponds to the Torah, the hadith is the equivalent of the Mishna and Talmud. The more valuable traditions were collected in the ninth century by Bukhari and five other scholars. Through these channels a great many of Mohammed's remarks have been handed down, such as: "What is the best kind of Islam? The Prophet replies: The best Islam is that you feed the hungry and spread peace among friends and strangers." Or the Prophet says: "When God completed the Creation, he wrote in the book that is preserved beside his heavenly throne: My mercy overwhelms my wrath."

HISTORY OF ISLAM

Embittered partisan struggles and the formation of rival sects marked the history of Islam soon after the death of the Prophet. The four first caliphs (from Arabic *chalifa*, "successor"), were the Koreishites Abu Bekr, Omar, Othman and Ali, whose reigns are regarded as the golden age of the Caliphate (632–661). Afterward there began to be factional fights that led, for political reasons, into a breakup of Islam into sects. A constitutional dispute raged along with disagreements over interpretation of the Koran. The majority of the Shiites (*shiah* means literally faction, party), who venerated Ali and Hussein as holy martyrs, insisted that the Imam, the holder of the Caliphate and spiritual leader, must be a direct descendant of Mohammed's cousin Ali and his son Hussein. The Sunnites adhered to the elected first three Caliphs, and later to the house of the Umayyads in Damascus, while the Shiites ignored the opinion of the community and insisted on the Imam from the Prophet's family. Later Shiite speculation held that the "glowing bright shadow" of Mohammed was the first created principle, thereafter revealing itself in the succession of Imams.

When Omar I, leading his armies under the green banner of the Prophet, speedily conquered Persia, Palestine, Syria and Egypt, thus laying the foundation for the Mohammedan Empire, the Shiites were already bitterly antagonistic to him. To this day "curse Omar" is still the strongest expression of Shiite hatred for the Sunnites. The struggle between the two schools continued down the centuries. Ever since the descendants of Mohammed died out—the twelfth and last Imam mysteriously vanished from the face of the earth in 912, at the age of eight—the Shiites have waited for Allah to send a *mahdi*, a leader of the Last Days, to bring salvation. The Shiites had great success in Persia, making many converts, and in 1501 the Shiah faith became the state religion in that country. Syria and Iraq have also long been Shiite strongholds. They are split into many sects, such as the Druses, the Nosairi and the Ismaili (of whose Indian branch the fourth Aga Khan has been forty-ninth Imam since 1957). Today they number between twenty and twenty-five million persons. Common to all is a rather esoteric interpretation of the Koran and a step-by-step initiation into the mysteries and doctrines of the creed.

Islamic history was determined largely by the Sunnite majority, which spread the rule of Islam by force of arms through the entire Near East and Central Asia, and over North Africa to Spain. In the seventh and eighth centuries the Caliphates of Damascus, Baghdad and Spain were set up. A hundred years after Mohammed's death all the land from Saragossa, Spain, to the Caucasus was in the hands of the Moslems. All of Europe might have fallen to them and become Mohammedan if the Franks under Charles Martel had not checked their onrush at the Battle of Tours in 732.

Although the central power of the Caliphate declined from the tenth century on, Islam continued to gain ground. From Gibraltar to the Himalayas the green flag of the Prophet waved for centuries. The Balkans, too, fell entirely into the hands of the Moslems. In 1453 Byzantium was conquered and the Osmans planted the crescent upon Hagia Sophia. In 1529 the victorious armies of Moslems stood before the gates of Vienna; it was not until the naval battle of Lepanto in 1571 and the battle on the Kahlenberg before the walls of Vienna in 1685 that the "Turkish peril" was at last banished. Between the eleventh and the sixteenth centuries northern India and Indonesia were also conquered by Islam. But gradually the secular power of the Mohammedans began to fade. Islam, internally disunited, lacked centralistic leadership.

THE PRESENT

Today Islam is again gaining ground in the areas that have been, historically, its outlying territories. In Indonesia some seventy of seventy-five million inhabitants are Mohammedans. Pakistan since 1947 has been a purely Mohammedan state, and the sixty million Pariahs in the rest of India are a huge reserve army of potential proselytes. Islam also exerts a strong attraction for people at earlier stages of civilization, such as the Negroes of Central Africa, among whom it conducts vigorous missionary activities. Today the power of technological civilization and industrialization is presenting Islam with wholly new problems. So also is the awakening nationalism among the African and Asiatic peoples, since religion and the state no longer simply coincide even in the Orient. Serious social tensions are coming to the fore; the monopoly of land by wealthy sheiks is no longer tamely accepted everywhere in the Mohammedan world. The Koran is frequently hailed as an "anticapitalistic book." There are strong movements seeking adaptation of Islam to the modern world without relinquishing the core of the old doctrines and traditions. A good deal of agitation for reform now proceeds from the principal seat of Islamic scholarship, the thousand-year-old El-Azhar Mosque in Cairo, although this most famous of Islam's theological universities is still steeped in conservatism.

Improvement of the legal position of women, and civil legislation on the European pattern, has been largely carried out in Turkey and Egypt, and partly in Persia. In Turkey Kemal Atatürk (1881–1938) abolished the Caliphate after the First World War, thus separating church and state. He also replaced the Arabic by the Roman alphabet and ordained that the Turkish language be used in the mosques. Now, however, this extreme laicism seems to have been somewhat softened; religious instruction has been reintroduced into the state schools. In Persia, too, the influence of the muftis (the interpreters of religious law) and the ulemas (Koran scholars) is once more on the increase.

The principal religious reform movement, puritanical and ascetic in nature, was that of the Wahabis, which started in the eighteenth century; its last uncontested leader was King Ibn Saud, who died in 1953. The Wahabis wanted to restore the original purity of ancient Islam, and therefore rejected all innovations, such as celebration of the Prophet's birthday, and the cult of saints, tombs and relics. Using strict military discipline, they waged a campaign against superstition and the cult of demons, with the result that Saudi Arabia was able to enter the modern age.

Syncretistic schools have moved further away from original Islamic doctrine. Among these are the Bahai religion, an outgrowth of Shiitism, which attempts to unite all religions on a pacifistic, humanitarian basis. It was founded in the 1950s by Beha-ullah (God's radiance). There is also the Ahmediyya movement in India (since 1880), which holds modernistic views and carries on missionary work in both Europe and America.

More than 550 million persons—an eighth of the total population of the earth—now profess Islam. In fifty-two nations, the doctrines of the Prophet have won a firm hold over the overwhelming majority of the people.

CHRISTIANITY

CHRISTIANITY is the religion of the majority of Europeans and Americans. That is our reason for a more detailed description of Christian creeds and Christian doctrines.

The faith of Christians of all denominations is founded on events in the ancient world at the beginning of our era, events connected with the life and death of a Jewish man believed to be the Messiah (Christ) of the stock of David: Jesus of Nazareth. Religious history regards this event, and the personality of Jesus, in terms different from those of theology. Unlike theology, religious history has neither to prove nor deny that God revealed himself in Jesus Christ; it accepts as a fact that revelation testified to in the creed of believers. The religious historian may therefore best begin with the experiences which underlay the creation of the Christian Church as expressed in the words of Paul the Apostle—who was also the greatest theologian of the age of Jesus.

Jesus, whose brief earthly life ended on the cross, rose from the dead. He appeared to Peter, then to a crowd of his disciples ("more than 500 brethren"), to James, then to all the apostles, and finally to Paul himself (I Corinthians 15: 3–8). Thereafter he was carried off into heaven, dwells with God, and will soon reappear as the Son of Man upon the clouds of heaven. This man Jesus was, when the time had fully come, born of woman (Galatians 4: 4), but designated Son of God in power by his resurrection from the dead (Romans 1: 4), and was God's Son in the likeness of sinful flesh (Romans 8: 3). He left behind the riches of divine glory and entered earthly poverty (II Corinthians 8: 9), assumed the form of a servant and humbled himself to the point of death on the cross. "Therefore God has highly exalted him and bestowed on him the name which is above every name," Kyrios (Lord), "that at the name of Jesus every knee should bow, in heaven and on earth and under the earth" (Philippians 2: 9–10).

Furthermore: "For our sake he made him to be sin who knew no sin, so that in him we might become the righteousness of God." The death of Jesus for our sins (Romans 4: 25) became the "mercy-seat" and purchased mankind's freedom from sin. God was in Christ, reconciling the world to himself (II Corinthians 5: 19). The death of the Son of God redeemed the cosmos and all mankind, for in Christ's death on the cross the world was crucified (Galatians 6: 14).

During the second century A.D. more and more pagans renounced the gods of Greece and Rome and turned to the "one God who created heaven and earth." Since by baptism they received a share in the Holy Spirit and became members of the Christian Church, there became established in Rome around 140 a tripartite baptismal profession which later became the basis of the Apostle's Creed. It expressed the fundamental elements of the Christian faith:

I believe in God, the Father, the Almighty;
and in Christ Jesus, his only begotten Son, our Lord,
born of the Holy Spirit and Mary, the Virgin,
who under Pontius Pilate was crucified and buried,
was resurrected from the dead on the third day, and rose to
    heaven,
sitting at the right hand of the Father, whence he will come
to judge the quick and the dead;
and in the Holy Spirit, one holy Church,
forgiveness of sins, resurrection of the flesh.

Amen

But a long road led to this first creed of the young Church. Its beginnings are to be found in Jesus' life on earth.

THE LIFE AND MESSAGE OF JESUS

From the beginning of the third century the Church acknowledged twenty-seven writings in Greek as "apostolic and canonical." Apostolic means that they could be traced back to the circle of Jesus' apostles; canonical that they were binding upon the entire Church and intended to be read aloud during divine services. The four Gospels or Evangels ("good tidings") of Matthew,

Mark, Luke and John formed the beginning of this collection. The first three of these Gospels form a group separate from the fourth. In spite of a good many differences on details, these three agree largely in essentials, so that they can be studied in terms of a "general view"—synopsis. Hence the term Synoptic Gospels, which has come into use for the past one hundred and fifty years. After extensive analyses of the texts, biblical researchers have come to the conclusion that Mark was the source of the other two Gospels, and that his work in turn was based on still another source. This was a collection of *logia*, or sayings of Jesus; it is usually referred to as Q. There is ample evidence that the first three Gospels were written earlier than the fourth. But even so, as we have them today they come from a relatively late period; they are separated from the event they report by generations and times of turbulence. The historical material in the Synoptic Gospels, however, derives from an original tradition which was passed on by the disciples. All the older evidence confirms this statement.

The Gospel of Luke has an introductory statement, the only such statement of a literary nature in the Gospels. It avers that "many have undertaken to compile a narrative of the things which have been accomplished among us, just as they were delivered to us by those who from the beginning were eyewitnesses and ministers of the word" (Luke 1: 1–2). Here we have evidence that there was indeed a tradition of the contemporaries of Jesus, and that this tradition had been set down in writing several times. Paul also refers to this tradition when he declares (I Corinthians 11: 23 and 15: 3): "For I received from the Lord what I also delivered to you; . . . for I delivered to you as of first importance what I also received." The second epistle to the Thessalonians (2: 15) also refers to oral tradition: "Hold to the traditions which you were taught by us, either by word of mouth or by letter."

The oral tradition was very much alive during the first two centuries, and spread in apocryphal gospels and acts of the Apostles until the Church decided to stop the proliferation of legends by decreeing the legitimacy of certain of the writings. On the nature of such traditions as sources, the following must be said: The Gospels cannot be equated either with modern or an-

cient biographies, whose authors portrayed the life of their heroes as they learned of it by personal experience or by research.
The Gospels' primary purpose was not to present a detailed
historical picture of the life of Jesus. And the non-Christian materials on the life of Jesus provide us with no essential new
knowledge beyond the accounts of the Gospels. The chief of
these non-Christian evidences are an account of the execution of
one "Chrestus" under Pontius Pilate in the *Annals* of Tacitus, a
similar report in Suetonius, passages in the *Antiquities* of the Jewish historian Josephus (some of which were later interpolations),
and some legendary echoes of the tragedy of the life of Jesus to
be found in the Talmud.

For the scientific historian, then, the situation in regard to
sources is highly unsatisfactory; legendary and historical accounts
are hopelessly intertwined. The historian must recognize that the
materials available to us do not enable us to reconstruct Jesus as
he really was. He has only the Jesus the early disciples saw, the
Christ who has survived in the beliefs of the Christian community.

JEWISH RELIGIOUS PARTIES IN THE TIME OF JESUS

When Jesus began his mission, the Jewish people no longer
held their ancient sovereignty. All the creative forces of the nation were by necessity directed inward, toward the shaping of
religious life. Political hopes were colored by chiliastic, messianic
aspirations. In the time of Jesus there was, however, a group of
political activists, the Zealots, who were rebelling against Roman
domination. From the death of Herod the Great to the uprising
of A.D. 66, which led to the final downfall of Jerusalem, there was
a constant succession of small rebellions by the Zealots. Among
the disciples of Jesus we find Simon the Zealot, evidently a former
adherent of the revolutionary party, who had been converted to
belief in Jesus. But Jesus had nothing to do with the Zealots; he
should not be regarded as a political candidate for the throne of
David.

The Jewish religious parties of the time were the Sadducees,
the Pharisees and the Essenes. The Sadducees were the ruling
group of priestly families, and highly conservative in religious

matters. They frowned upon anything that might be regarded as an evolutionary development of doctrine and accepted only the five books of Moses as binding. Since they concluded that nothing in these books justified the resurrection of the dead, they rejected this tenet in the doctrines of the opposing Pharisaic Party. But the chief difference between the two groups consisted in their attitude toward oral doctrine as such.

The Pharisees held that the will of God as revealed in the Torah must be applied to contemporary historical situations. They favored the principle of oral doctrine, that is, interpretation and extension of the laws of Sinai so that the commandments and prohibitions would be applicable to the daily life of men in their time. Without turning their backs on tradition, they claimed that their own interpretations of the Scriptures must be regarded as authoritative, equal in rank to the ancient Laws. These claims were the source of Jesus' conflicts with the Scribes and Pharisees.

The Pharisees were not only advocates of religious progress; they were also representatives of genuine piety. They should not be identified with narrowness, self-righteousness and conceit— only the worst of them had such traits. On the contrary, they aimed at attaining true faith. The Pharisaic movement sought to take sanctity seriously and to follow the word of God in daily life: "Consecrate yourselves therefore, and be holy" (Leviticus 11: 44). They wished to prepare the soil for the Kingdom of God, so that it would come.

An extreme group among the Pharisees were the Essenes ("saints"). They carried even further the principle of isolation advocated by the Pharisees, organizing themselves in small monastic communities. The brotherhoods of Essenes followed even stricter purification rites than other Jews. They endeavored to anticipate the Kingdom of God in their midst by sharing all their goods with one another in brotherly love. They rejected everything that seemed to them tokens of this transitory world: weapons, trade and luxury. They would not take oaths or sacrifice animals, and they set limits upon sexual intercourse. Asceticism intensified morality, they believed. The central feature of their community life was a sacred meal partaken in perfect silence by the brethren dressed in white clothing.

The famous Qumran finds of scrolls in almost inaccessible caves near the Dead Sea, which have been creating a great stir since 1947, have greatly added to our knowledge of the Essene sect. Half a century before the appearance of Jesus a "Teacher of Righteousness" in many respects similar to the Nazarene Messiah seems to have been active among the Essenes. The newly discovered Qumran texts throw light on a good many phrases in the Gospels and give us a better understanding of the origin of some New Testament views. But although these new finds are enormously important to scholars, their general significance should not be overdrawn.

Attempts have frequently been made to depict Jesus as a secret follower, or even a member, of the Essene sect. But there is no sound evidence for such theories. It is probable that some Essenes and some Essene ideas entered the early Christian community. Among these was probably the principle of common ownership of all goods, which prevailed for a time in early Christianity. And the later Ebionites demonstrably took Essene models as the basis for their community life and their theology.

JOHN THE BAPTIST

The oldest tradition of the Christian community links Jesus with the movement of John the Baptist (Mark 1: 1), which was in some respects akin to that of the Essenes. According to Luke 3: 1, John the Baptist emerged in the fifteenth year of Tiberius—A.D. 28. He lived as a hermit in the wilderness of reeds and shrubs along the Jordan, and dressed like the Prophet Elijah in a hide held together by a leather girdle. There is nothing unusual in the fact that John was an ascetic rebel against the Hellenistic urban culture of the time—the Essenes were that also. But his preaching was novel, as was his practice of baptizing even the "pious" in preparation for the end of time. He proclaimed the Lord's imminent Day of Judgment. The ax was already laid to the roots of the trees, he announced. One who was mightier than he would come to judge and to separate the chaff from the wheat. The only escape from this day of wrath was repentance and baptism. "I baptize you with water; but he will baptize you with fire," John is said to have cried—referring to the Jewish eschatological notion of a renewal of the world by fire.

We know what Jesus thought of John. Jesus said that John was more than a prophet, that he was indeed God's messenger Elijah who was to immediately precede the Savior. He referred to him as the greatest of all men born of woman. But when the Kingdom of Heaven would come, the smallest in this new age would be greater than John the Baptist.

Jesus evidently took the arrest of the Baptist as the beginning of the new times, and the sign that he was to undertake his ministry. Mark dates from this event the preaching of the gospel in Galilee, that is, the beginning of Jesus' own movement. The Baptist fell into the power of Herod Antipas, who had him executed. A comment by Josephus indicates that Herod regarded John as a politically dangerous troublemaker. Indeed, any preacher who announces that the coming of the Messiah is near is a danger to a monarch, for it is a threat that another is coming to topple him from his throne.

The movement of Jesus, which developed between A.D. 28 and 33, differed from the outset from that of the Baptist. For Jesus did not appear as an unworldly ascetic who called only for baptism. Instead, in announcing the Kingdom of God he assembled people—in this like Mohammed. He gathered around him fishermen, farmers, artisans, tax collectors of his native Galilee who were prepared to exchange their narrow occupations for the life of itinerant preachers. The twelve disciples he selected were in a sense representative of the Twelve Tribes of Israel. With this following, Jesus set out for Jerusalem to confront the powers of the country with this new movement and force a decision. The outcome of that venture we know. The Roman Procurator Pontius Pilate, in collaboration with groups in the Jewish administration who were concerned with political tranquillity and cooperation with the Roman occupying power, had the inconvenient troublemaker crucified. As John the Baptist was beheaded, Jesus was condemned to death on the cross like many another leader. However this fate, unlike that of the others, was no end but a new beginning, since the movement begun by Jesus lives on in the Church of Christ. Out of defeat on the cross a world-conquering religion was founded.

THE KINGDOM OF GOD

At first the primary message of Jesus was that the Kingdom of God was coming, that fulfillment of the promise was at the gates: "Blessed are the eyes which see what you see. For I tell you that many prophets and kings desired to see what you see, and did not see it, and to hear what you hear, and did not hear it" (Luke 10: 23–24). To doubters he said: "If it is by the finger of God that I cast out demons, then the Kingdom of God has come upon you" (Luke 11: 20). The promise of the prophets is being fulfilled: "The blind receive their sight, and the lame walk, lepers are cleansed and the deaf hear, and the dead are raised up, and the poor have good news preached to them" (Matthew 11:5).

The healings that Jesus performed, the exorcisms of demons and all the other miracles were, to be sure, not proofs of the approach of the Kingdom of God—for that would be too magical a conception. But the multitude of miraculous events was to be understood as a sign of its imminence. The simple accounts in the Gospels of the miracles of Jesus are intended as examples to illustrate his sermons on the Kingdom of God—and only as such. That sets them apart from other ancient miracle tales. Alien motifs, legendary material taken from popular folklore, feats attributed to Jewish and pagan miracle workers, may have been ascribed to Jesus by the myth-making impulse in the early Christian community—certainly critical modern research has shown a good many parallels in non-Christian sources. But none of that matters; not even the question of the historical actuality of the miracles is decisive. All that is important is that Jesus went about the land of Palestine healing, helping and proclaiming the imminent Kingdom of God.

The important aspect of it all has been beautifully put by Martin Dibelius in his little book on Jesus: "The transformation of the world is God's affair. What Jesus did was to make men feel this God, his will, his judgment and his grace. The forces of the Kingdom are already present, but not as the kind of power that transforms the world, rather as a force that radiates from the one, the only one, who knows and communicates them. What he made men see . . . was not the Kingdom but the signs of that King-

dom. To that extent certainly, but only to that extent, the Kingdom of God is in the midst of you. . . . He himself is the sign of
the last hour."

Jesus' message, then, was imbued with the certainty that the
Kingdom of God is coming, is coming now. Only for that reason
did he come to Jerusalem with his band and occupy the temple
courtyard, in order to purify it. In the course of the Passover feast
which he celebrated with his disciples in Jerusalem, he said
something that reveals his knowledge of the situation; the meaning gleams even through the accounts handed down by tradition:
that he would celebrate the next Passover in the Kingdom of God
(Luke 22: 15–18).

What, then, is the Kingdom of God? It is the beginning of the
end of time, of which dramatic events are expected—and first of
all the fulfillment of ancient national hopes: the collapse of foreign rule, restoration of the kingdom of David, the gathering of
the Jewish diaspora in the Holy Land. In addition, apocalyptic
literature predicted the miracles of the Last Days: the coming of
the Messiah, the resurrection of the dead, the expunging of evil
from the hearts of men. Secular restitution of the nation and
miraculous transformation of the universe, frequently viewed as
a return to the sinless beginnings in Paradise, were so intermin-
gled in men's minds in the time of Jesus that they can scarcely be
separated. When Jesus spoke of the dawning Kingdom of God,
he meant all these things together.

The national hopes of Jewish eschatology were, of course, not
fulfilled then or later. They are, moreover, less prominent in the
preaching of Jesus himself than in the minds of the disciples who
asked him: "Lord, will you at this time restore the kingdom of
Israel?" (Acts 1: 6). The apocalyptic expectations were not fulfilled either—at least not as was assumed by virtually all the
apostles of the primitive community, for they expected Jesus to
return in their lifetimes. Peter said (I Peter 4: 7): "The end of all
things is at hand"; John (I John 2: 18): "It is the last hour";
James (James 5: 9): "The Judge is standing at the doors"; Paul
(Philippians 4: 5): "The Lord is at hand." The ages run on and
human hearts have not changed. But a sign has been given them.
The person and the life of Jesus have revealed a sign of the

Kingdom of God and its coming to men who hitherto had not heard of the God of Israel. The reality of God in the world was manifested in Jesus.

In describing the life of Jesus, the evangelists dwell upon the scenes of the Passion, the death and resurrection. That is no accident, for the Gospel accounts already regarded his death as an atonement for the sins of man. Early Christian tradition looked back upon the earthly life of Jesus in the light of the miracle of the empty grave. The facts of his life were interpreted in terms of belief in his resurrection. What we have in the Gospels, therefore, are not the factual accounts of disinterested chroniclers, but the narratives of believers. Event and interpretation are so interwoven in the early depictions of the life of Jesus that there is no separating the two strands. If we are to try to render the picture of Jesus that emerges from the New Testament, we must take the viewpoint of the evangelists themselves and understand his life as they did: as a bringer of salvation by his death.

When Jesus came to Jerusalem, the spiritual center of the country, with his following, he knew, the Synoptic Gospels tell us, what his own fate was to be. The guiding idea is expressed in Mark, undoubtedly the oldest and least altered account: "The Son of Man goes as it is written of him" (14: 21). The events are too well known to need repeating. The execution was a Roman, not a Jewish, procedure. It may be added that according to Cicero, execution on the cross, with its prolonged agony, was the most terrible form of death. It was also the most shameful, and was intended to mark Jesus as a criminal. Scholarly researchers have calculated, with considerable probability, that the day of Jesus' death on a Sabbath which was also the first day of Passover must have been the fourteenth Nissan or April 3 in the year 33. But there are other datings. In any case, the Church annually marks the day on Good Friday.

All the features recounted in the story of the Passion correspond precisely to the Jewish expectation of the Messiah, as the Gospels clearly indicate by their quotations. The last words of Jesus: "My God, my God, why have you forsaken me," are not a cry of despair, but the opening words of Psalm 22, a Jewish prayer for the dying.

Two events are the true foundation of the religion on which the Christian Church is built: the Last Supper, and the events after the death of Jesus. Jesus assembled his disciples for a meal on that last evening. It was a farewell supper, obviously a *seder* such as pious Jews celebrate to this day on the eve of the Passover in memory of the exodus from Egypt. The accounts do not agree in the exact words he spoke for the *kiddush*, the blessing of the wine; but in the oldest version, preserved by Paul, he probably said: "This cup is the new covenant in my blood" (I Corinthians 11: 25). According to Mark 14: 25, Jesus added: "Truly, I say to you, I shall not drink again of the fruit of the vine until that day when I drink it new in the Kingdom of God." In other words, the Master's parting from his disciples, which is impending, is not to be the end; the group is to remain together until the day their companionship is renewed in the kingdom of the Messiah. The original community of Christians understood that as the foundation of a new *ecclesia*. Religious history can only observe that the foundation of the Christian Church is ultimately based on this Last Supper of Jesus with his disciples.

The other basis of this foundation, however, is something else again. It is not subject to research by religious historians or any others, because it concerns something which science cannot recognize: the events after the death of Jesus. The believers relate (Acts 13: 29–31): "They took him down from the cross, and laid him in a tomb. But God raised him from the dead; and for many days he appeared to those who came up with him from Galilee to Jerusalem." The Synoptic Gospels say that the stone was rolled away from the door of the tomb, and the grave was empty; the women who discovered this fled in terror. "And they said nothing to any one, for they were afraid." The Apostle Paul writes that he was told that Christ rose up on the third day in accordance with the Scriptures and appeared to Peter, then to the twelve (I Corinthians 15: 4–5). The traditions do not concur on all points, but they do agree that the life of Jesus did not end in a defeat. On those beliefs, the oldest community in Jerusalem was founded.

Questions arose immediately as to the meaning of the life and death of Christ; and the establishment of the Christian Church was possible only after those questions had been answered. The first communities had to settle upon an authoritative interpretation—and the process by which they arrived at it can still be recognized in the canonical writings of the New Testament. Let us first consider the beginnings of Christian theology, the writings of John and Paul.

The fourth Gospel occupies a special place. John sees the life of Jesus differently from the Synoptics. Although John is almost always represented in Christian art as a radiant youth, according to tradition he wrote his Gospel as a very old man—almost seventy years after the death of Jesus. It is the fruit of his meditations on the events rather than a report on the events themselves, even though it does contain a good many detailed descriptions and speeches of Jesus which are not to be found in the Synoptics, and which were perhaps known only to John. His Gospel is intended to answer the many questions on the nature of the Christ which had come up in the interval.

The peculiar character of John's picture of Christ is not easy to define. John was—if we accept the Catholic view of the authorship of the Gospel—set apart from the others as the favorite disciple of Jesus, and therefore had a special knowledge of him, a sense of the mystery in the essence of Jesus, which he repeatedly tried to express in fresh language. John's message is that in Jesus divinity had become present, the word made flesh.

First of all, John represents Jesus as being raised above the logic and the laws of this world; he stood in a unique, entirely different order of being, which was bound to be felt as offensive by the men of this world. The reality of divinity puts the world in the wrong. "If the world hates you, know that it has hated me before it hated you. If you were of the world, the world would love its own; but because you are not of the world, but I chose you out of the world, therefore the world hates you" (15: 18–19). This hatred on the one hand and profound loneliness on the other are necessary expressions of the particular existential structure of John's Christ.

Furthermore, there is the mystical element. To believe in Jesus Christ as the Son of God, the incarnate Logos, means to John "to live in him as in living truth, to be in the circulation of his blood and the current of his soul, to enter into him" (Guardini).

Here is the link between John and Paul, whose thinking is entirely dominated by the risen Christ in whom the believers participate to such an extent that they become members of his body, that Christ lives in them. The sacraments of baptism and communion do not merely symbolize this relationship; they *are* the relationship of the believer with Christ. Christian faith and Christian doctrine, as keenly formulated by Paul, see the living Christ as the medium in whom this relationship is accomplished throughout time.

PAUL'S VIEW OF CHRIST

Paul's view of Christ has become the most important one for Christendom because Paul was basically in the same position as all Christians after him, down to the present day, for unlike the evangelists, Paul did not see Jesus of Nazareth living and conducting his ministry on earth; he saw only the risen Christ, who appeared to him on the road to Damascus, summoned him to his service, and made him a disciple.

The Christ proclaimed by Paul has certain features borrowed, like those in the Gospels, from the Jewish Messiah of the Old Testament. But for Paul, Jesus is principally the Son of Man who was before the world was and will return at the end of time. His voluntary death expiates man's sins and binds man to God; the new principle of salvation is faith, which replaces observance of the Law. Through faith, men participate in Christ and enter into him.

These ideas of Paul became the fundamental doctrines of the Christian faith, and the basis of the Church's dogma. Paul was a sharply logical thinker, exceedingly aware of history. He drew the conclusion that with the appearance of Christ as the Messiah, a new era had begun. Until Christ came, the messianic expectations of Judaism were valid. But then the Messiah—Christ— arrived, lived, suffered, died and was resurrected and sits on the right hand of the Father in heaven. That means that we already live in the post-messianic age. The anticipated future is now in the past, and the world is only waiting his final return at the Last Judgment. Paul's theology really consisted in thinking through all matters in their relation to this transformation of the world, this new historical situation.

Paul thought that the post-messianic age would be short, that the return of Christ was imminent. In keeping with the messianic calculations of Judaism, he expected the end of this present age to come within the next forty years, and he believed that many of his contemporaries would witness that end. But it did not come; the return of Jesus was postponed, and the postponement has lasted to the present day. Thus the Church arose, and Jesus, who in his lifetime had only gathered a band of disciples around him, became the founder of a religion. The Church built in his name, which regards the Last Supper of Jesus with his disciples symbolically as the founding event, and which solemnly repeats that event in Communion, declares itself the representative of Christ until his return. The Church is the continuously living Body of Christ, and in the sacrament it gives this body to believers. Only in the light of this mystery can we understand what the Christian Church is. In the mystery of the faith the Church is an instrument of salvation, or in Protestant terms, an institution mediating salvation, and proclaiming to the whole world the gospel of Jesus as the incarnate Son of God. The whole history of the Christian Church, the development of creed, forms of worship and organization, is nothing but the extension of this view of Christ.

THE GROWTH OF THE CHRISTIAN CHURCH

Jesus did not intend to found the Christian Church, but it proceeded directly from his life and ministry when he called men to the approaching Kingdom of God. The original hearers of these tidings formed the nucleus of the first Christian community. The history of primitive Christianity illustrates the way a new messianic movement arose out of belief in the resurrection of Jesus. According to the account in Acts 3: 18 f., the original Christian community of Jerusalem began with the descent of the Holy Spirit on the first Pentecost, and was expressed by an actual speaking in foreign tongues. That was a sign to the community that they themselves belonged to the Last Days, for Jewish eschatology predicted this outpouring of the spirit in those days. The skepticism of the Jews isolated the community of the Kyrios Jesus, and thus established the independence of the early Church.

The first Christians early became convinced that the tidings of Jesus Christ, the Crucified and Resurrected, must be carried beyond the borders of Palestine to all the world. The origins of the ecclesiastical organization are to be found in this effort to bring the message of salvation to all men. The question of how this mission was to be carried out was discussed by the Apostles' Council of 49, and it was decided that believers among the pagans should not have to follow such Jewish laws and customs as circumcision and dietary practices. An unsettled question remained: whether the risen Christ was, as Paul taught, alive and present in his believers through the Spirit, or whether the believers were only entrusted with the task of proclaiming the revelation of the historical Jesus, as the Judaists held.

The Pauline view won out after the death of the twelve original apostles. The Judaeo-Christians or Ebionites ("the poor"), as they later called themselves, went into exile in Transjordania shortly before the destruction of Jerusalem. There they developed a number of peculiar dogmas; they also preserved a good many of the beliefs and practices of primitive Christianity which were early forgotten in the main Church, or which succumbed to the pressure of the "world." The author has discussed these matters in detail in his *The Jewish-Christian Argument* (New York: Holt, 1963).

Thenceforward, the Church was and remained a Church of the gentiles, although it always acknowledged its Jewish spiritual heritage. Underlying its opposition to the existing order of the world was the expectation of the Kingdom of God. On the other hand, as the end of the world was postponed, the Church was compelled to take an active part in the world in order to preach the Gospel. At last, anticipation of an imminent Second Coming had to be abandoned. Since world history went right on after the birth and death of Christ, it was decided that the end of time must be put off to the remote future, since to God a thousand years are as a day (II Peter 3: 8). In the interval the Church, as anticipation and embodiment of the coming kingdom, offered to believers the sacraments.

The first Christians had already made baptism in the name of Christ and celebration of the Last Supper a firm custom. Paul, however, transformed these customs into true sacraments. In Pauline doctrine, baptism meant real participation of the believer in the body of Christ, and in Christ's death and resurrection (Romans 6: 3–5; Colossians 2: 1–15; 3: 1f.). Baptism anticipates future salvation in the present, so that in it both the natural and supernatural conditions of the world are intermixed. Baptism by water assures the believer reception of the Holy Spirit; by it, Christians are buried with Christ and will be awakened from the dead.

Communion, also called Eucharist, was instituted by Jesus himself in memory of his last meal with the disciples. Paul gave to it the meaning of a communion of the celebrants with the exalted Lord. Believers participate in the physical being of Jesus; they eat his flesh and drink his blood—though in the form of "pneumatic" substance. "The cup which we drink, is it not a communion in the blood of Christ? The bread which we break, is it not a communion in the body of Christ?" (I Corinthians 10: 16). Christ himself must thus be conceived as present in the bread and wine. In this sense the sacraments communicate salvation; they accomplish the essence of Christian redemption: dying and being resurrected with Jesus Christ. The fate of the Savior is re-enacted in the participants—that is the sacramental meaning of the cult of Christ.

This conception has vast implications. If in the Eucharist the flesh and blood of Christ are actually eaten and drunk by the believers, the bread and wine are continuations of Christ's physical being. This belief, which had support in Hellenistic ways of thought, developed early in the ancient Church, and from the time of Ignatius of Antioch was taught by the great Church Fathers. In the Mass the elements of the actually present God are once again offered as sacrifice; the priest's sacrifice imitates the sacrifice on Golgotha, and is designed to reconcile man with

God. Martin Luther objected to this view, branding it a misunderstanding.

THE ECCLESIASTICAL OFFICES

The primitive Christian Church consisted of a number of fra-
ternally linked communities. But even in New Testament times
apostles, prophets, teachers, bishops and their aids (deacons)
were differentiated. Fixed organizations, definite offices and
statutes were as yet lacking. The Church thought of itself as the
living body of Christ under the direction of the Holy Spirit. But
the Spirit blows not always, but only when and where it lists.
Therefore institutions had to be established, all the more so since
the Last Days did not come. The result was the organization of
the Church, a special class of clerics, and later, under the influence of Roman legal thought, a distinct canon law and fixed
system for achieving salvation.

The administrative institutions of the Church developed in
Rome around the end of the first century. The office of the bishop,
originally overseer of a local church, was now reserved for the
leader of a larger congregation, and his deputies, the presbyters,
became priests. It was the bishop's task to confer their office upon
all priests. The whole life of the congregation, baptism, penance,
excommunication and absolution, was placed under his direction.
Thus the groundwork for an authoritarian rule of the Church was
laid. In the oldest times, however, every congregation had its
own bishop; we hear of parishes headed by priests only from the
fourth century on.

The influential office of deacons, who originally served at the
communion and cared for the sick, goes back to apostolic times,
as does the selection of deaconesses. From about 250 on there
were also subdeacons. Later, a number of lower ecclesiastical
offices were added, the minor orders. These were introduced in
Rome and only partly accepted in the Orient. Celibacy was an
old rule for bishops and priests; but in the early days continuance
of marriage was sanctioned if a married man was called to office.
Celibacy was legally introduced quite late, at the Second Lateran
Council in 1139. Tonsure was the external mark of the clergy
from the fifth century on.

The sharp division between clerics and laics, which was already to be found in Rome in the year 95 (First Epistle of Clement) was further sharpened by the development of the ecclesiastical doctrine of succession: that is, that Christ had appointed the apostles who in turn appointed the bishops and deacons. Henceforth, bishops as bearers of ecclesiastical authority could only be ordained by other bishops. Consecration conferred a special gift of the Holy Spirit which was permanent (*character indelibilis*), so that in the Catholic view a cleric could not be degraded to a layman.

The Church Fathers of around the year 200 and afterward (Irenaeus of Lyons, Hippolytus of Rome, Tertullian and particularly Cyprian of Carthage) developed this conception of the episcopal office and the "power of the keys" based on Matthew 16: 19 (to "bind and to loose" means approximately to decide what is banned and what is permissible). Cyprian said: "Every Christian must realize that not only is the bishop in the Church, but the Church is also in the bishop." Which means: without the office of bishop there is no Church, and "outside the Church there is no salvation"—a quotation from the same Father. Every episcopal see is a *cathedra Petri*.

Thus the Roman institutional Church was created and the principle of ecclesiastical obedience established. The office of bishop became monarchic. "No one can have God for Father who does not have the Church for Mother." But the Church speaks through the bishop. What the bishop declares is right is pleasing to God.

From the second century on, meetings of bishops (synods and councils) took place as expressions of the unity of the Church. At these assemblies, questions of a general character were dealt with. From 250 on we find regularly recurrent provincial synods at which the bishops of a particular province of the Empire met. Such meetings took place in the provincial capital (metropolis); the bishop of that city became the metropolitan and acquired jurisdiction over the bishops of the province. The Church as a whole now had an active organ, a form of representation, in these synods. And the Church ruled by the college of bishops purported to possess sole power of conferring salvation. The Christian episcopate should take credit for much of the work of forging the numerous peoples of late antiquity into a whole, and with checking the dangers of the Teutonic Völkerwanderung, which threatened to break down all the structures of society.

Thus, in the course of three to four centuries, there developed out of the free association of disciples of Jesus a tightly organized institution, linked to the state, which embraced the entire Roman Empire. This evolution from a spiritual to an institutional Church has often been deplored and condemned by Protestant critics. But it was only the inevitable consequence of the fact that the awaited Kingdom of God had not arrived, so that the Church had to adapt itself to the world. The Church became in St. Augustine's words a *corpus permixtum*, a mixed body, which therefore needed a legal organization. Much of the original spirit was lost in the process; but its historical importance to the transformation of the West was enormous. As F. Gregorovius, the great historian of Rome, put it in the nineteenth century: "The organized Church of the Empire saved Latinism and civilization, taking what was left of these under its care. It stood as the sole bulwark against which the surging waves of barbarian peoples broke. It was already an unshakable organism while the ancient Empire was falling to pieces—and this is one of the greatest facts of history."

THE PAPACY

One of the questions most disputed among the Christian denominations is that of the period at which Roman primacy, the supreme authority of the Bishop of Rome over all the bishops of the Empire, was first recognized. Probably we may give the years 190–191, when Bishop Victor of Rome threatened the church of Asia Minor with exclusion from the community of the Church for its deviations on the date of Easter.

In Catholic opinion, however, the time must be placed much further back, at the very beginning of the formation of the Christian Church. Jesus, it is said, addressed the Apostle Peter with the words in Matthew 16: 18: "You are the rock on whom I will build my Church." Those words stand written in golden letters on the inside of the dome of St. Peter's Cathedral in Rome. As Catholics interpret them, they mean that Peter was being given

full legal authority over the entire Church. Aside from the
Judaeo-Christians, who advocated the cause of the Lord's brother
James and who were later condemned as heretical, the earliest
Christians are said to have regarded Peter as head of the Church.
And, the Catholic argument continues, this dignity was unques-
tionably transferred to his successors in office, the bishops of the
Christian congregation in Rome. Certainly the successors of
Peter, after he had suffered a martyr's death as Bishop of Rome
in the year 63, seem very soon to have raised the claim to precedence over all other churches. Despite a good deal of resistance, the Roman Church and its bishops gradually won their
point.

According to the first epistle of Clement, the Roman Church
intervened authoritatively in the affairs of the Church of Corinth
as early as the end of the first century. Ignatius of Antioch (died
117) calls the Roman Church "head of the covenant of love."
But the first bishop who explicitly identified his office with that
of Peter was Calixtus I (217–222). By the end of the third century
we find the bishop of the capital, as "pope," in order to win
acceptance for his doctrinal decisions, raising the claim of being
vicar of Christ on earth. As such he claimed to possess supreme
authority in matters of belief and in the administration of the
Church when he made a pronouncement *urbi et orbi ex cathedra*
(to the city and the world from the episcopal seat), proclaiming
the will of Jesus Christ as Peter's successor. This dogmatic asser-
tion of the primacy of Peter and his Roman successors in office is
the ideological basis of the Roman papacy.

SPREAD AND PERSECUTION

The missionary spread of the Gospel among the pagans proceeded rapidly. The new teachings won adherents first of all in
the synagogues scattered throughout the range of Hellenistic
civilization around the Mediterranean—not so much among the
Jews as among the many so-called "God-fearing" pagans who
were already influenced by Judaism and other monotheistic religions. The tendency toward a monotheistic view had been stimulated by the widespread veneration of the sun god propagated
by the cult of Mithra; those with philosophical training were

especially hospitable to monotheism. But the whole age was
marked by a longing for saviors and ways of salvation, such as
the mystery cults taught. Above all the exploited and enslaved
poor were susceptible to the appeal of a new doctrine that promised human dignity and equality. So also were women, who in
much of the Roman world had very few rights. "There is neither
Jew nor Greek, there is neither slave nor free, there is neither
male nor female; for you are all one in Christ Jesus" (Galatians
3: 28). The charitable activities and mutual aid of Christians,
who called one another brothers and sisters, also attracted many
persons who found no such kindnesses in the heathen world. And
pagans were likewise impressed by the "witness" of the Christians, so many of whom suffered martyrdom when their beliefs
brought them into conflict with the laws of the state.

The Roman Empire, which ordinarily manifested great religious tolerance, early sensed in the Christians dangerous opponents, and not just because they refused to sacrifice to the
emperors and were thus withholding reverence from the Genius
of Rome. Special regulations might have been devised for them,
as were already provided for Jews, who were not required to
make such sacrifices. But the Christian claims to total direction
of the human person necessarily involved conflict with the state
power. For centuries the emperors did not trouble to settle the
legal position of Christians. But this indifference or toleration
ended with the cruel persecutions under the Emperors Decius
and Valerian in the middle of the third century. The waves of
persecution spread over the entire Empire and led to mass
martyrdoms.

The Christians were charged with enmity toward the world
and with contempt of men. Their rites were denounced as im-
moral orgies. Any mishap, any misfortune was laid to their door.
In the Roman Empire in those days the Christians were victimized in the same way that the Jews, as a defenseless minority,
have frequently been victimized. Tertullian described this general hatred of Christians thus: "When the Tiber floods over the
walls, when the Nile does not water the fields, when the weather
will not change, when the earth shakes and there is famine or
plague, the cry arises at once: the Christians to the lions."

After a brief interval of seeming latitude, there began the terri-

ble persecutions of Christians under the Emperor Diocletian
(284–305), who wanted to reorder and consolidate the Empire.
In 303 three edicts were issued, calling for destruction of the
churches, surrender of the sacred books, imprisonment of clerics,
and forcing Christians by torture to sacrifice to the gods. These
ushered in a general persecution that lasted for two years. Many
martyrs perished; there were, of course, many other lukewarm
Christians who became apostates. But as the ecclesiastical writers
phrased it: The wave battered in vain against the Rock of Peter.

The number of Christians had already increased too greatly
and their ecclesiastical organization was too solid to be destroyed. Moreover, the persecutions obviously no longer had
the support of the populace, as had been the case a few decades
earlier. In 313 the Emperors Licinius and Constantine issued an
edict of tolerance, after Constantine had defeated his rival
Maxentius at the Milvian Bridge. Legend has it that a radiant
cross appeared to him above the setting sun bearing the inscrip-
tion: *In hoc signo vinces* (by this sign you will win). Constantine
ordered the sign of Christ inscribed in Greek letters (XP) on the
standards of his legions. With that symbolic act, a new era in
world history began.

CHRISTIANITY AS THE RELIGION OF THE EMPIRE

The total population of the Roman Empire in the time of Constantine amounted to some eighty million, of whom about one-
quarter were Christians in 310. These were, however, very un-
evenly distributed. In some provinces (Phrygia, Bithynia, Pontus
and Asia Minor in general) about half the population supported
the Christians. In Africa and Numidia, Egypt, Rome, Lower
Italy and Spain, Christian congregations formed a respected and
active minority. In Gaul, Germany and Rhaetia the religion was
only beginning to gain a foothold. Eastern Christianity was thus
far stronger than Western—and that became an important factor
in the religious policy of Constantine.

Constantine's religious policies had distinct political ends: the
consolidation of imperial unity, and the winning of the Orient.
One act of his fraught with the most remarkable consequences
was the building of a second capital in the East, New Rome,

which was named Constantinople in his honor. The old city of Byzantium, now enlarged and embellished, became a purely Christian city, in which there were no sacrifices to the old gods. Since this was the usual residence of the emperor, the bishop of the city remained in a position of dependency, while Rome and the papacy were for a time freed from the proximity of secular rule, always a threat to the independence of the Church. In this situation lay the germ of the later schism between the Western and the Eastern Churches.

In Constantinople the emperor had a magnificent church built; later Justinian erected Hagia Sophia on its site. The building of churches was intended to make the Christian faith visible to all the world; out of the same impulse the Church of the Holy Sepulcher was erected in Jerusalem, the Church of the Redeemer in Rome, and above all the ancient St. Peter's Basilica, built on the site of Nero's Circus, where legend had it that Peter had suffered martyrdom. In creating this church for the glorification of a martyr executed by the Roman state, the emperor affirmed the victory of the Roman bishops over the secular state. Constantine also presented the Lateran Palace to the pope, conferring upon the Roman bishop a degree of secular recognition that was subsequently to affect that bishop's prestige within the Church.

Thus in the fourth century Christianity developed from one among other religions having equal legal rights to the sole religion recognized by the state, and under Emperor Theodosius the Great in 380 to the sole religion in the Empire. Theodosius declared paganism a crime against the state, and the pagan cults vanished rapidly from public life. With Justinian's closing of the Platonic Academy in Athens in 529, this operation was complete.

The significance of this can be appreciated by an aphorism of Tertullian written only a century earlier: "Two unalterable facts oppose a conversion of the emperor to Christianity: the fact that the world cannot exist without Caesars, and the fact that a Christian can never become Caesar." The great revolution wrought by Constantine proved that Tertullian had been wrong. But it created a new problem which was to become the theme of all subsequent centuries: the tension and the dichotomy between

Empire and Christianity, which in the Middle Ages became the struggle between pope and emperor, and in modern times the conflict between religion and politics.

SIN AND PENANCE: THE GREAT STRUGGLE

The ethical rigorousness of the early Church Fathers led to great difficulties in the daily life of Christians. The ideal of a "Church of the Saints" proved untenable; far too many Christians could not attain moral perfection. Of the three mortal sins that according to Tertullian and others meant permanent exclusion from the Church—idolatry, murder and unchastity or sins of the flesh—the latter in particular were too widespread for the Church to treat as unpardonable. Bishop Calixtus I in 220 introduced a revolutionary innovation by taking a more lenient view of unchastity and allowing those who committed sins of the flesh to be taken back into the fold if they did appropriate penance. His pastoral edict was soon accepted, despite opposition, in the practice of the Roman and the African Church. It was of crucial importance in the history of Catholic penance. The primitive Church of Saints, which irrevocably excluded a sinner, had become a memory by the beginning of the fifth century. The fact of human frailty was given official acknowledgment and the sinner was forbearingly granted the opportunity to return to the way of righteousness.

Soon it was discovered that other grave sins likewise had to be forgiven. Calixtus had already advocated receiving back the apostates (*lapsi*) who had fallen into heresy. Such leniency became a compelling necessity a few decades later, when the great persecutions began and many believers under torture or in fear of death sacrificed to idols and thus became apostates. Even the initially obdurate Bishop Cyprian finally agreed that a sincere penitent could atone for his wrongs by a strict three-year penance and be received back into the Church with full privileges. Thus the viewpoint of leniency and forbearance gradually won out. Christ's commandment of love became part and parcel of the history of the Church.

The milder estimation of mortal sins was afterward extended to lighter or venial sins, which did not come under the penitential power of the Church in general, but were subject to private penances or reprimands imposed by the bishop or priest. Increasing tolerance toward "ordinary" sins caused a reaction, however: the rise of monasticism, which took even such sins very seriously for the sake of the desired Kingdom of Heaven.

MONASTICISM

Penitential doctrine developed a two-stage ethics: one ethics binding upon all Christians, and the ethics of perfection, with strict ascetic requirements meant for a few. Catholic doctrine therefore distinguishes precepts and counsels. The argument runs: Because a few demand everything of themselves, the moral requirements on the many may be eased. This thinking led to the rise of monasticism with its ascetic ideal of sanctity.

Monasticism began with anchoritism (*anachorese* means withdrawal, retirement—i.e., from the world). The anchorites represented a select company of initiates and illuminates who sought moral perfection through asceticism. Monasticism developed a comprehensive penitential discipline in which every sin, whether minor or major, was considered disobedience to God. In order to combat hidden sins, secret confession was introduced into the monastic communities.

One New Testament root of monasticism was the deliberate aloofness from the world and its cares in imitation of the complete devotion of Jesus to his ministry. Another source was the hostility to the body which is alien to the spirit of the Bible, but which was characteristic of Gnosticism and other currents of thought in late antiquity: the idea that the body is the "prison of the soul" and that the sexual instinct as such is sinful.

From about the year 200 on a special group of ascetics existed in Christian congregations. Soon they retired from the world and became hermits (literally, desert-dwellers). Often their separation from the world ended in sheer eccentricity, some hermits, for example, preserving their sanctity from the contamination of the world by installing themselves on top of pillars. The first Christian monastery was founded between 314 and 317 by Pachomius on the eastern bank of the Nile. It united its members as *cenobites* (from *koinos bios*, "living together") in a close community under an abbot to whom obedience was due. The monastic cells were shut off from the outside world by a wall, the *claustrum,* whence our word *cloister.* The Rule of Pachomius, which served as the model for all subsequent monastic rules, laid down the standards for acceptance, the clothing, way of life, work and religious exercises of the monks. There was much emphasis on work of the hands and singing of psalms. From the fourth century on monasticism spread rapidly throughout the Church, and became associated with the philosophical ideals of the ancient world. Emperor Justinian by his legislation furthered monasticism as against more individualistic modes of achieving sanctity.

In the Eastern Church Basil the Great (died 379) proclaimed the monastic community the image of the true Body of Christ. Certain forms of exaggerated asceticism, such as were practiced by the pillar-saints, were repressed in the West by Benedict of Nursia (died circa 550). For the monastery of Monte Cassino, founded in 529 in the Campagna between Rome and Naples, Benedict composed the *Regula Benedicti.* The Benedictine Rule insisted on permanence of residence as a check upon itinerant monks, on renunciation of property and vows of chastity and obedience.

Work is valued even higher than asceticism; with his Rule and his *ora et labora* ("pray and work"), Benedict became the educator of European monasticism. His Rule owes its spread chiefly to Pope Gregory the Great (540–604); from the eighth to the twelfth centuries it was the dominant monastic Rule throughout the West. Benedictines such as Willibrord, Boniface, Ansgar and others performed tremendous missionary work among the Germanic tribes. Their Rule has been called "the greatest organizational achievement of the West." Along with the growth of monasteries, convents for women also arose. Nuns subject to the Benedictine Rule made major contributions to the education of women; some of them won fame as poets, such as Hroswitha of Gandersheim (circa 933–1002).

In the early Middle Ages many other monastic orders were founded—thus in the thirteenth century the mendicant orders of Franciscans (Francis of Assisi, 1182–1226) and Dominicans

(Dominic, 1170–1221), who made poverty the central concern of the community. Their members left the walls of the cloister and went out into the world. The sciences and arts owe a great deal to these orders, for the monastic ideal early became joined to the ideal of scholarship. Numerous reform movements in the Church started in monasteries. Always, however, the organized ascetic movement represented by the monks has been the most faithful and effective force within the Church. The close tie between the Church's secular rule and monasticism's flight from the world dominated Catholicism in the High Middle Ages.

DEVELOPMENT OF THEOLOGY AND DOGMA

The formulation of a canon of the New Testament and a defined creed was greatly spurred by the confrontation of early Christianity with numerous Gnostic schools and mystery organizations which in the second century threatened to flood the Church. Gnosticism has been rightly called an "impersonal religious mass movement," which developed approximately at the same time as Christianity and flourished especially in the second and third centuries. Around 375 Epiphanius, one of the Church Fathers, knew of more than sixty Gnostic groups. Most of the names in his catalogue of heresies must remain mere names to us. We can identify about twenty, the most important of them being the Valentinians, Basilidians, Carpocratians, Sethians, Ophites or Naassenes, Barbelo Gnostics and Archontics. Irenaeus' comment on the Valentinians applies to them all: "You cannot find two or three who say the same thing about the same subject; in names and matters they completely contradict one another." Nevertheless, we can state approximately what speculations were common to all of them. Earlier stages of Gnostic thought are recognized by some scholars in the writings of the Qumran sect.

Simultaneously with the Qumran finds, hitherto wholly unknown Gnostic original documents in Coptic dialects were found near Nag Hammadi in Lower Egypt. Among these was a Gospel of Thomas containing hitherto unknown sayings of Christ, and a Valentinian "Gospel of Truth" which has thrown much new light on Gnosticism.

If we attempt a cross section of the later systems, we find a complex, highly mythological picture of a universe which arose not by an act of Creation, but by continuous emanation from the supreme deity. In the beginning sparks of light mingled with matter, and those sparks, caught in the darkness of the world, strive for reunion with the primordial light. Since the sparks of light incarnated in certain men, the "pneumatics," these men are capable of recalling the divine origin of the soul's core. The ascent from the fetters of matter through the hostile planetary spheres (eons)—the Valentinians reckoned thirty of them—was called the "ascension of the soul." Certain mysteries purify the soul from the compulsions of destiny and prepare it to receive the Inaccessible Light.

This speculative view of the world was much colored by numerology and alphabetic mystification. It originated in a pessimistic sense of the dichotomy of soul and body. But since it taught that man must save himself, there were no hard-and-fast boundaries between it and Christianity. Yet Christianity could not very well compromise with it. The Gnostics did endeavor, by allegorical interpretations of the Bible, to fit Jesus Christ into their system as a cosmological savior figure—suggesting, for example, that the heavenly Christ had a pseudo-connection with the historical Jesus of the Gospels (Docetism). With its dualism of a world of light and one of matter, and with its abundance of intermediate beings, Gnosticism represents a wholly anti-Christian picture of the world, and a pagan feeling about life. There can be no mistaking that, in spite of the borrowings from the Gnostics that we find even in the Johannine writings of the New Testament, and later on in the Alexandrine Fathers of the Church.

The one case in which Christianity and Gnosticism mingled and merged was in the personality and thought of Marcion, the founder of a heretical church. Marcion strictly separated the God of the Old Testament, the Creator of the world, from the supreme God, the Father of Jesus Christ. This dualism led him to a radical dismissal of the earthly world, and a strictly ascetic ethics quite alien to Christianity and not justifiable by anything in the writings of Paul, from whom Marcion believed he had derived his doctrines. Marcion thought that the Judaistic "pillars" referred to in Galatians 2: 9 had corrupted the gospel of the good "Stranger God" announced by Jesus; he considered the Judaeo-Christians as the worst enemies of himself and the truth.

The Church expelled Marcion in 144. His doctrine of the "Stranger God," who dismissed the Creation of the God of the Jews as the work of a bungler, was held to be heretical. Marcion thereupon founded his own church, which had unusual success in spite of its stringent, antiphysical asceticism. Between 150 and 190, and in the Orient even up to the fourth century, it constituted a real danger to the main Church. The Church Fathers regarded the Marcionites as their chief foe. Ultimately, however, the new church fell victim to the imperial laws against heresy.

Marcion proved to be of great importance for the Catholic Church. Because he named a revised Gospel of Luke, the Acts of the Apostles, and the epistles of Paul to be the holy scriptures of his church, the growing Catholic Church was compelled to establish canonical scriptures for itself. In addition, Catholic theology made great strides during the second century out of efforts to refute this dangerous heretic. The baptismal profession was also introduced into liturgical use in answer to the Marcionites. The struggle with Marcion had more influence on the Catholic Church than the confrontation with all the other heresies that later arose.

After Marcion's attack upon the Old Testament had been fended off, a new crisis ensued somewhat later in connection with the apocalyptic writings. Disappointment over the postponement of the Second Coming had resulted in new annunciations by a Phrygian prophet named Montanus and two prophetesses. They predicted the return of Christ in the immediate future. On a plain near Pepuza in Asia Minor—so the prophecy ran—the Heavenly Jerusalem would descend. Montanus quickly gained followers, and a wave of prophecy swept the entire Church. The mood was a reversion to the earliest days of the Church, with prophecies of doom, speaking in tongues and strictest asceticism. Montanus considered himself the Paraclete and believed he was beginning a new era in the story of salvation. Even the sober African Tertullian joined the new movement in 202 and stayed with it for five years. The Church found it advisable to bar the gates against such ecstatic prophecies and such undisciplined testimonies to the presence of the Spirit. Aside from the Revelation of St. John, therefore, no other apocalyptic writings were accepted into the canon of the New Testament. Montanism was the last of the enthusiastic movements, and forced the Church to develop firmer forms of organization and to exclude independent thinkers from its ranks as heretics if they deviated from the apostolic Gospel by as much as a single point. Primitive Christianity may be said to have ended with the containment of the Montanist crisis at the end of the second century.

CHRISTOLOGICAL DOCTRINAL DISPUTES

There followed the involved dogmatic disputes within the Church from the fourth to the seventh centuries, which even students of theology are reluctant to discuss. There was an inner necessity underlying these quarrels, however. What was at stake was the correct formulation of the basic dogma on which the whole Christian Church stands and falls: Christ is the Lord and is God. It seemed requisite for salvation to defend this conviction against heresies. From the Council of Nicaea, called by Emperor Constantine in 325, to the Monothelite controversy in the seventh century, that was the single issue. The discussion had to run on until all possibilities of a solution had been thoroughly examined. The dogmatic decisions of the Church, whose purpose was to skirt any one-sided, heretical interpretation of Revelation, did not mean—as is often charged—the petrifying of Christianity. On the contrary, these decisions were of enormous and lasting religious importance. In their time, moreover, these disputes were burning contemporary issues. How else can we understand the story that for the sake of an *iota* (literally), the market women in Byzantium pounded each other on the head—the issue being whether Christ was *homousios* (of the same substance as God) or *homoiusios* (of similar substance), or, in other words, whether they sided with Athanasius or Arius on the nature of Christ. A man like Athanasius knew what was at stake. He would rather be driven from his episcopal see six times than give in on the phraseology he favored. For this formula was more than a formula; it alone concealed the right doctrine of the Redemption.

What is a dogma? It is a conceptually formulated tenet that the Church regards as binding on all men. By "conceptually formulated" we mean that a truth taken from holy scriptures is expressed in philosophical language. Theology, as the ecclesiastical discipline that deals with faith, is entrusted with the task of creating dogma. Carefully weighed and formulated, these tenets are meant to cancel the disagreements of men. They are arrived at by the Church sitting in council; the theory is that the Holy Spirit is present at such conferences. The process of formulating dogma has never really ceased in the Catholic Church. As late as 1870 the Vatican Council proclaimed the dogma of the infallibility of the pope when speaking *ex cathedra* as the successor to Peter. And in 1950 Pope Pius XII proclaimed the bodily Ascension of Mary as a dogma. But the great period in the formulation of dogma was the fourth to the seventh centuries. The chief questions were the Trinitarian and the Christological. That is, Revelation taught and the general belief of the Church professed:

One God; the Father = God, the Son = God, the Holy Spirit = God.

Jesus Christ = God and man.

On the one hand, the logically thorny problem of one deity in three Persons, together with the relationship of the Holy Spirit or Logos to the Father and to the Son, had to be elucidated. On the other hand, the complete equality of Christ with the Father and simultaneously his difference from the Father had to be proclaimed, and the divinity of the Logos emphasized, without equating him with the Father or lapsing into polytheism.

These questions were particularly acute in the more speculatively inclined Orient. Ultimately, the view of the Alexandrian priest Arius (died 336) was rejected. Arius regarded Jesus not as God, but as a creature endowed with divine powers and adopted by the Father as his son. The First General Council of Nicaea in 325 decided in favor of the opposing view held by Bishop Athanasius (died 373) that Christ as true Son of God was of the same substance with the Father. Nevertheless, this dispute was to rage throughout the fourth century. The migrating East Germanic tribes of the time (Vandals, Burgundians, Ostrogoths, Rugians, Lombards) had been converted to Arianism—and the Lombards remained Arians until the seventh century. Nevertheless, largely due to the intervention of the emperor, the Nicene solution won out. With the acceptance of the *homousia* formula, the equality of the Logos with God, which Athanasius had advocated, was also established.

The full humanness of Christ was asserted at the Third General Council of Ephesus (431), and it was also ordained that Mary was true Mother of God. Since the doctrine of the Savior's two natures repeatedly offended the intellect, the—rationally inexplicable—mystery of the Incarnation of God was again proclaimed as against the arguments of the Monophysites (advocates of the doctrine of a single nature of Christ) and the Nestorians, and at the Fourth General Council in Chalcedon (451) all the bishops present signed a statement in the presence of the emperor and empress: "We all unanimously teach one and the same Son, our Lord Jesus Christ, perfect according to divinity and perfect according to humanity . . . in two natures, unmingled and unchanged [against the Monophysites], unseparated and unparted [against the Nestorians], both coming together in one person. . . ." On this basis all the decisions of subsequent councils were taken; old heresies that cropped up in new forms (such as Monotheletism in the seventh century) were repeatedly disclaimed.

In the more practically minded West, the question of the process of salvation became the subject of controversy. How do divine Grace and the human will collaborate? In the dispute between Pelagius and Augustine, the fundamental opposition came into the open. Can man's free moral acts affect God (Pelagius), or is man in essence unfree and can God alone confer salvation (Augustine). Following Paul, Augustine taught that man is fundamentally incapable of good (original sin), and that the decree of God alone decides whether he is to be saved or damned (predestination). The disputes with the Pelagians over grace and predestination were extremely complex and difficult, but ultimately led to the victory of Augustine. Nevertheless, in practice the Church adapted an intermediate viewpoint (Semi-Pelagianism). Critics of the Semi-Pelagianism of the Catholic Church in the Late Middle Ages (Wycliffe, Luther, and, in the seventeenth century, Jansen) often invoked the "uncontaminated" views of Augustine.

AUGUSTINE

In the struggle with Pelagius, the greatness of St. Augustine (354–430) emerged. In influence, Augustine was the most important of all the Church Fathers. He was also one of the most prolific writers of the Church, as a systematic theologian (*On the Trinity*), as interpreter of the Bible (*On Christian Doctrine*), as preacher and adviser, as may be seen in his voluminous correspondence. The Bishop of Hippo—a port city in North Africa—held to his dualistic view of the universe, which had led him to Manichaeism and neoplatonism before he became a Christian, and which may well account for his great historical influence. As Erich Seeberg has pointed out, Augustine was not an armchair theologian like Thomas Aquinas, who perseveringly filed away at his system. Augustine's ideas grew out of his reflections on his life. He described his way to faith in his famous *Confessions*. The concentrated vision with which he confronted sinful man and the living God was the new element that distinguished him from all his predecessors. "Against Thee alone have I sinned." "Thou, O Lord, hast created us for Thyself, and our hearts are restless until they find rest in Thee."

Augustine placed the authority of the Church even above that of the scriptures. He once went so far as to say: "I would not believe the Gospel if the authority of the Catholic Church did not prompt me to." His concept of the Church was closely connected with the doctrine of Grace developed in the struggle against Pelagius, and with the doctrine of sin and justification that he derived from the epistles of Paul. Augustine also put forth the idea that within the Church, after baptism, there is forgiveness for all sins if appropriate penance is made. Outside the Church there is no forgiveness. To repudiate this is to commit the sin against the Holy Spirit.

Other new concepts to be found in Augustine are those of purgatory and the idea that survivors can help departed souls by intercessory prayer, alms and Masses. Purgatory is not infernal punishment, but an opportunity offered to the sinner after death to make up for insufficient penances in his lifetime.

One of the most important of Augustine's works was his *De civitate Dei*, which he wrote under the immediate impact of the capture of Rome by Alaric, King of the Visigoths, in 410. In this last great apology of Christianity against the pagans, Augustine drew a contrast between the unjust secular state based on power, which he called a "great robber band," with the Kingdom of God represented by the Church. Babylon and Jerusalem, the kingdom of the devil and the Kingdom of God, are forever struggling against one another. But in Augustine's opinion, the earthly state can, if it comes to the defense of peace and justice, also serve and prepare the way for the Kingdom of God. Christian emperors such as Constantine and Theodosius had, after all, placed their power at the service of God's majesty. On the other hand, Augustine warns Christendom against committing itself too deeply to any earthly structure. This point was to have far-reaching consequences. The policies of the medieval popes were based upon this tenet of Augustine's that the earthly state must be subordinate to the Kingdom of God.

BRIEF SKETCH OF MEDIEVAL CHURCH HISTORY

After the Roman Empire of the West had collapsed before the onslaught of the Germanic tribes in 476 and pagan antiquity was swallowed up by the Great Migrations, the "Middle Ages" may be said to have begun. The Catholic Church dominated the religious and intellectual life of the Romano-Germanic world. With the rise of the Frankish state, and its breakup in the ninth century, there gradually arose in place of the Church of the Empire provincial churches which held their own synods and developed their own idiosyncrasies. The Church countered such particularistic tendencies by exerting cultural and social influence. The common language of worship and culture had a large part in preserving the unity of the West, as did the idea of a single Christian republic of nations united into a superior whole by the Catholic Church. The rise of the papacy to a universal power in the Church and the world was essential to the fulfillment of this idea. For a time the pope became the overlord of the Western world;

the Church of the East, although it remained "Catholic" did not become "papal," and so remained dependent on the secular powers.

THE SCHISM

The great schism that has kept the churches of the East and West apart to this day was in the making for several centuries before it became an accomplished fact in 1054. In language, culture and character, the Easterners have always been another breed from the Romans. While the popes began to lean upon the Franks, and the Frankish king Pippin received his crown from the hand of the pope, while the imperial title was renewed in the West by Charlemagne, the course of events in East Rome ran in a different direction. There the emperor towered above the Church. The "ecumenical patriarchs" of Byzantium were virtually court bishops who could not criticize but only bless the ruler's secular actions. The Church of the East therefore remained passive toward emperors and tsars, abjuring the active role of penetrating and shaping secular society which became so characteristic of the Roman Catholic Church.

Thus two Christian churches formed, for these outward differences have kept them apart to this day. The Christianity of the Eastern Church is in many respects much more antiquated—in a neutral sense—than Roman Catholicism; for the former has remained at the stage of the eight ecumenical councils held between the fourth and ninth centuries, and has undergone no major developments since. By inflexibly clinging to the dogmas of the ecumenical councils, the Eastern Church has won the epithet "orthodox." Devoutness in this church is centered upon those rites which symbolize earthly closeness to God; those are orthodox, therefore, who properly perform these rites.

A dispute over excessive veneration of images, which broke out in Byzantium in 726, deepened the gulf between East and West. Ultimately the Eastern Church approved the veneration of images in several councils. Icons were declared revealed images of divine persons and events, and believers were urged to venerate them. The iconostasis, a wall adorned with icons of Christ, the

Blessed Virgin, angels and saints, separates the altar from the rest of the church in Greek Orthodox churches.

The final breach between East and West came in 1054, as the result of a dispute over the rights of the patriarchate in Lower Italy. But that was only the final occasion, not the primary reason for the ecclesiastical rift between East and West. In spite of several attempts at reunion, the split has remained unhealed to this day.

WORLD POWER AND POLITICAL DECLINE OF THE PAPACY

The basis for the universal power of the papacy was laid by two forgeries that were accepted as authentic throughout the Middle Ages. The first of these was the eighth-century Donation of Constantine, a forged document wherein the Emperor Constantine confirmed the precedence of the Church of Rome, and conferred upon the pope the imperial palace (the Lateran) and secular rule over Rome, Italy and all the provinces of the West. This "donation" was supplemented by the actual Donation of Pippin, King of the Franks, in 756, which led to the formation of the States of the Church—thus making the popes a factor in secular politics for the next eleven hundred years.

The other forgery dates from the first half of the ninth century, and is known as the False Decretals. Purporting to be statements of canon law, these decretals ruled that bishops were subordinate neither to the metropolitan of their own countries nor to the secular power, but only to the distant pope. By partly genuine and partly falsified synodal decrees, this forgery upheld papal claims to sole powers of leadership and nomination. The position of the episcopate as against the pope was decisively weakened in favor of papal centralistic power.

Charlemagne (768–814) to all intents and purposes ruled over the Church and reduced the pope almost to the status of a Frankish bishop. Even the fact that Pope Leo III put himself forward as transmitter of the imperial dignity on Christmas Day 800, when Charlemagne was crowned Roman emperor, in no way changed the actual power relationships. The disintegration of the Frankish Empire under Charlemagne's successors, however, offered wider opportunities to the papacy. The creation of numerous ecclesiastical principalities under the Ottos offered the pope a dangerous instrument for intervening in the internal politics of the Empire.

From the time of Louis the Pious the emperors conceded that the pope, as holder of the "power of the keys," exerted spiritual direction over themselves as persons. Until the late Middle Ages no German king contested the pope's right to confer the crown of the Holy Roman Empire of the German Nation, that vast congeries of territories that extended far to the east and west of Germany, though never including France, England or the Scandinavian countries. The popes repeatedly found themselves in difficulties with the Roman nobility, and had to appeal for help to the German rulers. Thus they became dependent on Otto the Great (936–973), who in 962 renewed the imperial dignity in the West, and on his successor. Henry III (1039–1056), one of the most powerful of the German kings, took steps to stem the decay. At the Synod of Sutri (1046) he began a program of spiritual rejuvenation by installing German popes. Nevertheless the papacy resisted the inroads of secular power upon the freedom of the Church, and a struggle began which was to last for centuries. A reform movement was born, emanating from the monastery of Cluny, which called for a curbing of undisciplined monasticism, celibacy of priests, and abolition of simony, that is, the sale of ecclesiastical posts, often to laymen. These reformist ideas came to a head over the question of the appointment of bishops and abbots (investiture) by the secular powers.

With Pope Gregory VII (1073–1085), who dreamed of transforming the world into an Augustinian *civitas Dei*, monasticism assumed the leadership of the Church of the High Middle Ages. Gregory took up the dispute over investitures with young King Henry IV, and in 1075 flatly forbade lay investiture. The king retaliated by having a synod of German bishops at Worms depose the pope. But the papacy had the devout souls of every land on its side; in this struggle for world rule, Gregory deposed and excommunicated the German king and released his subjects from their oath of allegiance. The ban of the Church was imposed upon Henry IV until he had stood in the court of the Castle of Canossa for three days, barefoot in the snow, and done penance on his knees. Nevertheless, Gregory VII did not emerge victorious; he died, embittered, in exile. The struggle over investitures ended in 1122 with a compromise (the Concordat of Worms), which permitted the popes to nominate bishops and imperial abbots, but allowed the kings—at least in Germany—certain rights of proposing candidates. At the consecration of a bishop, he received the ring and staff from the pope, and a scepter from the king or emperor, who were thereby acknowledged to have some part in the matter.

After a long contest replete with vicissitudes between Frederick Barbarossa (1152–1190) and the popes of his time, Pope Innocent III managed to make good capital of the struggles among Frederick's successors. Innocent (1198–1216) brought the papacy to the height of its secular power. For a time, at least, the papacy was able to decide the choice of the German candidate for the throne. The kings of England and France accepted his claim that they held their lands from him in fee. The world seemed to have become a great ecclesiastical state, with the pope as heir of the Roman Caesars. Karl Heussi describes this period of papal overlordship thus:

"The papacy now had attained an incomparable expansion of power and an unsurpassed conviction of power. The pope was the lord of the world and of the Church. He was no longer merely the successor to Peter, but the vicar of Christ and God on earth. He was sinless and infallible in his official acts. The emperor and kings were the pope's vassals; they were expected to do homage to him by kissing his foot and holding his stirrup. He could depose them and release their subjects from their oaths of fidelity. As the sign of his dignity he himself wore the tiara, which from the fourteenth century on consisted of a triple crown. In the thirteenth century the Church actually became the pope's Church. In legislation and in administration the pope became more and more the absolute lord of the Church."

The period of universal papal rule reached its climax with the victory over the Hohenstaufens and the destruction of the German imperium as the secular head of Christendom. In 1268 Konradin, the last Hohenstaufen, was beheaded at Naples. Pope Boniface VIII (1294–1303) proclaimed the principle of universal dominion in the words of Thomas Aquinas: it was necessary for the salvation of every living being to bow down to the Roman pope (the bull *Unam sanctam*, 1302). This bull was directed particularly at the German episcopate, which generally remained loyal to the emperors. But Boniface's successor had to pay a price for the crushing of Germany by himself bowing to a united France. From 1309 to 1377 the popes, stripped of their political but by no means of their ecclesiastical power, resided in French Avignon. In 1356 the Golden Bull at last excluded the popes from taking part in the election of the German king. A papal schism— for thirty-seven years there were two popes, one residing in Rome and the other in Avignon—was at last ended by the Council of Constance (1414–1418). Another council in Basel (1431–1439) attempted to carry out a "reform of the Church in head and limbs," but with no lasting result. The successive councils, however, could no longer seriously threaten papal primacy. If the reformist councils of the fifteenth century had been successful, the great schism of the sixteenth century probably would have been avoided. But they were not, and under the politically adroit Renaissance popes the Church entered a period of financial recklessness, intense exploitation and ethical decay, which led to the Reformation.

THE CRUSADES

Papal aspirations for universal power also precipitated the Crusades, which continued for two centuries (1095–1291). The seven major Crusades were conducted as a holy war against heretics and heathens. Their purpose was to rescue the Holy Sepulcher from the hands of the unbelievers; but along with the conquest of the Holy Land by the Christian nations, the power of the papacy was to be extended.

A variety of political, cultural and economic interests played their part in the genesis of the Crusades. All those preparing to give battle against the heathen pinned a red cross to their shoulders and received indulgence for their sins. In the beginning, the Crusaders were disorderly mobs who in Germany carried out pogroms against the Jews. Shouting "God wills it," inspired by eloquent preachers like Peter of Amiens, the armies of the First Crusade were strikingly successful. In 1099 they set up the Kingdom of Jerusalem under Duke Godfrey of Bouillon of Lorraine. But in 1244 Jerusalem finally fell into the hands of the

Turks, who held it until 1918. After a period of initial enthusiasm and genuine heroism, the Crusaders succumbed more and more to the demoralizing influences of Oriental customs.

One product of the Crusading movement were the Christian chivalric orders, which merged the ideals of chivalry and asceticism. The most important of these were the Order of Templars (1119), the Knights of St. John (circa 1120), and the Teutonic Knights (1198), who were responsible for founding the state of Prussia (circa 1250). Combat against unbelievers, protection of pilgrims, care of the sick and the wounded were the monastic and ecclesiastical tasks of these armed knights.

For the West, the major lasting effect of the Crusades was the greater contact with Islamic culture, the resumption of Oriental trade and extension of men's intellectual horizons. In spite of common ideals and actions carried out in common, the peoples of Europe emerged from the Crusades even more divided than before. Politically, the sacrifices of blood and treasure had been in vain.

CHRISTIAN ART AND SCHOLARSHIP

The spirit of the Christian Middle Ages found lasting expression in the great churches and cathedrals all over Europe. From about 1000 to 1200 the monumental Romanesque style richly transformed Roman formal elements, especially in France and Germany. Among the great German Romanesque churches are the cathedrals of Speyer, Worms, Mainz and the abbey church of Maria Laach. From about 1150 on the Romanesque yielded to the Gothic, with its pointed arches, soaring pillars and cross-ribbed vaulting. Shortly before 1500 the Gothic passed into the Renaissance style; in architecture, the pointed arch was replaced by the rounded arch, and the cross-ribbed vault by the barrel vault. Domes, such as the dome of St. Peter's in Rome, became much more common. Grandiose conceptions of space and emphasis on the central structure characterize the architecture of the Renaissance. By the sixteenth century painting had reached a high stage of development and vied with its sister arts of sculpture and architecture in glorifying the Church.

Like the arts, the scholarship of the Middle Ages was ecclesiastical. Its sole purpose was to contribute to a philosophical understanding of Christian revelation. Scholasticism was an elaborate intellectual system for expounding the traditional, authoritative subjects taught at the universities, and at the cathedral and monastic schools of the period. Scholastics were not allowed to teach anything that ran counter to the doctrines of the Church; philosophy was regarded as the "handmaiden of theology."

The great period of scholasticism came in the thirteenth century, when the complete works of Aristotle became known in Europe by way of Jewish and Arabic scholars. The task of integrating Aristotle with the dogma of the Church was performed particularly by the Domican monk Thomas Aquinas (1225–1274), whose *Summa theologica* remains to this day the great compendium of Roman Catholic theology. According to Thomas, man's God-created reason can recognize the divine elements in the world and in the plan of salvation. Essential points in this doctrine were opposed by the English Franciscan John Duns Scotus (1266–1308), who taught the superiority of the will to the intellect. Many other disputed questions, which cannot be discussed here, led to long contentions in the schools.

In late scholasticism (fourteenth and fifteenth centuries), subtle disputations became the rule. Rigidities set in, and sterility threatened to overtake the system until the new school of Jesuits introduced new vitality into it in the age of the Counter Reformation. However, a good many of the questions of modern philosophy were first raised by the scholastics—especially in logic. William of Ockham (circa 1285–1349) attempted to prove that reason is incapable of grasping the supernatural. That proposition was the beginning of the end of scholasticism. It ceased to be the sole form in which Occidental man cast his philosophical speculations.

Scholasticism provided the intellectual foundation for the cultural unity of the Middle Ages within the Church. That unity rested on three propositions: 1) Faith is in accord with science; 2) the harmony of the theological tradition is demonstrable; 3) the insights of faith can be grouped systematically around certain central points.

SYMPTOMS OF DECAY

In the "autumn of the Middle Ages" there grew out of the unsatisfied needs of popular piety new movements, some of them potentially explosive, which gradually brought about the dissolution of the unified culture of the Church. The end of the Crusades, and the excesses of papal imperialism, which led to papal downfall and the exile in Avignon, contributed to this process. When the Renaissance popes resorted to simony in order to meet the everlasting financial exigencies of the Church, the moral authority of the papacy rapidly decayed. Great preachers called for repentance and inveighed against the corruption within the administration of the Church, the secularization of the higher clergy, and the general moral decline. Savonarola (1452–1498), for example, declared in a Lenton sermon in February 1498: "The shamefulness begins in Rome and passes through the whole; they are worse there than the Turks and Moors. Go look in Rome and you will find that they have all obtained their spiritual benefices by simony. Many search for benefices for their children or their brothers. . . . Their greed is monstrous; they do everything for money. Their bells ring for avarice; the priests go to the choir for money, to vespers, to Mass for money. They sell the sacraments, barter with the Mass; in short, everything is done for money. . . . As soon as evening comes, one goes to gamble, the other to his concubine. Where they ought to pray quietly for the dead, they eat and drink abundantly, chatter excessively. . . ."

These symptoms of degeneracy, at which Savonarola lashed out, reflect a disintegration within the Church that had long since given rise to countermovements, for public criticism of the moral ills of the Church had been going on for centuries. In 1176 the Waldensians had appeared; they strove for a simple and purified Christianity of apostolic poverty, but were cruelly persecuted in a veritable "crusade." Remnants of them have remained to this day in northern Italy. In 1383–1384 John Wycliffe, professor of theology at Oxford, denounced the pope as Antichrist. So that all the people might read the true Gospel, he translated the Bible into English. No measures were taken against him in his lifetime, but he was condemned as a heretic posthumously; forty-four years after his death the pope had his bones burned. Wycliffe influenced John Huss (circa 1370–1415) and Jerome of Prague, whose religious reform movements gave rise to the Hussites and the Bohemian Brethren.

John Huss, who preached against the secularization of the clergy and the ownership of property by monasteries, sought to make spiritual office dependent upon the moral worth of the holder. Aside from its practical implications, this principle violated the Catholic concept of the Church as an objective institution. Called to the Council of Constance in order to defend his doctrines in person, he was arrested in spite of his imperial safe-conduct and burned at the stake as a heretic, for violence and trickery were permissible against heretics as "enemies of God." The Inquisition had been organized in 1251 to track down apostates and heretics and subject them to death by fire in order to purify them of their sins. Since Huss had also called for ecclesiastical independence for Bohemia, he became the martyr and national hero of the Czechs, who rose up in revolt and were crushed in the bloody Hussite wars (1420–1436).

The intensified religious feeling of the late Middle Ages was also expressed in a movement toward contemplation and solitary mystical experience. The Dominican monks Meister Eckart (died 1327) and his disciple Johannes Tauler held that the goal of Christian devotion was the birth of God as an inner light within the soul. Isolation from the world and tranquillity of soul ("surrender to God") would lead to that goal. In the Netherlands Thomas à Kempis (1380–1471), to whom is ascribed the *Imitation of Christ*, was a representative of this mystical school; and an unknown author in Germany wrote a small mystical book, probably around 1400, which was later to be published by Luther under the title of *German Theology*.

With the onset of the fourteenth century, Europe was swept by the twin movements of the Renaissance and humanism, which looked back to classical antiquity for models of human achievement. Their birthplace was Italy, but their impact was felt throughout Europe. Along with a remarkable flowering of the arts, there was an enthusiasm for the learned study of ancient languages. Classical clarity of form became, for the humanists and the men of the Renaissance, the standard of a superior humanity. A new cultural goal arose: cultivation of all the spiritual qualities within men, in order to develop the individual personality. Man as the measure of all things stood in the center of an overwhelmingly optimistic view of the cosmos.

With the watchword *ad fontes*, "to the sources," men turned above all to a study of the Bible in the original languages. The art of printing, which began around 1450, made it possible for every man thirsty for knowledge to possess a New Testament in Greek and his own language.

Out of German humanism erupted the first powerful movement to break with Rome. The German freedom for which such a man as Ulrich von Hutten (died 1523) called meant freedom from the Roman Church, freedom for the national church to develop after its own fashion. Hutten was one of the co-authors of the notorious *Letters of Obscure Men*, which mocked the opponents of humanism and voiced that humanistic battle cry: "O century, O science! It is a joy to live! Studies flourish, minds stir!"

Erasmus of Rotterdam (1465–1536) sought to reconcile Christianity and culture; but came to view religion in entirely humanistic terms independent of Church and dogma. While protesting abuses in the Church, Erasmus remained Catholic. Humanism and the Renaissance made formidable contributions to the premises on which the Reformation was based. In calling for religion to turn "back to the sources," the Reformers were following the example of the humanists—who, to be sure, never comprised more than an intellectual elite. Humanism as a cultural movement was only one element of the epoch which reached its apex in the Reformation.

THE REFORMATION

The beginning of the Reformation can be dated precisely to October 31, 1517, when the Augustinian monk Martin Luther posted his famous ninety-five theses on the portal of the palace church in Wittenberg, a small country town of two thousand inhabitants "on the frontier of civilization," as Luther himself once said. There was already widespread dissatisfaction with the traffic in indulgences, the sacrament of penance having degenerated into a moneymaking device on the part of ecclesiastic interests.

Though Luther had not meant it so, the time was so apposite that the posting of the theses became the signal for a general storm.

News of the theses spread like wildfire through Germany. Disputations, first within Luther's own order (at Heidelberg in April 1518), then with the Ingolstadt preacher Dr. Eck in Leipzig in the summer of 1519, then a denunciation by the Dominicans in Rome, which preluded the trial of Luther for heresy, were the first consequences. Martin Luther answered the papal bull threatening him with excommunication by publicly burning the document. That revolutionary act kindled greater flames than had the imposition of the ban, which in the past had brought Peter Waldo, Huss, and their followers to the stake. Luther was the first man to burn a papal bull without being himself burned. At the request of his overlord, Electoral Prince Frederick the Wise of Saxony, Luther appeared at Worms for a hearing before the emperor and the Diet of the Empire. The momentous hearing took place on April 17 and 18, 1521; Luther refused to recant various theses he had written in the meanwhile, in which he had taken issue with the papacy and the infallibility of councils. They, too, could err, he contended, and averred that he would be imperiling his soul to do anything against conscience— "God help me, Amen." On the way back from the Diet he was "captured" by the Prince of Saxony's mounted men and carried off to the Wartburg, where his overlord could keep him safe from the imperial ban and the hands of his enemies.

The third decade of the sixteenth century saw the really stormy years of the Reformation: the uprising of the knight Franz von Sickingen against the power of the princes, and the social revolution of the peasants in 1525. Luther, though first favoring their cause, furiously denounced the insurgents in a pamphlet entitled "Against the Thievish and Murderous Hordes of Peasants." In thus disassociating himself from this movement, Luther saved the Reformation from the danger of being crushed along with the peasants, but he did so at a high price. After 1525 it became clear that the Reformation could not be a cause of the entire Empire, nor could it become an all-embracing popular movement. After the collapse of their uprising the peasants were rather inclined to look to the Anabaptists for religious identity.

Martin Luther himself had meanwhile performed another

iconoclastic act by his marriage to Katharina von Bora. This double breach of celibacy—an apostate monk marrying a runaway nun—was the height of offensiveness to the medieval sensibility.

The Emperor Charles V, whose ideas had remained medieval, attempted in vain to exterminate the new heresy; his efforts came too late. The Protestants, as they had been called since their protest at the Diet of Speyer (1529), demanded recognition of their creed in the law of the Empire. The decision on this question was to be taken in 1530, at the Diet of Augsburg. Martin Luther himself could not attend this diet, since the ban of the Empire had been imposed upon him. The burden of the struggle was born by his conciliatory fellow fighter, Philipp Melanchthon (1497–1560), who formulated the Augsburg Confession. This was originally intended to pave the way for a reconciliation with the Catholics; it provided for retention of the episcopate, the sacramental order and the liturgy of the old Church. But agreement could not be reached; by the end of the Diet the religious factions in Germany were far apart. The Protestant territories joined together in the Schmalkaldic League (February 1531) in order to defy any attempt to suppress their faith by force. Thus Protestantism became organized as a political party and the emperor had to consent to a truce.

After years of struggle, during which the cause of Protestantism was sometimes brought to the verge of extinction, a valid basis for religious peace was at last found at another Augsburg Diet in 1555. The principle of religious "liberty" was established, the basis being that the sovereign of a given part of the Empire could decide its religion: *cuius regio, eius religio.* "The Catholics, however, made the stipulation that an ecclesiastical prince must renounce his office if he changed his religion. This provision saved Catholicism in Germany, for otherwise the supporters of the old religion would scarcely have retained a single ecclesiastical territory. . . . Thus the great goal was achieved. The Protestants had obtained imperial recognition. The German estates had settled the religious question without consulting the pope or a council. The Augsburg religious peace was, of course, very far from establishing religious liberty in the modern sense. Only the estates of the Reich, that is, the princes or the magistrates of the cities, had free choice, and even they could choose only between

Catholicism and the Augsburg Confession. The sects, among which was reckoned Calvinism, had no protection. Subjects who did not share the creed of their sovereign were accorded only the right of emigrating" (Johannes Paul).

The Religious Peace of Augsburg, which concluded the Age of Reformation proper, provided for a new order on the basis of a political compromise. It was to lead to a great variety of disputes and, ultimately, to the outbreak of the Thirty Years' War. Gradually, however, the hostile confessions were more and more compelled to tolerate one another.

If we now regard the Reformation in terms of religious history, we must ask: What was Martin Luther's principal concern? The answer is to be found in the first of the ninety-five theses on indulgences: "When our Lord Jesus Christ says, 'Do penance, the Kingdom of Heaven draws near,' he wishes that the whole life of believers should be penance." According to Luther, neither the indulgence which the priest confers out of the Church's store of grace, nor any vicarious authority, opens the way to salvation. What does open the way is man's living entirely for his faith, showing that his whole life has become a penance. Almighty God, whose requirements shame all our efforts, all our good works, does not reject us in his righteous wrath, but justifies us, sinners though we are, unmeritedly, out of pure grace. We cannot choose God, but the *Deus absconditus,* the hidden God, chooses us, and transforms us, useless as we are, into a fitting instrument for his works. In requiring that Christian life be lived solely in terms of faith, Luther confronted man with the solitude of inner decision in the presence of God. But man does not possess belief or unbelief; rather, these are events that happen within him. For Christian belief will never be man's secure possession; it is always wavering in an eternal dialectic of having and not-having. "I believe, Lord, help Thou my unbelief," Luther's prayer, *Simul peccator, simul justus*—sinner and just man at one and the same time: that is the Christian in Luther's eyes.

Luther wrestled with a problem that for the most part has become very remote from modern man, namely, the distance between God and man, God's infinite sanctity and justice, and man's insurmountable sinfulness and injustice. The solution involved the concepts of *sola gratia* (by grace alone) and *sola fide* (by faith alone). God's justice, however, cannot be demanded by man, or obtained through good works or dutiful worship. Rather, God of his free choice confers upon men the gift of being able to believe.

Justification through faith alone was the heart of the Reformation. From his studies of Paul's epistles, Luther had concluded that salvation is an unearned gift of God, conferred by belief in the divine promise that Christ by his death had atoned for all sins. Justified man, however, has free access to God without the mediation of the sacraments, priests or saints. Thus Luther's doctrine led to acceptance of the universal priesthood of believers and, necessarily, to rejection of the infallibility of popes and councils, and to emphasis on holy scripture as the sole and sufficient basis for doctrine.

The impact of Luther's translation of the Bible upon the development of the German language is too well known to need further discussion. Luther placed the Bible in the hands of all the people. His *Songbook* made the Protestant Church a singing Church. The Lutheran choral is a unique blending of doctrine, worship and praise, in vigorous words and often with magnificent melodies. And the Lutheran catechism for instruction in the biblical truths proved to be a novel form of teaching, and a fundamental force in the religious education of the populace. The Catholic Church imitated it by instituting the *Catechismus Romanus* (1566).

Luther also introduced a wholly new occupational ethic. All honest work devoutly done is sanctified, he declared. Every secular occupation, high or low, is fulfillment of a divine assignment; for everyone can and ought to be God's co-worker, from stable hand to highborn sovereign. In view of original sin, he regarded the state—or as he put it, "authority"—as essential to keep the masses in check. If all men were Christian, he argued in a sermon, no authority would be needed. But "we serve in a tavern where the devil is master and the world is mistress." That will never change; there will never be a Kingdom of God on earth. "The world is a stable full of wicked rascals; therefore one must have laws and authority, judges, executioners, the sword, the gallows, and all such things, to keep down the wicked rascals."

Luther wrote indefatigably on a vast variety of subjects—the Weimar edition of his complete works runs to ninety volumes. But perhaps he may be said to have summed up his lifework in the famous note found after his death: "No one can understand Virgil's *Bucolics* unless he has been a herdsman for five years; no one can understand the letters of Cicero unless he has lived and moved in a great commonwealth for twenty-five years. Let no one think he has tasted enough of the Holy Scriptures unless he has ruled the congregation with Prophets like Elijah and Elisha, John the Baptist, Christ and the Apostles. . . . We are beggars —that is true."

Hanns Lilje has construed these words thus: "For more than two centuries men have sought to proclaim and to live the autonomy of man. Today it is plain to all that this human attempt at rebellion has gone astray. The individual who made himself the measure of all things has now begun to doubt himself, and finds himself homeless as never before in the cosmos that he wanted to dominate without God and without any supernatural allegiances. As opposed to all man's 'achievements,' which in the end have become a deadly menace to him, these last words of Luther serve as admonition and warning. He was right and the whole modern world wrong. 'We are beggars—that is true.' But in the end it does not matter that we are beggars; for behind Luther's last words stands that faith in God which is the hope of the lowly, the consolation of sinners, the life of the dying, and which fills the empty hands of beggars."

ZWINGLI AND CALVIN

Alongside the dynamic and tormented Martin Luther, who throughout his life wrestled with the question of how sinful man can find a merciful God and partake of salvation, stands the far more gracious personality of Huldreich Zwingli (1484–1531), the Zurich Reformer. His humanistic background and the special political conditions of Switzerland led him to transform Lutheran ideas into a more practical and rationalistic form. Communion, in particular, had a different meaning for Zwingli; unlike Luther, he viewed the presence of Christ in the sacrament only in a spiritual sense. He was anxious to prevent any possible perversion of the sacrament into magic. The two men parted ways over this question.

Zwingli, who in some respects stood quite close to Erasmus of Rotterdam theologically, attempted to effect a union between the Reformation and humanism. In the course of a Swiss civil war, he fell on the field of battle in 1531, fighting for the cause of Protestantism. Luther took this death as a judgment upon Zwingli for his having wielded the sword, although a man of God. Zwingli, however, had regarded himself as a soldier of Christ; he was thus the prototype of the political Christian and the Christian politician under Protestantism.

John Calvin (1509–1564) was a Reformer of the second generation. The marks of his legal training were never quite erased from his character, which remained cool and intellectual. Expelled from his home, he published at the age of twenty-seven the *Institutio religionis Christianae*. Up to the end of his life he worked on a systematic presentation of Protestant doctrine, with emphasis upon the dominion of God and the power of God's unalterable will. This work was one of the most remarkable intellectual feats of the Reformation. Calvin extended the Pauline or Augustinian doctrine of predestination to the conclusion that both the election of the saved and the rejection of the damned arises from an unalterable decree of God. From this doctrine of "double predestination" Anglo-Saxon followers of Calvin concluded that God's election will be demonstrated in worldly happiness and prosperity. It has been asserted that the economic attitudes of modern capitalism had their roots in these teachings.

To Luther good works were signs and fruits of faith. To Calvin they were signs of divine election—for which reason he, too, placed the greatest emphasis upon them. Not the justification of God, but public witness to the honor of God occupied the center of his thinking. In Geneva Calvin succeeded in building a community of remarkable discipline, which was intended to be a forecasting of the Kingdom of God. Calvin himself became the overlord of this Protestant city-state and exercised the strictest control over the moral life of his community. He firmly believed that the Kingdom of God had been advancing toward realization in the course of history, and that secular states had their contribution to make to it. This idea continues to exert political effects to this day, for the Geneva Reformation—in spite of what can be said of Calvin's inclinations toward tyranny—did in fact link religious with political freedom. Geneva became a model of public responsibility for Western Europe—and has remained so to this day.

All his life Luther was the subject of a prince, not master of Wittenberg as Calvin was master of Geneva. Luther preached under the protection of his sovereign and favored an ethics of obedience which all too frequently led him and his followers to withdraw from public responsibility to the privacy of their own consciences. On the other hand, Calvin's lofty aspirations to create a Kingdom of God here and now helped to shape the English and American national mentalities, and to give to Western democracy, secularized though it is, a religious emotionalism such as is unknown in Germany. The crusade of Christian soldiers against the enemies of freedom and democracy became a political and religious reality to England and America. That, too, must be set down among the world-historical consequences of the Reformation.

Why did Luther's conviction that man can be justified by faith alone lead to a split in the Church which has persisted for more than four hundred years? Could not the "freedom of a Christian" have been attained within the one great Catholic Church? The question has been debated for centuries. It cannot be proved that the Reformation necessarily had to lead to the formation of a new Church, nor can it be proved that such an outcome could have been avoided if Luther had encountered a more conciliatory response on the part of the mother Church. The scandal erupted, the schism took place; and in spite of many ecumenical efforts a reunion of the Reformation churches with Rome still seems utterly inconceivable. The dogma formulated ex cathedra by Pope Pius XII on November 1, 1950, of the physical Ascension of Mary seems only to have deepened the gulf between faith and dogma. The true Protestant again feels himself to be what Luther was, a lifelong rebel protesting against the doctrinal authority of an infallible church and contending that only what Christ himself taught has validity. To be sure, the modern Protestant would scarcely regard the pope as the incarnate Antichrist that Luther saw; but he believes today as Protestants believed four hundred years ago that the papal church has diverged from the pure teachings of the Word of God.

On the other hand, Catholic theologians, historians and apologists have repeatedly pointed out that the Reformation represents the greatest breach of tradition in all time, that it not only destroyed the religiously determined, unified culture of the Middle Ages, but also caused that chain reaction of political revolutions and upheavals which have continued from 1789 down to our own time. Moreover, from the Catholic point of view, the Protestant concept of the Church is its weakest point, providing as it does neither for succession of offices nor for coherent hierarchical organization. Since he himself imminently expected the Second Coming, Luther contented himself with improvisations and emergency solutions in questions of ecclesiastical organization. These subsequently became permanent institutions. It has been said that the Reformation ground to a halt in the Old Lutheran orthodoxy of the sixteenth and seventeenth centuries, and that even then Protestantism began misunderstanding itself. But it is also true that it suffered the penalty of its origins. Having arisen out of protest, it engendered more and more sects and independent churches which were in protest against it.

While no further sects appeared in Catholicism, Protestantism spawned a great many more during the seventeenth century. Basically, the doctrine of universal priesthood bore its natural fruit; the laity had escaped from wardship and were asserting their independence. This process had a tremendous influence upon the individualization of the newly developing bourgeois world.

The splintering of Protestantism, however, also brought to light many tensions that had been inherent in the movement from the beginning. Innumerable tendencies and their related theologies have sprung up, from "verbal inspiration"—belief in the divinity of individual letters of the Bible—all the way to "demythologization" of the Bible by rational, scientific textual criticism; from joyful affirmation of civilization to sharpest criticism of civilization and a view that a divine judgment is leveled against all the works of man. The history of the Protestant church from the Religious Peace of Augsburg to the present day has been shaped both by developments in different nations and by the great intellectual currents of the modern age.

In the age of religious wars Protestantism tended to develop a rigid dogmatism of its own. By the end of the Age of the Reformation, the fierce emotion and shock that had given rise to the faith of the Reformers had considerably diminished, giving way to a new, more tranquil self-assurance. The struggle for purity of doctrine frequently became petrified in formalistic self-righteousness, and sterile denominational bickerings were commonplace.

The Enlightenment unleashed the forces of rationality, philosophical idealism, romanticism and revivalism during the eighteenth and nineteenth centuries. The age of individualism and secularism, which has continued to the present day, gave rise to a variety of theological doctrines and movements in ecclesiastical politics. The Enlightenment, which led politically to the French Revolution of 1789, successfully established beneficent principles of tolerance, and the right of the individual to develop his own religious personality. But its rationalistic tendency also undermined the old church-oriented piety and prepared the way for modern man's unbelief, his lack of a spiritual dimension and conviction that he no longer needs divine mercy.

Common to all schools of Protestantism is the belief that the authority of the holy scriptures is superior to that of the Church, and that the message of the Church must be constantly derived anew from the Gospels. Proper understanding of holy scripture ought to reveal the depths of Christianity. Faith is the precondition for grace; it is never a human achievement, far less a magically effective sacrament, but a divine gift. The churches of the Reformations are congregations of believers in which the Gospel is rightly preached and the sacraments obediently administered.

THE COUNTER REFORMATION

The Counter Reformation, which might better be called the Catholic Reformation, resulted in the creation of a number of new monastic orders (Capuchins, Ursulines, etc.). The most important of these was the *Societas Jesu,* founded by Ignatius de

Loyola (1491–1556). The decisions of the Council of Trent, which met from 1545–1563, abolished many of those abuses within the Church to which the Reformers had objected—among them the sale of indulgences and of livings. Along with holy scripture, the traditions of the Church were declared to be sources of the dogma, and a Catholic doctrine of justification was, in answer to Luther, attached to the sacrament. The doctrine of the Catholic Church was formulated in the Tridentine Creed of 1564. This was the definitive and only valid creed which henceforth every priest had to affirm.

The Jesuits, strictly organized on military lines under a general of the order, proved to be a major instrument in spreading the faith and regaining lapsed territories. The order placed itself unconditionally at the service of the Chair of St. Peter. Jesuits served as confessors at the courts of many sovereigns, as educators of upper-class youths, for whom they founded excellent schools throughout Europe, and as missionaries in the Far East (India, Japan, China) and in the New World. The *Spiritual Exercises*, a textbook by Ignatius that is used to this day, exerted enormous influence; it taught men to approach a given spiritual goal by strict exercises of the will and also trained novices in that unconditional obedience to their superiors which was so vital to the order.

As a result of the Catholic Reformation, which was propagated principally by the Society of Jesus, a large part of Germany was won back to the influence of Rome. In France the flourishing Calvinist Church was almost annihilated on bloody St. Bartholomew's Night in 1572. In Poland, Bohemia, Moravia and Hungary Protestantism was forced back; in Spain and Italy Reformist tendencies were crushed by the Inquisition, which had been newly organized at Trent and subordinated to a congregation of cardinals (the Holy Office). But the real goal, the extermination of Protestantism, could no longer be achieved. One political result of the age of the Reformation was that Spain lost her dominant position, and that alongside of France, the Catholic great power in Europe, there appeared several Protestant great powers: England, Holland, Sweden, Denmark and, in the following century, Prussia.

"The piety of post-Tridentine Catholicism was characterized by mystical and crudely superstitious overtones. Many new saints and relics were adopted. The confessional, the Mass and communion acquired intensified importance. Everlasting worship of the Host, frequent enjoyment of the sacrament, the cult of the Heart of Jesus and the Heart of Mary arose. Cultivation of this type of religiosity, with its fondness for the miraculous and its sensual, narcotic features, deepened the gulf between Catholicism and Protestantism" (Heussi). Everywhere, and especially in South Germany, new pilgrimage churches were founded. Ritual became pompous and was elaborated in many ways. Many of the elements of religion that the Enlightenment later mocked as foolish became popular at this time, such as the practice of displaying effigies of healed limbs in churches. The use of the confessional was greatly increased—all emphasis was placed now on the outward forms of religion.

The further development of the Catholic Church was bound up with its political future in various nations. There was none of that frequent splintering, such as became commonplace in Protestantism, nor did national churches independent of Rome take shape. The anti-Jesuit Jansenists in seventeenth-century France remained within the Church, even though their Augustinian doctrines were condemned. Blaise Pascal (1635–1662), the great religious thinker, was close to the Jansenists. Of the more important groups, only the Old Catholics left the Church because they would not accept the dogma of papal infallibility. (Today they have some 225,000 members in Europe and 550,000 in America.) With that decree in 1870 Catholicism achieved its seemingly conclusive hierarchical form. The heresies with which Catholicism has had to deal in modern times have been chiefly political and ideological; and the papacy has, in numerous bulls and encyclicals, dealt with these as well as with the inadequacies of our social order. One example among many is the bull *Rerum novarum* of Pope Leo XIII in 1891.

CATHOLICISM TODAY

The Roman Catholic Church is by far the largest of all the Christian churches. Statistics on its world membership hover be-

tween 393 and 470 million. The first figure—that is, 50.7 per cent
of all Christians—seems more probable. According to its own
dogma, the Catholic Church is the Mystical Body of Christ, that
is, the visible union of all orthodox Christians. Catholic belief
holds that the Church is *holy* because it leads men to holiness by
its holy doctrines and sacraments. As an instrument of redemption it is necessary to the salvation of all men. There are two
classes in the membership of the Church: the hierarchically organized clergy, and the great mass of laity. Furthermore, the
Church is *catholic* (extending over the whole earth), because
it has spread through all countries and because its blessings extend to all men—that is, it seeks to make all partake of Christ's
work of Redemption. There is only one Christian Church that
merits the epithet catholic, in Roman belief, even though historical developments have abridged the Catholic absolutistic
claim ("there is no salvation outside the Church"), since there
are now many churches independent of Rome which preach the
tidings of Christ. Finally, the Church is *apostolic* because it derives from the Apostles and because the pope and the bishops,
through the sacrament of consecration, constitute an unbroken
succession of bearers of ecclesiastical office.

The Church administers the holy sacraments, whose purpose
is to unite the believer with the Body of Christ, and which ob-
jectively, of their own accord, make for salvation. At the Council
of Trent the number of the sacraments was definitively fixed at
seven: Baptism, confirmation, communion, penance, consecration of priests, marriage, extreme unction. The Catholic view
holds that all the sacraments were instituted by Christ himself
and that their effect is independent of the mind of the giver or
the receiver, so long as the latter does not impose any inward
barrier to their reception.

Since the Reformation the number of Catholic orders has increased greatly. Many congregations, most of them with educa-
tional or missionary assignments, have sprung up alongside the
older monastic communities.

After the First Vatican Council the Catholic hierarchy comprised 15 patriarchs, 1,340 resident archbishops, 70 prelates directly subordinate to the Curia, and 12 apostolic administrators.

At the head of this pyramid stands the pope as the receptacle of all spiritual powers. Among his titles is "Sovereign of the State of Vatican City." Of his secular power, the States of the Church, only Vatican City has been left him. Yet it has a symbolic significance that this tiny state possesses its own army, police, coinage, judiciary, railroad station, radio, post office and daily newspaper (*Osservatore Romano*).

The Curia Romana ("Roman Court") constitutes a regular government of the Church authorities residing in Rome. The present Curia includes eighty-six cardinals, who are divided into cardinal-bishops, cardinal-priests and cardinal-deacons. In 1586 the number of cardinals was fixed by Pope Sixtus V at seventy, and this limit was not breached until 1958. Within the College of Cardinals there are thirty-three curial cardinals and fifty-two cardinals who reside outside of Rome. The pope appoints cardinals from among the bishops; along with the cardinal's purple, they then have the right to participate in the election of the pope, which takes place in a conclave in the Vatican. At other assemblages of cardinals, only crowned heads and royal princes are permitted to participate as equals. Cardinals, with the title of "prefects," head the "congregations," which may be compared to secular ministries. There are a dozen of these to deal with various aspects of Church life from the Holy Office to the Congregation for the Eastern Churches, the title of which is self-explanatory. In addition there are curial courts, penitential courts, a supreme court of appeal. "Furthermore, there are five papal offices. The foremost of these is the Secretariat of State, which deals with matters of world politics. Its holder, the Cardinal Secretary of State, is the pope's confidant and alter ego; his tenure ceases with the pope's death. He is more or less the prime minister and foreign minister at once. Papal envoys are subordinate to him, especially the nuncios who enjoy the courtesy of precedence over all other ambassadors." (W. Philipp.)

This imposing organization reflects the Vatican as a world power. But in spite of all the pomp, it ultimately serves only spiritual ends and is considered by the Church as needful to the fulfillment of Christ's commission to Peter: "Pasture my lambs!" (John 21: 15).

THE SECOND VATICAN COUNCIL[*]

On January 25, 1959, a few months after his accession, Pope John XXIII (Angelo Roncalli) surprised his own Curia, Christendom and the world by announcing the holding of a General Council, which has already gone down in history as the Second Vatican Council (the First was held in 1869–1870 under Pius IX). In his diaries the pope records that, absorbed in prayer, he heard "in the intimacy and simplicity of our mind a divine invitation to convoke an ecumenical council." The response to the announcement of the council was on the whole favorable.

In the course of the preparations for the council, a secretariat for the unity of Christians was set up under the direction of the German curial cardinal Augustin Bea, S.J. This secretariat was a novel creation which had no precedent within the curial organization. Bea was responsible for quietly preparing contacts with non-Catholic Christian churches and for inviting observers. It was largely due to his work that most non-Catholic churches sent observers to the council.

In the bull convoking the council, which John XXIII issued on December 25, 1961, he called upon the members of the council to "go to work now joyfully and fearlessly and confer upon this age-old, eternal doctrine a meaning that corresponds to the conditions of our time." This program of modernization, summed up in the word *aggiornamento*, quickly became a settled concept. John XXIII was calling for more than a retracing of the well-worn ruts of doctrine and repetition of formulas from theological textbooks. He was determined to have a new unfolding and illumination of Catholic truths for modern man in a language he can understand.

The first session of Vatican II, as it was soon popularly called, opened on October 11, 1962, and lasted until December 8, 1962. At the first plenary session, the council fathers were presented with more than seventy texts which had been drawn up by the numerous preparatory commissions. Before the end of the second session these had been reduced to seventeen schemata, as they

[*] The author is indebted to his assistant, Kurt Töpner, who contributed this chapter on the Catholic Church during the Second Vatican Council.

were called; because of the abundance of material, culled from 8,972 separate suggestions of the higher church dignitaries throughout the world, it became essential to formulate central topics around which peripheral matters were grouped. In the course of the council, all the texts were greatly reduced. The schema "On Catholic Schools," for instance, was compressed to one and one-half pages and transformed into a simple declaration of principles. Whether the abbreviated version of the schema "On Marriage" can be retained seems questionable, since the debate on birth control and contraceptive pills has begun to stir vigorous concern even in the Catholic Church, and will certainly be brought to Rome by many of the council fathers. Only one of the schema was not drawn up by the preparatory commissions, but proposed during the council itself. That is the schema "On the Effective Presence of the Church in the World of Today." The schemata "On the Mass Media" and "On the Liturgy" were passed during the second session of 1963, and by 1965 the reformed liturgy, with parts of the Mass in the vernacular, had been introduced in most of the world.

The first session in 1962, held under the pontificate of John XXIII, yielded no results in the sense of fully formulated and accepted schemata. Among the subjects debated were the liturgy, the sources of revelation, the means of communication, and the unity of the Church. Thus early in the council the factions were clearly defined. The conservative curial party had a disproportionately large influence because its members for the most part sat in key posts on the commissions. Confronting them were far larger numbers of would-be reformers. Heated debates were quite common at the council. The most famous of them was the clash between Cardinals Ottaviani and Frings over the question of the Index of Forbidden Books. Majorities shifted frequently over different questions. While during the first two sessions the wedge of reformers consisted chiefly of German and French bishops, in the discussions on religious freedom and the relationship of the Catholic Church to the Jews, the English and American episcopates became the foremost advocates of *aggiornamento*.

The schema "On Ecumenism" was largely the work of Cardinal Bea. The original draft, however, was shortened from five chapters to three. The excised chapters were those dealing with freedom of religion and conscience, which encountered opposition from members of the Curia and had to be discussed as independent declarations during the fourth session of the council in 1965. The so-called "declaration on the Jews" in particular aroused sharp criticism by conservative forces at the council and also—on opposite grounds—by Jews. The first draft had stated that no blame for the death of Christ on the Cross could be ascribed to "the Jews of our time." The revised declaration blames the death of Christ neither on the "Jews of our time" nor the Jewish people of that time, but on "the leaders of Judaism in Jerusalem." In spite of the desire to arrive at a reconciliation with Judaism manifested by these words, the response by leading representatives of religious Judaism was highly critical in connection with other issues. Thus, for example, Rav Isser Jehuda Untermann stated: "From the start we did not believe in a change of mind on the Vatican's part in regard to Judaism. But what particularly offended me about this declaration was the proposal that the Jews convert to Christianity. To make such a proposal to the Jews today! Now, after they have remained true to their faith in spite of rivers of blood."

The constitution "On the Church," together with the decree on ecumenism, was passed on November 21, 1964, and solemnly proclaimed by Pope Paul VI. It concerned chiefly the upgrading of the office of bishop and the participation of the bishops in the government of the Universal Church—although in an advisory capacity, for papal privileges were retained. Nevertheless, the trend was clearly in a direction opposite to that of Vatican I.

Pope John XXIII died on June 3, 1963. On June 21, 1963, Giovanni Battista Montini, Archbishop of Milan, was elected to succeed him. Montini took the name of Paul VI. He was regarded as a moderate reformer. The character of the council was stamped by these two popes, John and Paul. John XXIII has sometimes been portrayed as a rather coarse, peasant personality who stumbled into the papacy and had no deeper insight into the nature of the office. Such a view does not do him justice. Along with a natural charm, he had intuition and keenness of intellect, wisdom and kindness. His encyclical *Pacem in Terris* of 1963 took the world by surprise. He spoke directly of nuclear disarmament, called off the battle against communists and secularists and nevertheless emphasized the Catholic point of view toward these modern phenomena. Above all, for the first time a pope affirmed the individual's right to subjective religious convictions, no matter what the teachings of the Catholic Church might be.

John may be compared to an open fire, Paul VI to a steely blue acetylene torch with a high utility value. Paul is a clear, sharp thinker with a bias for caution and restraint. He does not have the capacity for the global view, and he lacks the quality of natural force. His trip to the Holy Land in January 1964 was not the fruit of a personal inspiration, but was due to the influence of the French priest Pierre Gauthier, who lives in a kibbutz on Lake Gennesaret. One of the high points of this trip was the meeting with Athenagoras I, the Patriarch of Constantinople and honorary primate of the Orthodox Churches. On that pilgrimage Paul proved himself a diplomat of a high order; all possible consequences of his words and actions were carefully thought out. He is scarcely likely to be capable of the spontaneity that his predecessor displayed when he convoked the council, but he is quite able to carry on the work that has been begun.

Both popes, as well as the council, are too close to us to permit any final judgment upon them. For the Catholic Church, however, the "revolution from above" initiated by John XXIII and continued by the council can no longer be reversed. It is an epoch-making event in the history of the Church.

CHRISTIANITY TODAY

The second great branch of Christianity consists of the Orthodox Churches of the East, most of which are divided up into smaller units on a national basis. Orthodox Christians make up about eighteen per cent of Christendom; there are about 150 to 160 million of them, although the figures of the largest body of all, the Russian Orthodox Church, are obscure nowadays. Orthodox Churches outside the USSR have a membership, according to recent estimates, of about fifty-five million.

All these churches have developed out of the old church of Byzantium, the Eastern half of the Roman Empire, and are linked to one another by common dogma and ritual. Even after the fall of the Eastern Roman Empire in 1453, the Patriarch of Constantinople retained honorary precedence among the heads of the so-called autocephalous churches; but his actual powers diminished steadily with the decay of Turkish rule. Today the Patriarch of Moscow, who historically has no claim to the distinction, seeks precedence within the world Orthodox Churches. Since 1917 the Russian Church has suffered severe persecution; but during the Second World War, when the new Russian-Soviet patriotism flourished, it was able to consolidate its position once more by throwing its support behind the government. It is, however, not free to make its own decisions.

The four great patriarchates of the Orthodox world are those of Constantinople, Alexandria, Antioch and Jerusalem. Numerous national churches are subordinate to these four, but there are also autonomous and partly autonomous churches, as well as special churches of emigrants in Europe and America. A special case are the "Orthodox Catholic Churches" in the Orient, which are Monophysite—that is, they split off in the course of the struggle over the Creed of Chalcedon: the Coptic Church in Egypt (approximately 1.5 million members), the Ethiopian Church, originally dependent on it (approximately 8 million members), and the Armenian Church (approximately 3 million) are the most important of these. They are generally referred to collectively as the Oriental Churches.

The churches of the Reformation represent the third section of Christendom. Some 224 million or 28.9 per cent of all Christians belong to them. Almost eighty million are Protestants in lineal descent from Martin Luther, most of whom are in Europe; about forty-five million belong to the Reformed or Presbyterian Church; the remaining seventy to eighty million are divided among Methodists (about forty million) and a wide variety of denominations: Adventists, Baptists, Jehovah's Witnesses, Salvation Army, Christian Scientists, and others. The Anglicans (about twenty-six million) count only their regular *communicants*, while the larger churches count all the baptized, so that statistics are difficult to compare. Finally there are Theosophists and Anthroposophists—marginal groups.

THE PRESENT SITUATION AND THE NEED FOR TOLERANCE

Here, at the end of our discussion, let us look at some of the statistics on religions, since the notions about the distribution of religions over the globe are often wholly erroneous. It must be stated, however, that the figures are only approximate, and that most of them date back to the era between the two world wars, since at present only estimates are available for great regions of the world. Moreover, for the Far Eastern religions all the figures are inexact because millions of Asiatics respond to such questionnaires by declaring themselves adherents of several religions, since they do not distinguish among religions in terms of "either-or," but rather in terms of "both this and that." Thus many Japanese are Shintoists on happy occasions; on sad occasions they prefer to be Buddhists. We must keep this factor in mind when we consider our statistics. Half of the approximately 3.2 billion human beings on earth today are Asiatics; the whole of Europe has a smaller population than China. Given all these reservations, we may divide the religions of humanity approximately as follows:

Christians	950,550,000	= 29.4%
Mohammedans	456,000,000	= 14.2%
Jews (prewar 16,000,000)	13,000,000	= 0.4%
Chinese folk religion	390,000,000	= 12.2%
Hindus	395,000,000	= 12.3%
Buddhists	162,000,000	= 5%
Taoists	51,000,000	= 1.6%
Shintoists	67,000,000	= 2.1%
Primitive tribal religions	170,000,000	= 5.3%
Other, uncertain or no religion	560,000,000	= 17.5%

It is apparent from this table that the Far Eastern religions are numerically superior to Christianity, whose share, proportionally, in the earth's population, has long been gradually diminishing. Moreover, it must be considered that the population of the USSR, though ascribed to the Russian Orthodox Church, is to an unknown extent no longer attached to any church at all. What the percentage is cannot be determined. In 1939 there were, to be

sure, only six million organized atheists; but the number of un-
organized atheists in Europe and America—including those pur-
portedly Christian—does not appear in any statistics and cannot
be established with any degree of accuracy.

The present situation is characterized by a restive searching in
all the world's religions, an attempt to translate the original
message of each religion into the terms of a world transformed
by technology, so that modern man will once again be able to
understand the ancient tidings of salvation. Now that modern
communications have brought the five continents closer and
closer together, intellectual and spiritual contacts and attempts
at interpenetration between the great religions have become
much more common than in the past—even though China and
India entered the purview of cultivated Europe in the sixteenth
and seventeenth centuries. Nowadays, however, there is a distinct tendency in the West to extend a cordial welcome to religious ideas from India and China. Widespread pessimism about
the future of civilization, and an unsatisfied longing for new ways
to salvation, have even produced eclectic religions drawing upon
both the Christian and Hindu spiritual heritages, such as theosophy and anthroposophy. There is also Bahai, which springs from
a union of Christian and Persian religious ideas.

On the other hand, Christian concepts, both good and bad,
linked with European technology and civilization, have been
penetrating the Far East with increasing force. However, there
is a distinct limit to all attempts at a religious rapprochement between the West and the Far East. As we have already seen, given
the fundamental differences in the conceptions of reality and
attitudes toward the world, no real synthesis can be expected.

If we compare the religions we have discussed in this book in
terms of the essential core of each, we will most easily perceive
their incompatible elements. None of these religions can really
accommodate to or draw closer to the others; each must claim
to be the way, the truth and the life at least for its own believers,
and Christianity actually makes that claim for all men. No world
religion can seriously consider abandoning its absolutistic claim.
If it did, it would scarcely have the right to call itself a religion.

Nevertheless, there are certain signs of the times that seem to
favor some reconciliation among the world religions. In Europe

and America especially, all churches and denominations of Christianity must contend with the growing godlessness, with a conscious denial of supernatural forces and relationships. Judaism and Islam face the same problem. Godlessness has evolved out of a sense of being and a view of life that in the past several centuries has come to be considered typically modern. Since men no longer acknowledge sin and no longer feel the need for divine mercy, many men in their daily lives tend more and more to ignore doctrines, ethical commandments and forms of worship, although without ever necessarily making a formal break with the religion they were born into.

This tendency, that has manifested itself in all spheres of life, along with the recurrent attacks and excesses of militant atheism, cause grave concern to responsible persons in all religious groups. The monotheists of the biblical religions, in particular, are more inclined to listen to one another, and to join forces against the common enemy. A first groping effort toward an ecumenical council of world religions was undertaken in 1952 in Sagorsk in the USSR, where spiritual leaders of Orthodox, Roman Catholic, Protestant, Jewish, Islamic and even Buddhist religious communities met to confer on the question of whether and to what extent there exists in the present day a common foundation for all world religions.

In this light the modern idea of tolerance acquires a special importance. That idea was first developed by the "left wing" of the Reformation, among the subsidiary sects such as the Baptists, Spiritualists and Enthusiasts. In the Age of the Enlightenment, tolerance was provided with philosophical and legal footing—out of which the modern parliamentary-democratic state arose. Thus in 1625 Hugo Grotius argued that tolerance was based on a "natural sense of justice" which is "inscribed in men's hearts," and which as a matter of principle defends the rights of the individual against society. As the philosopher Wilhelm Dilthey has finely put it: "Only the ignorant can mock the sacred and devout ring that such words as natural religion, enlightenment, tolerance and humanity had to the men of those days. For that tone contains a sigh of relief from a world crushed by denominational pressures." It was a long struggle, however, before these ideas became firmly established in the constitutions of European states.

Among the states of the age, the most modern was Prussia. Electoral Prince Johann Sigismund of Prussia converted to Calvinism in 1615; but he renounced his rights under the Religious Peace of Augsburg and permitted his subjects to retain their Lutheran faith. In his proclamation he declared: "Moreover, His Grace the Elector does not wish to compel any subject openly or secretly to adopt this confession, but commends the course and current of the matter to the truth of God alone, because it is dependent not on racing and running, but on God's mercy." These remarkable words represented a great step toward the development of modern tolerance. Subsequently, too, Brandenburg-Prussia—as the Potsdam Edict of 1685 on the reception of French Huguenot refugees indicated—remained a home of religious peace, for the crown stood above all the churches and protected equal rights for all of them. The Bohemian Brethren could sing their hymn of gratitude:

> The folk which sate in darkness dire,
> With error all around,
> Are granted here a warm hearth fire
> And freedom now have found.

Frederick the Great had been asked on his accession in 1740 whether a Catholic might acquire citizenship, and had replied: "Everyone in my country can believe what he likes, so long as he is honest." Later, in keeping with the spirit of the Enlightenment, he found more rational justifications for tolerance as an aspect of *raison d'état*. Thus in his Political Testament of 1752 he wrote:

"I am neutral between Rome and Geneva. If Rome tries to harm Geneva, it will suffer for it. If Geneva represses Rome, Geneva is condemned. In this way I can regulate religious hatred, by preaching moderation to all parties. I am, however, also seeking to promote union among them by pointing out to them that they are fellow-citizens of one state, and that a man in a red frock can be loved as much as one in a gray robe."

After Frederick's death tolerance was incorporated into the Prussian civil code of 1794. Part II, Title 11 on the rights and duties of churches and spiritual associations provided that no inhabitant of the state could be subject to coercion in regard to his ideas about God and divine things, religion and forms of worship. Every inhabitant of the state was granted complete freedom of religion and conscience, and no one was to be molested, mocked or persecuted for his religious opinions. By contrast, the Edict of Toleration of Emperor Joseph II, issued for Austria on October 20, 1781, had a different end in view: to establish a state church independent of Rome. Nevertheless, it did provide toleration for the Protestants, who previously had been subject to punishment or expulsion.

In the other countries of Europe the idea of tolerance likewise became more firmly established during the seventeenth century. In the Protestant Netherlands, which had wrested their independence from Spain during a forty-year struggle in the latter part of the sixteenth century, Catholics and Lutherans, sectarians and spiritualists of all sorts found a new home. During the Thirty Years' War the honorary name of Eleutheropolis was conferred upon Amsterdam. There such free-thinking Marrani as Uriel Acosta, Juan Prado, and Baruch Spinoza could publicly renounce not only the faith of their fathers, but even the God of the Bible, without having to bend their heads to the executioner's sword. Spinoza's *Political-Theological Tract* of 1670 anticipated many aspects of the kind of political tolerance which was to develop fully only a century later.

In England, after bitter religious struggles, the Acts of Tolerance of 1689 crowned the "Glorious Revolution." They assured all Dissenters full religious freedom outside the state church so long as they swore fealty to the King of England and repudiated papal power. Henceforth, in England and America, the idea of tolerance remained one of the fundamental tenets of Protestantism, and later an essential element of modern democracy, insofar as protection was offered to the individual against arbitrariness of all kinds. The Bill of Rights and the declarations of rights written into the constitutions of the several states named religious freedom among the inalienable human rights. Freedom of conscience and separation of Church and State were incorporated into the Constitution of the American Union.

With the French Revolution of 1789 these ideas returned to

Europe and gradually found their way into all Continental constitutions, so that by now they are part and parcel of the European mentality. Since the *droits naturels et inscriptibles de l'homme* were proclaimed by the French Revolution, freedom, property, security and resistance to oppression have been considered the very essence of human and civil rights (Article 2 of the Declaration of July 26, 1789). Tolerance had been extended from those of different creed to minorities and nonconformists of all sorts.

The influence of the political theories of Thomas Hobbes (1588–1679) and the ideas of tolerance propagated by John Locke (1632–1704) in his letters *Concerning Toleration* built the bridge from the English to the French Revolutions. Locke proclaimed the duty of tolerance on the part of Church and State, equal treatment of different creeds, and freedom of conscience as natural rights, to be the lessons of the Revolution of 1688. He frequently employed utilitarian arguments to justify these principles philosophically. Locke denied to Christianity any right to secular domination, which to his mind was exclusively the concern of the secular authorities. Similarly, Pierre Bayle (1647–1706) in France drew lessons from the persecution of the Huguenots under Louis XIV and arrived at the principles of separation of Church and State and tolerance even toward atheists —ideas that Locke, in the spirit of the British Acts of Toleration, had not yet come to. Voltaire developed Bayle's skeptical criticism of religion into a virtual system and offended many sensitive souls by the caustic wit with which he offered psychological explanations for religious phenomena. His religion of reason became the common property of many French intellectuals; it was in the spirit of Voltaire that Robespierre erected a monument in Paris to the goddess of Reason. Napoleon Bonaparte had a more matter-of-fact conception of the utility of Christianity and its fundamental compatibility with state power. As emperor he declared: "As far as I am concerned, I regard Christianity not as the Mystery of the Incarnation, but as the mystery of the social order. Religion links an anticipation of equality with heaven, thus preventing the poor from killing the rich" (remark of March 4, 1806). The epigram was entirely in the spirit of the nineteenth century.

The popular philosophy of the German Enlightenment generally kept aloof from radicalism, in spite of strong French influences, and was thus able to develop a program of tolerance with
great effectiveness. G. E. Lessing in his *Education of the Human
Race* (1780) reconciled the ancient quarrel between Revelation
and reason with his conception of Revelation as reason disguised
for pedagogical purposes; and in his famous drama *Nathan the
Wise* he preached the idea of tolerance as a gospel of active humanitarian love. He went even further in his memorable parable
of the three rings—a tale borrowed from Boccaccio: all three rings
are false because the genuine one has been lost. In this parable
he represented the moral effect as the only earmark of true religion and pronounced man the lawgiver and judge in matters of
morality and religion. Moses Mendelssohn in his book *Jerusalem,
or on Religious Power and Judaism* (1783) skillfully supported
him, arguing that the essence of religion is to promote human
happiness and that Judaism, which possesses no ecclesiastical
power, well accords with the principles of secular government
in making a clear distinction between the separate authorities.
Freedom of thought is only possible, he pointed out, when every
man is granted the right to appeal to God in "his or his fathers'
own way." Therefore the state must recognize the variety of religious persuasions.

Civil equality of the Jews, which was the result of this recognition, was introduced into Europe and legally fixed by the French
Revolution. It became the touchstone by which Christian Europe
proved the sincerity of her humanitarian ideas. The Jews were
the first group for whom the principle of equal rights for all human beings could be proclaimed and implemented, just as today
Negroes and mulattos are the last. But the idea of tolerance is
eternally imperiled, and the existence of the modern state based
on justice is, in the age of the masses, forever threatened. That
has been amply demonstrated to our generation. Today there
is scarcely anyone who cherishes the belief in continual moral
progress held by the liberal advocates of tolerance and humanity
in our grandfathers' generation. Tolerance must be fought for
anew in every generation.

Yet it would be unjust to make the Enlightenment responsible
for all of its consequences, among which must be counted the

unbelief of the enlightened modern man. Since the rise of political substitute-religions, which have exerted their absolutistic
claims more cruelly than the religions of biblical revelation ever
did, modern man is confronted with the question of whether he
wishes to cling to that area of spiritual freedom which the generation of 1800 won for him when it moved from dogmatic contentions to religious dialogue and thus established a new apprecia-
tion of both religious and philosophical adversaries. Since then
the issue has been whether man can summon up the psychological willingness to live amid tensions, to listen to others, to brook
the claims and demands of his fellowmen and to curb his own,
instead of coping with discord by gagging his beloved neighbor
or even physically annihilating him. The most precious treasure
of modern liberalism consists in the assurance of an area for encounters, in which all partners to a dialogue can openly declare
the truth they desire to witness, without fear that they may suffer
personal harm or uselessly dash against walls of insuperable
prejudices.

As for the encounter of Christianity with alien religions, there
is still great truth in the words of old Matthias Claudius addressed "To my Son Johannes": "Despise no religion, for it is of
the spirit, and you do not know what may lie hidden beneath
inconspicuous symbols."

INDEX

Acosta, Uriel, 308
Adalbert of Prague, 114
Aesthetics (Hegel), 133
"Against the Thievish and Murderous Hordes of Peasants" (Luther), 286
Akkadians, 53 ff
Alaric, King, 275
Alcibiades, 131
Alexander the Great, 64–65, 118
Amenophis IV, King, 70–72; renames himself Ikhnaton, 70
Annals of Spring and Autumn (Confucian writing), 188
Apollonius of Rhodes, 129
Aquinas, St. Thomas, 274, 279
Archaic Period, Greek, 118
Asoka, Emperor, 161
Ataturk, Kemal, 241
Augustine, St., 3, 274–75
Augustus, Emperor, 142
Aurelian, Emperor, 85, 143
Aurobindo, Shri, 158–59
Aztec religions, 91–94

Babylonia, extinct religions of, 53–62; Akkadians, 53 ff; "Babel-Bible," 59–60; gods, 54–56; morality, 58–59; mythology, 56–58; piety, 58–59; Sumerians, 53 ff; West Semites, 60–62
Baetke, Walter, 103, 108
Barbarossa, Frederick (Frederick I), 279
Basil the Great, 267
Bayle, Pierre, 309
Benedict of Nursia, 267
Biblical revelation, religions of: Christianity, 242–311; Islam, 227–41; Judaism, 207–26. *See also* separate listings

Blavatzky, H. P., 159
Boccaccio, Giovanni, 310
Boniface VIII, Pope, 279, 280
Book of the Dead, 63, 74
Book of Historical Documents (Confucian writing), 188
Boor, Helmut de, 105
Bora, Katharina von, 287
Bousset, Wilhelm, 60
Brahminism. *See* Hinduism
Brosses, Charles de, 14
Brun of Querfurt, 114
Buber, Martin, 221, 224–25
Bucolics (Virgil), 290
Buddhism, 37, 39, 40, 41–42, 47, 49, 50, 77, 148, 151–52, 161–75; Burmese, 174; Caodaism, 174; Ceylonese, 174; Chinese, 173, 174, 181–83; Communist peril, resistance to, 174; developments in, 172–74; doctrine of the Buddha, 165–67, 169–72; evaluation of Buddha's doctrine, 169–72; "Four Noble Truths," 165–68; Hinayana, 172–75; history of, 161 ff; Japanese, 173, 182, 197–99, 203; life of the Buddha, 162–65; Mahayana, 172–75, 177, 181 ff; monasticism, 168–69; suffering, negative concept of, 171; in Thailand, 174; in Tibet, 176 ff, 198; value attached to non-being, 170–71; Vietnamese, 174
Buddhistische Geisteswelt (Mensching), 173
Burckhardt, Jakob, 133
Burmese Buddhism, 174

Caesar, Julius, 142
Caligula, Emperor, 143
Calixtus I, Bishop, 265

Calvin, John, 290–94; builds Geneva community, 291–92

Calvinism, 31, 47, 288, 290 ff

Caodaism Buddhism, 174

Caracalla, Emperor, 143

Carmarvon, Lord, 72

Carter, Howard, 72

Catholicism, 31, 115, 172, 177; Christian art, 281–83; Christian scholarship, 281–83; Counter Reformation, 294–96; Crusades, 280–81; degeneracy, symptoms of, 283–85; dogma, continuing process of formulating, 272; importance of Marcion to, 270; mysticism literature, 35; papacy, political decline of, 277–80; priests' "indelible character," 47; Protestantism, organization of, 287 ff; Reformation, 285 ff; schism between East and West, 276–77; Second Vatican Council, 299–303; today, 296–98. *See also* Christianity; Jesus Christ; Luther, Martin

Celts, extinct religions of, 110–12

Ceylonese Buddhism, 174

Chang Tao-ling, 194

Chanina, Rabbi, 217

Chan school of Buddhism (Japanese Zen), 182, 198–99

Charlemagne, Emperor, 109, 276, 277

Charles V, Emperor, 287

Charmides, 131

Chassidism. *See under* Judaism

Chiang Kai-shek, 178, 195

China, religion in: Buddhism, 173, 174, 181–83; celebrations and festivals, 184–85; Chan school of Buddhism (Japanese Zen), 182, 198–99; Confucianism, 41, 49, 50, 77, 181, 186, 188–96; folk, 183–85; Lao-tse, 184, 185–88, 192–94; Mahayana Buddhism, 173, 174, 181–83; Taoism, 24, 36, 41, 49, 50, 181, 183–89, 191–96; Tao-te-king, 185–88; Tsing school of Buddhism (Japanese Jodo), 182

Chinese People's Republic (Mao Tsetung's), 180, 196

Chinese Revolution, 195

Christ. *See* Jesus Christ

Christianity: acceptance by the Slavs, 114 ff; acceptance by the Teutons,

108 ff; art, 281–83; beginning of Christmas, 101; Catholic Counter Reformation, 294–96; Catholicism today, 296–98; creed of, 242–43; Crusades, 280–81; degeneracy, symptoms of, 283–85; denunciation of early Persian sects, 88; doctrinal disputes, 271–74; dogma, development of, 268–71; ecclesiastical offices, 258–60; founders in, 41; Gospel of John, 253–54; growth of, 255–57; guilt, negative concept of, 171; history of, 65, 75, 79; John the Baptist, 247–48; and Judaism, 223–26, 228, 234–35, 245 ff, 261–62, 301; Kingdom of God, 249–51, 255–56; life of Jesus, 243–45; medieval history, 275–76; merger with Persian religions, early, 90; message of Jesus, 243–45, 249–51; missionary spread of the Gospel, 261 ff; monasticism, 266–68; papacy, 260–61, 277–80; papacy, political decline of, 277–80; the Passion, 251–53; Paul's view of Jesus, 254–55, 256; penance and sin, 265–66; persecution of, 111, 262–63; positive view of being, 170; proportion to Eastern religions of, 304; Reformation, 285 ff; of the Roman Empire, 263 ff; sacraments, 257–58; St. Augustine, influence of, 274–75; schism between East and West, 276–77; scholarship, 281–83; Second Vatican Council, 299–303; sin and penance, 265–66; theology, development of, 268–71; today, 302 ff; tolerance, need for, 304; under Theodosius, 86. *See also* Catholicism; Jesus Christ

Christmas, beginning of, 101

Cicero, Marcus Tullius, 3, 142, 143

Classical Period, Greek, 118

Codrington, Robert Henry, 14

College of Cardinals, 298

Commodus, Emperor, 86

Communism, 21, 179; Buddhist resistance to, 174

Concerning Toleration (Locke), 309

Concordat of Worms (1122), 279

Confessions (Aquinas), 274

Confucianism, 41, 49, 50, 77, 181, 186, 188–96

Constantine, Emperor, 86, 263, 264, 271; Donation of, 277
Cordovero, Moses, 219
Cortez, Hernando, 91–92
Counter Reformation, Catholic, 294–96
Cretan-Mycenaean Period, Greek, 117–18
Critas (Plato), 132
Crusades, 280–81; effects of, 281
Curia Romana, 298
Cyprian of Carthage, 259, 265

Darwin, Charles, 7
Decius, Emperor, 262
Deity. *See* Man and deity, modes of relationship between
Deutero-Isaiah, 77
Dibelius, Martin, 249
Dilthey, Wilhelm, 5–6, 20, 306
Ding of Lu, Prince, 190–91
Diodetian, Emperor, 263
Diodorus, 63
Donation of Constantine, 277
Dongrub, Pabo, 178
Dostoevsky, Fyodor, 220
Druidism, persecution by Rome of, 111
Duns Scotus, John, 282

East, religions of the: Buddhism, 37, 39, 40, 41–42, 47, 49, 50, 77, 148, 151–52, 161 ff, 197 ff; in China, 181–96; Hinduism, 30–31, 45, 50, 83, 90, 148–60, 173; Indian world-view, 147; in Japan, 197–204; in Tibet, 176–80. *See also* Extinct religions outside of Europe; separate listings
Eastern Jewish Chassidism, 37
Eckart, Meister, 45, 284
Education of the Human Race (Lessing), 310
Egypt, extinct religions of, 24, 63–75; decipherment of Rosetta Stone, 63; gods, 65–70; history, 63–65; King Amenophis IV, 70–72; monuments, 72–75; pharaohs, 72–75; priests, 72–75; pyramids, 73–74
Egyptian Islam today, 241
Elagabalus, Emperor, 143
Eliezer, Israel ben, 220
Epictetus, 143
Erasmus, Desiderius, 285, 291

Etruscans, 134–35
Euhemerus, 132
Extinct religions outside of Europe: Babylonian, 53–62; Egyptian, 63–75; Persian, 76–90; pre-Columbian America, 91–96. *See also* separate listings
Extinct religions within Europe: Celts, 110–12; Greeks, 117–33; Romans, 134–44; Slavs, 112–16; Teutons, 99–109. *See also* separate listings

Fifth Buddhist World Congress (Rangoon), 174
First Vatican Council, 297
"Four Noble Truths" in Buddhism, 165–68
Frazer, Sir James G., 23, 28–29
Frederick I. *See* Barbarossa, Frederick
French Revolution, 222, 308–9

Gandhi, Mahatma, 151, 157, 158–59
Gautama, Prince Siddhartha, 162–63, 164, 168, 174, 198
Gauthier, Pierre, 302
Geibel, Emmanuel, 102
Geometric Period, Greek, 118
Germania (Tacitus), 99
German Theology (Thomas à Kempis), 284
Ghazali, al-, 236
Glasenapp, Helmut von, 152, 153, 154
Gnosticism, 39, 86, 88, 132, 143, 266, 268–69
Godfrey of Bouillon, Duke, 280
Gospel of John, 253–54
Gothic War (Peocopius of Caesarea), 113
Greek Orthodox Church, 38, 115, 277
Greek religious evolution, 9
Greeks, extinct religions of the, 117–33; Archaic Period, 118; classical enlightenment, 130–33; Classical Period, 118; Cretan-Mycenaean Period, 117–18; Geometric Period, 118; gods, 118 ff; Hellenistic Period, 118, 132; heroes, cult of, 129–30; mysteries of gods, 124–27; the polis, 127–29; Roman Period, 118; six major periods, division of, 117–18; worship, organization of, 127–29
Gregorovius, F., 260

Gregory VII, Pope, 278

Hadrian, Emperor, 136
Hajj (pillar of Islam), 237. *See also* Islam, five pillars of
Hamann, Johann Georg, 207
Hegel, Wilhelm Friedrich, 3, 66, 74, 99, 133, 139, 147
Heiler, Friedrich, 34–35, 36
Heliand (Old Saxon version of the Gospels), 109
Hellenistic Period, Greek, 118, 132
Heraclitus, 131
Herod Antipas, 248
Herod the Great, 245
Herodotus, 63, 74, 121, 128
Hesiod, 118, 132
Heussi, Karl, 279
Hinayana. *See under* Buddhism
Hinduism, 30–31, 45, 50, 83, 90, 148–60, 173; Atharvaveda (section of the Veda), 149; the *Bhagavadgita*, 150–51; caste, 153–55; combined Hindu-Moslem religion, 156; developments in, 155–58; gods, 151–52; karma, doctrine of, 152–53; the *Mahabharata*, 150; modern, 158–60; Rigveda (section of the Veda), 148; Samaveda (section of the Veda), 149; and the Sikhs, 156; the Veda, 148–49; Yajurveda (section of the Veda), 149
Hippocrates, 131
Hirohito, Emperor, 204
Hobbes, Thomas, 309
Homer, 118, 122, 124, 132
Horace, 142
Hroswitha of Gandersheim, 267
Huss, John, 284, 286
Hutten, Ulrich von, 285
"Hymn to Brother Sun" (St. Francis), 71
"Hymn to the Sun" (Ikhnaton), 71

Ibn Saud, King, 241
Idea of the Holy, The (Otto), 11
Ignatius of Antioch, 257
Ikhnaton. *See* Amenophia IV, King
Imitation of Christ (Thomas à Kemppis), 284
Inca religions, 91
Index of Forbidden Books, 300

Indian Islam today, 240
Indonesian Islam today, 240
Innocent III, Pope, 279
Institutio religionis Christianae (Calvin), 291
Iranian dualism, 80–83
Iranian Islam, 241
Islam, 49, 50, 77, 79, 148, 156; book, religion features of, 229–30; combined Hindu-Moslem religion, 156; in Egypt today, 241; five pillars of, 237; foundations of, 227–28; history of 238–40; in India today, 240; in Indonesia today, 240; in Iran today, 241; the Koran (holy book), 237–38, 239, 240; life of the prophet, 229–34; message of the prophet, 234–36; Mohammedan mysticism, 236; origin of, 229–34; Orthodox, 90; in Pakistan today, 240; in Saudi Arabia today, 241; today, 240–41; in Turkey today, 241. *See also* Mohammedanism

Jacob, Rabbi, 218
Jainism, 148, 163–64
Japan, religions in, 197–204; Buddhism, 173, 182, 197–99, 203; Shintoism, 197, 199–204; Zen Buddhism, 182, 198–99
Jerome of Prague, 114, 284
Jerusalem, or on Religious Power and Judaism (Mendelssohn), 310
Jesus Christ, 9, 31, 42, 88, 104; death of, 251, 256, 257; expiatory offering, 33; farewell addresses, 41; Gospel of John, 253–54; growth of Christian Church, 255–57; and Jewish religious parties, 245–47; and John the Baptist, 247–48; life of, 243–45; message of, 243–45, 249–51; missionary spread of the Gospel, 261 ff; the Passion, 251–53; Paul's view of, 254–55, 256; resurrection of, 251, 252, 256, 257; the sacraments, 257–58; Teutonic idea of, 108–9. *See also* Catholicism; Christianity
Jewish Academy (Stuttgart), 224
Jewish-Christian Argument, The (Shoeps), 256
Jodo, Japanese (Tsing-tu), 182. *See also* Buddhism, Japanese

John, Gospel of, 253–54
John, St., 253–54
John XXIII, Pope, 299–300, 301, 302
John the Baptist, 247–48
Jones, Peter, 27
Joseph II, Emperor, 308
Josephus, 63, 248
Judaism, 34, 38, 40, 49, 50, 81, 86, 89, 171–72, 207–9, 228, 310; Chassidism, 220–21, 223, 224; and Christianity, 223–26, 228, 234–35, 245 ff, 261–62, 301; creed, 209–11; dietary bans, 211, 231; Eastern Jewish Chassidim, 37; ethics, 214–16; festivals and holidays, 212 ff; meaning of, 207–8; mysticism, development of, 218–21; and Nazi persecutions, 222; orthodox, 32, 212; recent religious history, 221–23; rejection of Mohammed, 231; ritual, 211–14; the Talmud (holy book), 216–18; worship, 211–14
Julian, Emperor, 86
Justinian, Emperor, 65, 264, 267

Karma, Hindu doctrine of, 152–53
Kempis, Thomas à. *See* Thomas à Kempis
Kierkegaard, Sören, 220
Kingdom of God. *See under* Christianity
Koran, the (Islam holy book), 237–38, 239, 240
Krickeberg, Willy, 92
Kung-tse. *See* Confucianism
Kuomingtang government (Chiang Kai-shek's), 178, 195, 196

Lang, Andrew, 8
Lao-tse, 184, 185–88, 192–94
Last Things, Persian doctrine of, 79–80
Leeuw, Gerard van der, 9, 38
Leibnitz, Gottfried Wilhelm, 192
Leo III, Pope, 277
Leo XIII, Pope, 296
Leon, Moshe ben Shemtob de, 218
Lessing, Gotthold E., 310
Letters of Obscure Men (Hutten), 285
Licinius, Emperor, 263
Lilje, Hans, 290
Locke, John, 309
Long, J., 27
Louis XIV, King, 309

Loyola, Ignatius de, 294–95
Lucian, 60
Lun Yu (Confucian writing), 188, 189, 191
Luther, Martin, 284, 285 ff; hearing of 1521, 286; marriage to Katharina von Bora, 287; *Songbook*, 289; theses on indulgences, 288; writings, 288 ff. *See also* Reformation, Christian
Lutheranism, 31, 35, 47–48, 197, 258, 285 ff

Mahalel, Agabya ben, 217
Mahavira, 163
Mahayana. *See under* Buddhism
Maimon, Rabbi Moses ben. *See* Maimonides
Maimonides, 210
Man and deity, modes of relationship between: expiatory offering, 32–34; gift offering, 30–31; offering, 30–34; prayer, 34–37; primitial offering, 32; ritual, 37–39; sacramental offering, 31–32
Manichaeism, 40, 41, 86–88, 108, 274
Mao Tse-tung, 180, 196
Marett, R. R., 8
Martel, Charles, 240
Marxism-Leninism, 196. *See also* Communism
Maya religions, 91, 94–96
Melanchthon, Philipp, 287
Mendelssohn, Moses, 222, 310
Mensching, Gustav, 48, 173
Michizane, Sugahare, 201
Mithra, cult of, 85–86, 89
Mohammedanism, 30, 34, 40, 41–42, 44, 45, 156, 159, 171, 227 ff. *See also* Islam
Montezuma, 91
Montini, Giovanni Battista, 301
Moslems. *See* Hinduism; Islam; Mohammedanism
Mtesa, King, 18
Müller, Max, 14
Mutsuhito, Emperor, 17
Mycenaean-Cretan Period, Greek, 117–18

Nanak, 156
Napoleon Bonaparte, 309

Nathan the Wise (Lessing), 310
Nazi persecution of the Jews, 222
Nehru, Jawaharlal, 159
Nero, Emperor, 264
Nichiren, 198
Nietzsche, Friedrich, 133
Nilsson, M. P., 143
Nirvana. *See* Buddhism

Omar Khayyám, 37
Origin of religion: animistic theory of, 7–8; original monotheism theory, 8–10; preanimistic theory of, 8
Otto, Rudolf, 11–12, 23, 45, 156
Ovid, 142

Pacem in Terris (Pope John XXIII), 301
Pakistan, Islam in, 240
Pantheon (Rome), 135–38
Parseeism, 148
Pascal, Blaise, 296
Passion, the, 251–53. *See also* Christianity; Jesus Christ
Paul, Johannes, 288
Paul, St., 254–55, 256
Paul VI, Pope, 301, 302
Persia, religion in, 76–90; doctrine of Last Things, 79–80; end of, 89–90; funeral customs, 83–84; Iranian dualism, 80–83; Manichaeism, 86–88; Mithra, cult of, 85–86, 89; ritual, 83–84; Zervanism, 84–85; and Zoroaster, 76–79, 81–86, 87–88, 89. *See also* Zoroastrianism
Persian Wars, 130
Peter of Amiens, 280
Petrazzoni, R., 9
Petronius, 12
Phaedo (Plato), 74
Philo Judaeus, 60
Philosophy of History (Hegel), 99
Pinchas, Rabbi, 221
Pippin, King, 276; Donation of, 277
Pius IX, Pope, 299
Pius XII, Pope, 272, 292
Pizarro, Francisco, 94
Plato, 74, 132
Plutarch, 60
Political-Theological Tract (Spinoza), 308

Porphyry, 63
Prado, Juan, 308
Pre-Columbian America, religion in, 91–96; Aztecs, 91–94; Incas, 91; Mayas, 91, 94–96
Primitive peoples, thinking of: early age-classes, 26–27; leagues of men, 26–27; magical thinking, 20–23; magic and religion, 23–25; shamanism, 25–26; totenism, 27–29
Procopius of Caesarea, 113
Propertius, 142
Prophetic religion, 42–44
Protestantism, organization of, 287 ff. *See also* Calvin, John; Luther, Martin; Reformation, Christian

Quakers, 38

Radhakrishnan, Sarvepalli, 158, 159
Ramakrishna, 158, 159
Ramanuja, 47, 156
Reformation, Christian, 285 ff
Regula Benedicti (Benedict of Nursia), 267
Religion: basic ideas of, 11–19; definition of, 3; origin of, 7 ff
Religion, typical personalities in: the founder, 40–42; the mystic, 44–46; the priest, 46–47; the prophet, 42–44; the reformer, 47–50
Resurrection of Christ, 251, 252, 256, 257. *See also* Catholicism; Christianity; Jesus Christ
Robespierre, Maximilien de, 309
Roman Period, Greek, 118
Romans, extinct religions of the: character and organization, 138–40; development, 140–44; Etruscans, 134–35; gods, 135 ff; Latins, 134–35; the Pantheon, 135–38
Rosetta Stone, decipherment of, 63
Runes, magic of the, 103–5
Russia, Christianization of, 115–16
Russian Orthodox Church, 302–3, 304

Sa'am (pillar of Islam), 237. *See also* Islam, five pillars of
Saga of Burnt Njal, 102
Salat (pillar of Islam), 237. *See also* Islam, five pillars of

Samuel the Small, 218
Samyuttanikaya (Buddhist book), 168
Sankara, 155–56, 158, 159
Saudi-Arabian Islam today, 241
Savonarola, Girolamo, 283
Schelling, Friedrich Wilhelm Joseph von, 149
Schleiermacher, Friedrich, 3, 34
Schmidt, Karl Ludwig, 224–25
Schmidt, Wilhelm, 8–9
Schopenhauer, Arthur, 149
Second Vatican Council, 299–303
Second World War, 222, 303
Seeberg, Erich, 274
Semites, West, 60–62
Seneca, 143
Shahada (pillar of Islam), 237. *See also* Islam, five pillars of
Shah Namah (Persian "Book of Kings"), 90
Shamanism, 25–26
Shinran, 47
Shintoism, 197, 199–204
Sickingen, Franz von, 286
Sigismund, Johann, Prince, 307
Sikhism, 148, 156
Silesius, Angelus, 45
Silvanius, Johannes. *See* Jerome of Prague
Sixtus V, Pope, 298
Slavs, extinct religions of the, 112–16
Societas Jesu, 295–96
Socrates, 131–32
Söderblom, Nathan, 9, 13, 16, 23, 177, 188
Songbook (Luther), 289
Song of Igor, The, 113
Song of the Nibelungs (Tronje), 102
Spinoza, Baruch, 308
Spiritual Exercises (Loyola), 295
Stanley, Sir Henry Morton, 18
Sumerians, 53 ff
Summa theologica (Aquinas), 282
Sun Yat-sen, 195

Tacitus, 99
Talmud, the (Jewish holy book), 216–18
Tantrism. *See* Tibet, religions in, Mahayana Buddhism

Taoism, 24, 36, 41, 49, 50, 181, 183 ff, 191–96
Tao-te-king, 185–88
Tarquinius Superbus, 134
Tauler, Johannes, 284
Tersteegen, Gerhard, 35, 39
Tertullian, 259, 264, 265
Teutons, extinct religions of: acceptance of Christianity, 108 ff; conversion of people, 108–9; death, idea of, 105–7; fate, belief in, 101–3; gods, 100–1; runes, magic of, 103–5; ultimate end, idea of, 105–7; and Valhalla, 105–6, 109
Thailand, Buddhism in, 174
Theodosius the Great, Emperor, 86, 264
Theosophical Society, 159
Thirty Years' War, 288
Thomas à Kempis, 284
Tibet, religions in, 176–80; Buddhism, 176 ff, 198; Lamaism, 177–80; Mahayana Buddhism (Tantrism), 177, 198
Timaeus (Plato), 132
Töpner, Kurt, 299 n
Totenism, 27–29
Totenism and Exogamy (Frazer), 28
Tronje, Hagen, 102
Tsing school of Buddhism (Japanese Jodo), 182
Turkish Islam today, 241
Tylor, Sir Edward Burnett, 7–8

Untermann, Rav Isser Jehuda, 301

Valerian, Emperor, 262
Valhalla, 105–6, 109
Vatican Councils: First, 297; Second, 299–303
Veda (Hindu holy writings), 148–49
Vietnamese Buddhism, 174
Virgil, 142, 290
Vladimir, Grand Duke, 115–16
Voltaire, François Marie, 192, 309

Waldo, Peter, 286
Weber, Max, 31
West Semites, 60–62
Widengren, G., 9
William of Ockham, 282
Winckelmann, Johann, 133
Wolff, Christian, 192

World Brotherhood of Buddhism, 175
Wulfilas, Bishop, 108
Wycliffe, John, 283–84

Xenophanes, 130

Yehuda ha-Nassi, Rabbi, 216
Yin and Yang. *See* Taoism
Yochai, Simon bar, Rabbi, 218
Yoga, 44, 167

Zakat (pillar of Islam), 237. *See also* Islam, five pillars of
Zen Buddhism, 182, 198–99. *See also* Buddhism
Zervanism, 84–85, 88, 89
Zevi, Sabbatai, 219–20
Zimmer, Heinrich, 44
Zoroastrianism, 41, 44, 46, 47, 50, 76–79, 81–85, 86, 87–88, 89
Zwingli, Huldreich, 290–94